D1738019

JUNCTION OF FRANKSTOWN AND LUCKAHOE BRANCHES OF THE JUNIATA BELOW ALEXANDRIA.

HISTORY

OF THE

EARLY SETTLEMENT

OF THE

JUNIATA VALLEY:

EMBRACING AN

Account of the Early Pioneers,

AND THE TRIALS AND PRIVATIONS INCIDENT TO THE SETTLEMENT OF THE VALLEY,

PREDATORY INCURSIONS, MASSACRES, AND ABDUCTIONS BY THE INDIANS DURING THE FRENCH AND INDIAN WARS, AND THE WAR OF THE REVOLUTION, &c.

By U. J. JONES.

PHILADELPHIA:
PUBLISHED BY HENRY B. ASHMEAD,
GEORGE ST., ABOVE ELEVENTH.
1856.

Copyright 1997
Heritage Books, Inc.

Entered according to an act of Congress, in the year 1856, by
U. J. JONES,
in the Clerk's Office of the District Court of the United States for the Eastern
District of Pennsylvania.

A Facsimile Reprint
Published 1997 by

HERITAGE BOOKS, INC.
1540E Pointer Ridge Place
Bowie, Maryland 20716
1-800-398-7709

ISBN 0-7884-0807-0

A Complete Catalog Listing Hundreds of Titles
On History, Genealogy, and Americana
Available Free Upon Request

Dedication.

***

TO

MAJOR B. F. BELL,

BELL'S MILLS, BLAIR COUNTY, PENNSYLVANIA.

***

DEAR SIR:--I hope your well-known modesty will not be shocked when your eyes encounter this notice. In dedicating to you the fruits of my first historical labors in the field of literature, allow me to say that I am governed by reasons that will justify me. In the first place, I may cite your well-known and often-expressed veneration and esteem for the memory of the brave old Pioneers of our Valley, their heroic deeds, and their indomitable energy and perseverance, under the most discouraging circumstances, in turning the unbroken wilderness into "a land flowing with milk and honey." Secondly, you are the son of one of those self-same old pioneers, (now in his grave,) who, if not a direct actor in some of the scenes portrayed in the pages following, lived while they were enacted, and trod upon the ground where many of them occurred, while the actors in them were his friends and his neighbors. Manifold, indeed, were the changes he witnessed during a long and useful career; but the common lot of humanity was his, and he now "sleeps the sleep that knows no waking," where once the lordly savage roamed, and made the dim old woods echo with his whoop, many, many years ago.

Lastly, it was through your encouragement that I undertook the task;

3

and it was through your kind and liberal spirit that I was enabled to make it any thing more than an *unpublished* history, unless I chose to let others reap the benefit of my labors. These things, sir, you may look upon as *private*, but I cannot refrain from giving them publicity, since I acknowledge that your liberality has entailed upon me a deeper debt of gratitude than I can repay by merely dedicating my work to you.

Allow me, therefore, to dedicate to you, as a small token of my esteem for you, the "History of the Early Settlement of the Juniata Valley." If there is any thing in it to interest the present generation and enlighten posterity, I am willing to divide the honor and glory of its paternity with you, for I am neither afraid nor ashamed to confess that, although I *wrote* the *history*, it was through your generosity that I was enabled to *publish* the *book*.

A careful perusal of the work will, no doubt, convince you that I have labored studiously to make it interesting, not only to the resident of the Valley, but to the general reader, who must admit that, if I have failed, it has not been for lack of the best exertions on my part.

In conclusion, should the book prove a failure, and not come up to the expectations of my friends, you can console yourself with the reflection that you made a mistake by inciting the wrong man to an undertaking for which he was unqualified. A pleasant reflection! I have said, that, as you were the *originator* of the book, you should share all the *honor* that might arise from it. I will be more magnanimous still; if the History proves a mere catchpenny swindle, let the odium and execrations of a humbugged public fall upon

THE AUTHOR.

HOLLIDAYSBURG, PA., *Nov.* 1855.

PREFACE.

THE design, object, and aim of the following pages can be summed up without any circumlocution. Some ten or twelve years ago, a large volume of "Historical Collections of Pennsylvania" was published by Sherman Day, which gave a brief history, among others, of the counties composing the Valley of the Juniata. This work was followed by a compilation, by I. D. Rupp, Esq., entitled "A History of Northumberland, Huntingdon, Mifflin, Centre, Union, Clinton, Juniata, and Columbia counties." The last, as far as our valley was concerned, was almost a reprint of the first, with some few additions gleaned from the Colonial Records and the Archives of the State. Both these works were most liberally subscribed for; in fact, the compilation of the counties had upwards of a *thousand* subscribers in Huntingdon county (Blair not then formed) alone! The inducements held out, in order to gain such an extensive list, were, that the works would be graphic histories of the *early* settlement of this country. In this they signally failed. True, here and there they gave an account of some early occurrence; but they were exceedingly brief, lacked detail, and in many instances were found grossly inaccurate. Of course, they gave universal dissatisfaction, because the subscribers looked for a faithful record of the stirring events which occurred when this portion of the land of Penn was "the dark and bloody ground." The descendants of many who figured in the trials incident to the settlement of the valley are still living. The fireside recitals of these events made them "as familiar as household words" among those who are now fast passing away; but they search *all* histories in vain to find a faithful account of more than a moiety of the struggles, trials, and personal adventures of the pioneers, as well as the many cold-blooded Indian massacres and depredations which spread desolation through the land, and laid waste the homes and firesides of so many who located in what was then a wilderness. Let me not be understood as attempting to deny the merits of the works of which I have spoken. As *modern* histories, giving accounts, or rather descriptions, of the country as it was at the time they were issued, they were faithful records. Indeed, I will do Mr. Rupp the justice to say that I consider his compilation all it professes to be, according to his preface, in which he says: "A full and minute history of these counties can only be expected after a greater accumulation of historical facts is extant for that purpose."

The facts necessary to give a minute history of the early settlement of the Juniata have been accessible, although it must be admitted that those who could give them from reliable personal recollections have nearly all passed into "the valley and the shadow of death."

Some ten or twelve years ago, Judge M'Cune, Judge Adams, Michael Maguire, and Edward Bell, Esq., met at the mansion of the latter gentleman, in Antes township, Blair county, by invitation. These were all old settlers, whose memories dated back to the struggle of the infant colonies for freedom; and most vividly did they recollect the Indian butcheries when brave Old England paid a stipulated price for rebel scalps. The reunion of these veterans was an epoch in their lives, for they had been children together, had travelled the same rugged path, and, with stalwart frames, sinewy arms, and willing hearts, had earned for themselves names, reputation, and earthly competence. Well may we conjecture that, in fighting the battle of life over again in story, some interesting incidents were related. During this reunion, a history of the early settlement of the upper end of the valley was written, and the manuscript transmitted to the Historical Society of Pennsylvania, in the expectation that it would be published in some of their works. This, however, never was done; and when application was made to the society for a return of the manuscript, it was either lost or mislaid.

Since then, one by one, these old patriots have passed from time to eternity, and the woods and valleys that knew them for three-quarters of a century shall know them no more. With them would, in all probability, have been buried many important facts, had not the author of these pages called upon the last survivor, Michael Maguire, in October last, and taken down, at length, all his early recollections. The time was most opportune, for he was even then upon his deathbed. The sands of a long life were evidently ebbing fast, and he knew it, for he gave it as his solemn conviction that the proposed recital of the past was the last he should ever make to mortal man. Although enfeebled by age, and his body wasting away, his intellect was vigorous and unclouded, and his memory fresh as it was fourscore years ago. Indeed, I soon found that he had the most retentive memory of any man I ever knew, because, in narrating incidents, he gave days, dates, and names, with such ease as almost to stagger belief. Of course, to him I am mainly indebted for the material of that part of the History treating of the upper end of the valley, especially the occurrences between 1776 and 1782. Mr. M. died on the 17th inst.

From a manuscript memoir of E. Bell, Esq., I have also been enabled to glean some useful information. He commenced it a short time before his death, and it is to be deeply regretted that a violent attack of rheumatism in the hand compelled him to abandon the work after writing some six or eight pages.

I am also indebted to a number of persons for information that has been of value to me, whose names will be mentioned in another place in the work.

If this volume fails to meet the expectations of those kind friends who have interested themselves in my behalf, it will not be for lack of zeal or perseverence on my part. I am free to confess that the language of the book is not clothed in that attractive garb which makes books popular in the age we live in; but then it must be remembered that I am not, worthy reader, submitting to your judgment a romance, but a History, based upon immutable and undying TRUTHS.

U. J. JONES.

HOLLIDAYSBURG, *Nov.* 1855.

CONTENTS.

CHAPTER V.

CHAPTER VI.

CHAPTER VII.

CHAPTER VIII.

CHAPTER IX.

CHAPTER X.

CHAPTER XI.

CHAPTER XII.

CHAPTER XIII.

CHAPTER XIV.

CHAPTER XV.

CHAPTER XVI.

CHAPTER XVII.

CHAPTER XVIII.

CHAPTER XXXIII.

CHAPTER XXXIV.

APPENDIX.

EARLY SETTLEMENT

OF THE

JUNIATA VALLEY.

CHAPTER I.

THE ABORIGINES OF THE VALLEY—THEIR HABITS AND THEIR CUSTOMS.

WHEN the persevering and adventurous Anglo-Saxon first entered the wilds of the Juniata, his eye, as far as it could reach, beheld nothing but a dense forest; but his quick penetration observed its natural beauties, its advantages, and the fertility of its soil. Hence he did not long stand upon the crest of the Tuscarora Mountain, debating the advantages to be derived from making it his home, or the risk he was taking upon himself in doing so, but plunged boldly down into the valley and called it his own. He found it peopled with dusky warriors and their families, who received him with open arms; and the golden hues of hope for the future lightened his cares, and made his privations no longer a burden. On the banks of the beautiful river the

2

majestic stag trod, a very monarch; and the pellucid
stream, from the bubbling brooks that formed it, to its
mouth, was filled with the noble salmon and sportive
trout, with little to molest them; for the Indians did
not possess the penchant for indiscriminate slaughter of
game which characterized their successors. They held
that the land was given to human beings by the good
Manitou for a dwelling-place, and not for the purpose
of being broken up and cultivated for game. The fish
and game were also a free gift from the same spirit, for
the support of his people. Hence hunting and fishing
for more than what would supply immediate and
absolute wants were held in supreme contempt by the
red man.

The Indians found in the valley, when the whites
first invaded it, belonged to three or four tribes—the
Delawares, Monseys, Shawnees, and probably the Tuscaroras; all of whom, with the exception of the latter,
belonged to one of the eight great Indian confederations
scattered over the land, from the Rocky Mountains to
what they called, in their figurative language, the rising
of the sun. These Indians called themselves the *Lenni
Lenape*, or "original people," of which the Delawares and
Monseys were by far the most numerous of the tribes
settled in the valley. The Shawnees, a restless, lawless,
and ferocious band, were threatened with extermination
by a powerful foe in Florida, when they came to Pennsylvania and craved the protection of the *Lenapes*, which
was granted to them, and they were permitted to settle
upon the lands of the Delawares. The Delaware Indians
soon discovered that the Shawnees were quarrelsome and

treacherous neighbors, and their company not desirable. Notice was given them to quit, and they settled upon the flats of the Susquehanna, near Wilkesbarre, and from thence they found their way to the Juniata; and there is little doubt but that they were first and foremost in the depredations committed during the French and Indian wars, as well as during the American Revolution. The Tuscaroras did not claim to belong to the *Lenape* tribes, yet a large portion of them lived in their territory. They came from the South, and joined the *Aquanuschioni,* or "united people," known in history as the Six Nations. As they did not speak the language of either the "united people" or the "original people," it would appear that they were people on their own account, enjoying a sort of roving commission to hunt the lands and fish the streams of any of "their cousins," as they styled all other tribes.

The Conoy Indians settled in the valley in 1748. They left the Delaware on the strength of a promise made them by the proprietary government that they should be remunerated. The debt, however, we presume, must have been repudiated, for we find that an Indian orator named *Arruehquay,* of the Six Nations, made application to Governor Hamilton, during a "talk" in Philadelphia on the 1st of July, 1749, for something for them. The governor, quite as much of an adept at wheedling the savages as the proprietors themselves, returned the Conoy wampum, and "talked" the Seneca orator out of the belief that they owed the Conoys a single farthing, in consequence of their having left their land and settled among the nations of the Juniata of their own free will and accord. He ruled out the Conoy claim, and confirmed his opinion by sending them a string of government wampum. Whether this satisfied the Conoys or not does not appear upon the record. We think not—at least we should not suppose that they were half as well satisfied as the Six Nation deputies, who carried away, among other plunder, a quantity of tobacco and pipes, fifty ruffled shirts, and a gross and a half of brass jewsharps!

The Nanticokes settled about the mouth of the Juniata in 1748 or 1749, and in after years spread westward toward the Ohio. This portion of the tribe, when it first came to the Juniata, was not very formidable; but it increased and became powerful.

A number of Mengues, Mingoes, or Iroquois, of the Six Nations, settled a few years afterward in Kishacoquillas Valley, now Mifflin county.

Of all the savages in the valley, the Mingoes were probably the most peaceably disposed, although it is a well-attested fact that they were a brave and warlike band. The fathers of the principal chiefs of the Mingoes, settled in the Juniata Valley, had been *partially* (if we may use the term) Christianized by the teachings of the · Moravian missionaries, Heckwelder, Zinzendorf, and Loskiel; and this may account for their desire to live on terms of amity and friendship with their pale-faced brethren.

As the Delawares, or Lenapes, claimed to be the original people, we must come to the conclusion that they came toward the east before the Iroquois. They probably came from a northern direction, while the united people worked their way from the northwest to the northeast. To call these men original people, in the sense in which they applied it, may have been right enough; but to apply the term to them of *original*, as occupants of the country, is a misnomer, not only according to their own oral traditions, but according to the most indubitable evidence of antiquarians and geologists.

The traditions of the *Lenapes* were, in effect, that their ancestors were a mighty band of fierce warriors, who came from the setting of the sun, part of the way by canoes, and the balance of the way over land,—through dense forests, beautiful valleys, over lofty mountains. In their triumphant march they met but one foe, whom they trampled under their feet as the buffalo does the grass under his hoofs, and that this weak and effeminate foe was entirely exterminated.

These traditions, vague as they are, and as all oral traditions forever must be, have certainly a foundation in fact. Drake, whose Indian history is regarded as the most reliable, gives it as his opinion, formed only after all the facts could be collected and all the traditions fully digested, that the Indians originally came from Asia, by way of Behring's Straits.

The patient investigations made by antiquarians have long since settled the fact, to the entire satisfaction of most people, that a race did exist in this country prior to the advent and on the arrival of the Indians. The relics of this race, consisting of vases, pipes, earthenware, etc., found during the last century, indicate not only a race entirely different from the Indians, but one much farther advanced in civilization. The Indians, however, it would

appear, either scorned their handicraft, or never took time
to examine thoroughly the habits of these people before
they exterminated them in order to possess their country.
These relics bear a marked resemblance to those dug from
ruins in Egypt, as well as those found in Peru.   In fact,
the vases, and some of the earthenware, bear such a strong
resemblance to the Peruvian antiquities, that it is the
settled conviction of some that the earlier settlers of both
North and South America were identical, and that the
original stock was a tribe of Egyptians.

Some writers have asserted that these early inhabitants
were non-resistants. This is most unquestionably an
error.   The traditions of the Indians say that their ancestors fought many battles before they conquered the
country; but that they *always* were victorious. Of course,
this might be mere vain boasting by the Indians of their
ancestors' prowess and skill in war, and such we would
look upon it, if their oral history was not strengthened by
the fact that, on the banks of the Miami, Muskingum,
Kanawha, and Ohio Rivers, ancient fortifications, or at
least well-defined traces of them, have been found.   Nor
is this all; tolerably well-executed implements, evidently
intended for warlike purposes, have been taken from
mounds, as well as many unmistakable stone arrow-
heads.

Whether this anterior race existed to any considerable
extent along the Juniata we are not prepared to say;
but that some of them once lived here is more than probable, although antiquarians have failed to extend their
researches to the valley.   Among the evidences to induce
the belief that these ancients once occupied our land, we

shall refer to the most prominent, leaving the reader to make his own deductions.

When the excavation for the Pennsylvania Canal was going on, a laborer dug up, near Newport, a stone shaped like a Greek Cross. The formation of the stone bore unmistakable evidence that it was not a mere freak of nature. This attracted attention, and the stone was thoroughly cleansed, when the transverse was found to contain hieroglyphics, plainly marked with some sharp pointed instrument. Persons who saw it supposed that the French might have given it to the Indians, and that they used it for a purpose similar to that for which the Standing Stone was used, and that they brought it from Canada to the Juniata. This supposition was based upon the formation of the stone; but, strange to say, the hieroglyphics bore no resemblance to any thing pertaining to the modern Indians. It *may*, therefore, have belonged to the anterior race, and the person who shaped it may have been utterly ignorant of the fact that it was the symbol of the Christian religion. The cross was sent to Philadelphia to be submitted to the inspection of the *savans* of the Historical Society, but was lost on the way; at all events, it never reached its intended destination.

Speaking on the subject of antiquities with a physician some years ago,—probably the late Dr. Coffey,—he informed us that a skeleton was dug up near Frankstown, which he did not believe belonged to any of the tribes of Indians whose mounds are scattered so profusely along the Juniata. He arrived at this conclusion from numerous personal observations he made. In the first place, the body retained a portion of dried withered flesh, and portions of papyrus or bark-cloth enveloped the body, so that it must have undergone some species of embalming before sepulture. Embalming was unknown to the Indians. Secondly, the body was in a horizontal position, north and south, whereas the Indians always buried in a sitting posture, with the face to the east. And, finally, the body was buried alone, while the Indian method was to have one common grave for all who died for years. Some articles were found when the skeleton was exhumed; but they were so much corroded as to be useless even for scientific investigation.

In breaking up a piece of new ground in Kishacoquillas Valley some twenty-five, or probably thirty, years ago, traces of a well-defined wall were discovered, which was traced, and found to enclose about an acre of ground. Although the stones that formed this wall were the ordinary stones found along the stream, fashioned and shaped by the great Architect of the world himself, it is certain that human hands placed them in the position in which they were found. The whole thing was destroyed before any mention was made of it.

In addition to these evidences, we have heard of arrowheads and pottery being dug up in other sections of the valley; but, taking it for granted that they were all Indian relics, no effort was ever made to have a thorough investigation of their origin.

How long this continent was occupied by the Indians found here on the arrival of the Northmen is a mooted point, on which no two historians can agree. The Indian method of computing time by moons is rather vague to base a calculation upon. Those who contend that they originated from one of the lost tribes of Israel, endeavor to prove that they have been here for many centuries; while others, basing their calculations upon the usual increase of the human family, think that the numbers found here on the discovery of the continent would indicate that they had been here but three or four centuries. This we think a reasonable conclusion, for it is an undisputed fact that the Indians, previous to the advent of the whites, multiplied quite as rapidly as their civilized brethren; while the tender care and solicitude they evinced for children and aged people induces the belief that the deaths among them were not in proportion as one to six to the births.

We now come to the religious belief of the savages found in the Juniata Valley. The general impression of persons who have not read Indian history is that they were idolaters. Such, however, is not the fact. They worshipped no "graven image." Their belief was based upon a supreme good and an evil *Manitou* or spirit, and their subordinates,—the former of which they worshipped, while the anger of the latter was appeased by propitiatory offerings or sacrifices. It is true they had images, in the form of a head carved out of wood, which represented the good *Manitou*, and which they wore around their necks as a talisman against disease and to insure success in great undertakings; but even Loskiel, who spent a long time among them as a missionary, makes no mention of their worshipping their inanimate gods. Their worship generally consisted of sacrificial feasts, sometimes by the entire tribe, and at other times by single families. In the fall they invariably had a sort of general harvest-home gathering,

when bear's-meat and venison were served up,—the universal custom being to eat all prepared.　When provisions
were scarce, such an arrangement was no doubt satisfactory; but we can well imagine that when there was an
undue proportion of meats to guests the custom must
have proved exceedingly irksome.　After the meal, the
monotonous drum and the calabash with pebbles were
brought out, and those who had not gorged themselves to
repletion joined in the dance.　One of the chiefs usually
chanted a hymn, or rather song, of irregular measure, in
praise of the *Manitous,* and extolling the heroic deeds of
the ancestors of the tribes.　A second religious performance consisted of a sacred dance, in which the men alone
appeared, in almost a state of nudity, with their bodies
covered with pipe-clay.　This was probably a dance of
humble contrition.　A third feast, or religious observance,
consisted of some ten or a dozen of the oldest men and
women of a tribe enveloping themselves in deer-skins, standing with their faces to the east, and petitioning the good
Manitou to bless all their benefactors.　There were other
religious rites and sacrifices, which can be of little general
interest to the reader, such as a sacrificial feast in honor
of fire, another to propitiate the *Manitou* before going to
war, &c.　We shall, therefore, conclude this part of the
subject by giving the story of an old trader who traded
through the valley in 1750.　Of course we did not get it
direct from his own lips, for he has been dead and in his
grave for many years; but, even if we did get it second-
hand, it is nevertheless true.

Some time in the spring of 1750, the old trader, whose
name has now escaped our memory, received a pressing

invitation to visit Standing Stone a day or two before the
first full moon in September, as a grand feast was to come
off at that time, which would be attended by six or eight
tribes. The trader, foreseeing the chance of brisk barter,
brought a large quantity of goods from Lancaster, on pack-
horses, and arrived a day or two before the sports commenced. He found preparations made for a large company; and he accordingly pitched his tent on the hill,
while the wigwams of the Indians stood upon the flat near
the mouth of Stone Creek. On the day on which the
feast was to commence, the trader was awakened at an early
hour by the loud whoops of the savages already arriving to
take part in the ceremonies. The day wore on; and when
the sun reached the zenith a thousand warriors and their
squaws, in their best attire, had gathered upon the greensward. At the hour of twelve o'clock precisely, a chief,
whom the trader supposed to be at least a hundred years
of age, arose from the ground, while all the rest retained
a cross-legged, sitting posture. The trader understood
enough of the Delaware language to ascertain that the
feast was one which took place every hundred moons, to
render thanks to the *Manitou* for preserving them a great
people. After congratulating the different tribes, and
welcoming them to this friendly reunion, an immense
pipe was brought into the arena, which passed from mouth
to mouth, each man taking but a single whiff. Of course
the women formed the outer circle, and took no further
part in the proceedings than merely looking on. Two
half-grown lads followed the big pipe with a small bag of
Kinnikinique, and ever and anon replenished the bowl.
This consumed an hour, during which time there was pro-

found silence. The old sachem then arose, and said the balance of the day would be given up to festivities. The assemblage broke up into small parties, and as each tribe had their medicine-men, musicians, and prophets along, the tum tum of the drum and the wild chant were soon heard, and the dusky sons and daughters of the forest went into the dance of the gay and light-hearted with a thousand times more vigor than the beau and belle of the modern ball-room.

Many of the Indians called upon the trader, and were anxious to barter for "*lum;*" but, notwithstanding that he had five kegs of rum, and the most friendly feeling existed between himself and the tribes, he refused to deal. In fact, he was a prudent man, and did not consider it altogether safe. The festivities of the day and part of the night were kept up with dancing, singing, and howling. The next day, religious exercises followed; and on the third a very solemn and impressive ceremony was to take place, to wind up the meeting, at which the trader was urgently invited to be present, and in an evil moment gave his consent to do so. Accordingly he sold all of his barrels or kegs of rum, packed up the balance of his goods, and started his pack-horse train to Aughwick, himself and horse alone remaining behind.

At the appointed time in the evening for the feast, a large fire of dry wood was built, and the savages commenced dancing around it, howling, and throwing their bodies into the most violent contortions, first stepping three or four feet forward, with the body inclined in the same direction; then, throwing the body backward, moved on, keeping time with the drum and the chant. As one party got tired, or probably roasted out, they danced away, and another set took their places. When the fire burnt fiercest, and the lurid flame lit the surrounding hills, a wild chorus was sung in unison that might have been heard for miles. This, the trader was told, was the *loud* hymn of adoration. He did not dispute the assertion. The rum he had sold the Indians began to work, and the old fox was enjoying some funny scenes not set down in the bills of the day. Occasionally a chief, under the wild influence of the *fire-water*, would make a misstep and tramp upon the burning coals. To see him quitting in a hurry afforded the trader an infinite deal of amusement. At length the pile was reduced to coals, when an Indian brought forth from a wigwam a live dog, and threw him upon the burning embers. Another and another followed, until ten dogs were thrown upon the fire. Of course they tried to escape, but the Indians hemmed them in so completely that this was a matter of impossibility. They set up a dreadful howl, but the Indians drowned the canine noise by another stave of their loud chorus. The odor of the roasting dogs did not sit well upon the trader's stomach, and, bidding adieu to his immediate acquaintances, he expressed a determination to leave for Aughwick. This his friends would not permit, and insisted most vehemently that he should see the end of it. As he had seen considerable fun, he thought he might wait and see it out, as the carcasses of the dogs would soon be consumed. In this, however, he was mistaken, for the medicine-men drew them from the fire, placed them upon wooden platters, and cut them into pieces. Five or six of them carried them around among the auditory, offering to each chief a piece, who not only took it, but eagerly ate it. The conclusion of this feast we give in the trader's own words :—

"At last they came where I was sitting, among the only sober chiefs in the party. The stench of the half-roasted dogs was awful. One of them came with his trencher to me, and offered me a piece,—a choice piece, too, as I was an invited guest, being a piece of the most unclean part of the entrails. 'Thank'ee,' said I; 'never dine on dog.' But this did not satisfy them. One of the prophets, laboring under the effects of about a quart of my rum, insisted on me eating what was offered to me. I again declined, when one of the chiefs informed me that it was a very sacred feast, and unless I partook of my allotted portion I would highly insult the Indians, and some of those intoxicated might deprive me of my scalp. The thing was no longer a joke, and I seized the piece of dog entrail and put it in my mouth, in hopes of spitting it out; but they watched me so close that by one mighty effort I managed to swallow it. I did not wait to see the end of the feast; I had my portion, and thought I might as well retire. I started in the direction of Aughwick, and every half mile the nauseous dog served every purpose of a powerful emetic. I was a much sicker man next day than if I had drank a gallon of my own rum; and, in all my dealings with the red men, I took particular care never again to be present at any dog feast!"

Of the social and general character of the savages we have many contradictions. Heckwelder, the old Moravian Missionary, whose innate goodness found

> "Tongues in trees, books in the running brooks,
> Sermons in stones, and God in every thing,"

intimated that some of their social habits, such as their tender solicitude for infants and the great deference and respect they paid to the aged, were noble traits in their character. Loskiel says that "in common life and conversation, the Indians observed great decency. They usually treated one another, and strangers, with kindness and civility, and without empty compliments. In the converse of both sexes, the greatest decency and propriety were observed. They were sociable and friendly. Difference of rank, with all its consequences, was not to be found among the Indians. They were equally noble and free. The only difference consisted in wealth, age, dexterity, courage, and office."

Their hospitality to strangers knew no bounds. In some instances it was carried to extremes. An Indian who would not hospitably entertain a stranger under his roof, and attend to all his wants as far as lay within his power, was held in supreme contempt by all his acquaintances. Indeed, the offence was deemed so grievous, that the offender was not only detested and abhorred by all, but liable to revenge from the person to whom the common and acknowledged rights of hospitality were denied.

Lying, cheating, and stealing, as well as adultery and fornication, were deemed scandalous offences, and were punished. They did not exist to any great extent until the parent of them—drunkenness—was introduced by the white man.

To these commendable traits in a savage people there were sad offsets. The savage was cruel and exceedingly bloodthirsty. He never forgave a premeditated injury; and if no opportunity offered to avenge himself, he enjoined upon his descendants, "even to the third and fourth generation," to revenge him. A hatred once formed against an enemy could only be quenched with his blood. He would treasure up a wrong for years, and it would rankle in his heart until he got his enemy into his power, when flaying, roasting, or killing by inches, was not too cruel a death to mete out to him. Nay, more than this,—in their wars neither age, sex, nor condition, were taken into consideration; and the proud warrior who sang the great and heroic deeds of his ancestors for a thousand moons was not too proud to carry in his belt the scalp of an innocent babe! But then the savage was untutored, and it unquestionably was a part of his religion to put to death an enemy by the most cruel torture; neither did he expect any other treatment if he fell into the hands of a foe.

In ordinary life, there undoubtedly was some honor in the Indian, but in war no trait of it was perceptible in his composition. To slay an enemy while asleep, or destroy him by any stratagem, was a feat to boast of, and claimed quite as much glory as if it had been accomplished by the prowess of arms. To shoot an enemy from ambuscade, or lure him to destruction by treachery that would be branded as most infamous among civilized nations, were looked upon as exceedingly cunning by the Indians.

As a general thing, they professed to abhor war among themselves, and only declared it when aggravating circumstances absolutely demanded;—that the question was deliberately debated by the tribe, and if, after mature deliberation, a majority of the chiefs and captains favored a war, speedy preparation was made for it; a red hatchet or club was sent to the offending tribe, or one of them was caught, scalped, and a war-club, painted red,

SCENE EAST OF PATTERSON.

laid by his side. Hostilities were then commenced, and the war waged with the greatest fury until one or the other party succumbed.

Now it happens that *professions* do not always accord with *practice*, and in this case we are quite sure they did not. The whole tenor and bearing of the savages must lead us to believe that there was no avenue open to the aspiring Indian to attain honor and distinction, except through feats of arms and daring; and it is only too true that he shared the common weakness of humanity in loving the " pride, pomp, and circumstance of glorious warfare." The proof of this is that some of their most bloody conflicts were caused by the most trivial circumstances.

That they had many fierce and sanguinary struggles among themselves is well authenticated. A battle almost of extermination was once fought between two tribes at Juniata,—now known as Duncan's Island,—within the memory of many Indians who were living when the whites settled among them. This island must have been a famous battle-ground—a very Waterloo—in its day. When the canal was in progress of construction, hundreds of skeletons were exhumed; and to this day stone arrow-heads can be found upon almost any part of the island.

The Indian traditions also chronicle a fierce battle between two tribes near Millerstown; another in Tuscarora, and another at Standing Stone. The truth on which these traditions are based is made evident by the fact that at those places, for years, Indian war-relics have been found.

There existed for years the most intense and bitter

feuds between the Six Nations and the Lenape Indians, commonly called the Delawares. How long the feud existed, or how many bloody conflicts they had to gain the ascendency, cannot now, either by tradition or record, be made reliable history. From the best information we can gather, it is highly probable that these confederations had buried the hatchet a short time previous to the landing of Penn. And we may also readily assume that the final declaration of peace was sued for by the Delawares; for the Iroquois always boasted that they had reduced them to the *condition of women* by their superior bravery and skill in war. This the Delawares denied, and declared that "by treaty and voluntary consent they had agreed to act as mediators and peacemakers among the other great nations; and to this end they had consented to lay aside entirely the implements of war, and to hold and to keep bright the chain of peace. This, among individual tribes, was the usual province of women. The Delawares, therefore, alleged that they were *figuratively* termed women on this account." This cunningly-devised story the Delawares palmed upon the missionary Heckwelder while he labored among them, and he was disposed to give them great credit. The Iroquois, having formed an early alliance with the Dutch on the Hudson, received fire-arms, and by the liberal use of them soon brought refractory tribes out of their confederation to terms, and reduced others to vassalage, and exacted from them an annual tribute or an acknowledgment of fealty, permitting them, on such conditions, to occupy certain hunting-grounds; and there must, therefore, have been at least *some* truth in the allegation of the Iroquois that the Delawares were "conquered by their arms, and were compelled to this humiliating concession as the only means of averting impending destruction." It is said, however, that the Delawares were finally enabled to throw off this galling yoke, through the influence of Zeedyusung, a powerful chief, who extorted from the Iroquois an acknowledgment of their independence at a treaty held at Tioga in 1756.

"The humiliation of tributary nations was, however, tempered with a paternal regard for their interests in all negotiations with the whites; and care was taken that no trespasses should be committed on their rights, and that they should be justly dealt with."

So says the record; and yet we find that the sachems of the Six Nations, who had evidently learned from the whites both the use and abuse of money, in July, 1754, at Albany, sold all the lands in the State, not previously purchased, "lying southwest of a line beginning one mile above the mouth of Penn's Creek, and running northwest-by-west to the western boundary of the State." This sold the land from under the feet of the Delawares, Shawnees, and Monseys, of the Juniata Valley, notwithstanding the Six Nations had guaranteed it to them forever as a sacred hunting-ground. This act of treachery on the part of the Iroquois, and the insatiate appetite of the proprietors to add broad acres to their extensive domain, caused many of these homeless tribes to go over to the French, and, as a writer truly adds, "the blood of Braddock's soldiers was added to the price of the land."

But to return to the original settlement of the valley. The Indians unquestionably received the white adventurers with open arms, and extended to them such a hearty welcome as must have banished all fears for the future. The savages looked upon the death-dealing rifle with superstitious awe; and the saw, the axe, the plane, and other implements of handicraft in the possession of the whites, made them a high order of beings, endowed with peculiar gifts by the Great Spirit, in the eyes of the Indians, and their persons were regarded as sacred. They shared with them their rude huts, and left nothing undone within their power to render them comfortable.

And for this noble and magnanimous conduct on the part of the Indian, what return did the white man make? Such a one only, we regret to say, as makes no bright page in their history. They were taught all the vices of civilization, but to teach them its virtues was deemed a work of supererogation. The ignorant Indian and his primitive habits were treated with disdain, and he was deemed a fit subject for robbery whenever opportunity offered—this more especially by the lawless, who considered themselves out of the reach of government and its officers. A gradual encroachment upon the Indian's sacred hunting-grounds, and the refusal of the white man to look upon him as any thing but a degraded being or to associate with him on an equality, soon taught the Indian that he had taken into fellowship the crafty white man only to enable him to suck out his existence by his superior skill and his subtle cunning. The keen penetration of the savage soon discovered the position he occupied by the side of his white brother. Smarting under the indignities offered, and foreseeing the degradation to which he would be subjected in time, the red man and the white man did not long dwell together in unity. While the latter commenced tilling the land and surrounding himself with the comforts of civilization, the former fled before him to the mountains and valleys where he was monarch of the land,—where the council-fire could blaze, the green-corn dance and song be heard, and the calumet of peace be smoked without the presence of the white man.

Yet, with all the encroachments upon their rights by the settlers, the Indians exercised great forbearance. They knew the warlike appliances in the power of the proprietary government; hence they repeatedly declared their wish to " keep bright the chain of friendship;"—in less figurative language, they did not want to go to war. No depredations were committed upon the whites, of any consequence, before the French tampered with them and the Six Nations perfidiously sold the land they had given "their cousins" as a sacred hunting-ground. Nor even then, although the aggravation was great, did all the Indians leave the valley to join the French. Many who were friendly toward the proprietary government remained until war broke out between the colonies and Great Britain; and some few peaceably-disposed fragments of tribes even lingered in the valley until the close of the Revolutionary war.

During the French and Indian war, and at its close, many of the Indians returned, and lived for some years in the valley unmolested. But in 1761–62 the footprints of the white man were seen in their paths, and civilization began to crowd them. The white adventurers crowded so thick upon them, that, after the war of 1764, the greater portion of them left; nor did they return again until 1777, when they appeared as allies to the British crown, to massacre and scalp the unprotected frontier-men. To stimulate them to this inhuman warfare, the British not only impressed it upon them that they were redressing grievances, but they actually paid them a stipulated price for every scalp, of child as well as adult, brought to the Canadian frontier.

The Indians who figured in the predatory incursions from 1776 to 1781 were probably Delawares, Monseys, Nanticokes, Shawnees, and Tuscaroras; but they were then only known as Delawares, all other titles having been merged into that of the most powerful tribe. That these tribes were the ones who committed most of the depredations, we judge from the fact that the elder chiefs and captains emigrated to the Canadian frontier from the Juniata Valley, and consequently knew every foot of the valley, from the base of the Alleghany Mountains to the very mouth of the river.

CHAPTER II.

HISTORY OF THE EARLY SETTLERS.

I⊤ appears from all authentic evidence that white traders ventured into the valley as early as 1740, but always left again after transacting their business. It was about the year 1741 that bold and daring men pushed into the valley with the evident determination of making it their home. They were nearly all Scotch-Irish,—a hardy race of devout Christians, whose ancestors had been persecuted in the north of Scotland, by Charles I., and driven to the north of Ireland, and who, fearful of the provisions of the Schism Bill, in their turn fled from Ireland to America, between the years 1714 and 1720. The first of them located near or about the line (then in dispute) between Maryland and Pennsylvania. Logan, the secretary of the province, who was probably an adherent to the religion professed by the proprietors, was very much annoyed at the Scotch-Irish assumption and maintenance of "squatter's rights." In a letter to the Provincial Government, in 1724, he said, "They (the Scotch-Irish and Scotch) have generally taken up the western lands; and as they rarely approach me to propose to purchase, I look upon them as bold and indigent strangers, giving as their excuse, when challenged for titles, that we had solicited for colonists, and they had come accordingly."

Notwithstanding this, they were not molested, for they were exempted from the payment of rents by an ordinance passed in 1720, in consequence of their being frontier-men, and forming a cordon of defence to the colony.

Logan, it must be admitted, had no friendly feeling toward the new comers. In 1725 he stated that they had taken possession of one thousand acres of land, resolutely sat down and improved it without having any right to it, and he expressed himself much at a loss to determine how to dispossess them. On this occasion he admitted that among them were a number of Germans.

In 1730, Logan wrote to the government, or probably the proprietors, complaining of the Scotch-Irish, in an audacious and disorderly manner, possessing themselves of the whole of Conestoga Manor, of fifteen thousand acres, being the best land in the country. In doing this by force, they alleged that it was against the laws of God and nature that so much land should be idle while so many Christians wanted it to labor on and raise their bread. They were finally dispossessed by the sheriff and his posse, and their cabins, to the number of thirty, were burned.

These men apparently held in contempt the sham purchases of Penn from the Indians; asserted that the treaties by which the lands were secured to the proprietors were nothing more than downright farces; and they justified their course by assuming that if the Penn family had a right to "*fillibuster*" on an extensive scale, the same right to enjoy enough land to support their families should not be denied them. If the disciples of George Fox, by craft and cunning, could obtain from the Indians thousands upon thousands of acres of land by a royal grant and the presentation of baubles that shamed the idea of a purchase, the disciples of John Calvin thought they had an equal right to possess themselves of at least a portion of the acres wrested by stratagem from the Indians. They considered the Penns usurpers and pretenders, and despised their feudal prerogatives which gave them pomp and circumstance, and refused to pay them the quit-rents, which enabled them to rule by deputy, and riot in the luxury of aristocratic life in England, rather than adopt the unostentatious manners of the new world.

Logan's successor was Richard Peters. He, too, was deeply devoted to the proprietors, and used his utmost exertions to get quit-rents out of the squatters. Failing to do so peaceably, he went to Marsh Creek, then in Lancaster county, for the express purpose of dispossessing them, and measuring the lands of the manor. This occurred in 1743. The squatters assembled in great force, notwithstanding the secretary was accompanied by the sheriff and a magistrate, and forbade Peters to proceed. On his refusal, the chain was broken, and demonstrations of a riot made, whereupon the surveying party retired. The settlers were afterward indicted, but the matter was compromised by the secretary granting them leases on very favorable terms.

From the counties of Chester and Lancaster, these settlers gradually worked their way to the west, and about 1748 the Kittochtinny Valley was tolerably well settled. The influx of emigrants from Europe—embracing Irish, Scotch, Scotch-Irish, German, and a few English—was so great, that it followed, as a matter of course, that the Juniata Valley was in its turn soon invaded.

There, in all probability, the proprietors would have suffered them to remain, as they knew little of, and cared less, about the land; but the Indians made complaint of the aggressions. The Six Nations took the matter in hand, and declared that usurping the lands they had guaranteed to their cousins, the Delawares, as a sacred hunting-ground, was a breach of faith, and that the settlers must be removed; or, if the settlers persisted in their encroachments, the Delawares would take up the hatchet against them. Only too glad to get rid of their settlers in the lower counties, the government made little effort to remove them from the Indian lands. True, to satisfy the Indians, they issued proclamations warning squatters to keep off these lands, under certain penalties which they knew could not be executed.

These usurpations of land, and the contumely with which the settlers treated the Indians, at length threatened serious consequences. The Delawares, as well as the Six Nations, made complaints such as could not be misunderstood. The proprietors, at length alarmed at the probable consequences of letting their squatters usurp the lands or hunting-grounds of the Indians, sent Peters and others to dispossess them. The following is Secretary Peters's report, sent to Governor Hamilton in 1750:—

TO JAMES HAMILTON, ESQ., GOVERNOR OF PENNSYLVANIA.

May it please your honor, Mr. Weiser and I having received your honor's orders to give information to the proper magistrates against all such as had presumed to settle on the lands beyond the Kittochtinny Mountains not purchased of the Indians, in contempt of the laws repeatedly signified by proclamations, and particularly by your honor's last one, and to bring them to a legal conviction, lest for want of their removal a breach should ensue between the Six Nations of Indians and this Province, we set out on Tuesday, the 15th of May, 1750, for the new county of Cumberland, where the places on which the trespassers had settled lay.

At Mr. Croghan's we met with five Indians,—three from Shamokin, two of which were sons of the late Shickcalamy, who transact the business of the Six Nations with this government; two were just arrived from Alleghany, viz., one of the Mohawk's nation, called Aaron, and Andrew Montour, the interpreter at Ohio. Mr. Montour telling us he had a message from the Ohio Indians and Twightwees to this government, and desiring a conference, one was held on the 18th of May last, in the presence of James Galbreath, George Croghan, William Wilson, and Hermanus Alricks, Esqrs., justices of the county of Cumberland; and when Mr. Montour's business was done, we, with the advice of the other justices, imparted to the Indians the design we were assembled upon; at which they expressed great satisfaction.

Another conference was held, at the instance of the Indians, in the presence of Mr. Galbreath and Mr. Croghan, before mentioned, wherein they expressed themselves as follows:—

"Brethren,—We have thought a great deal of what you imparted to us, that ye were come to turn the people off who are settled over the hills; we are pleased to see you on this occasion; and, as the council of Onondago has this affair exceedingly at heart, and it was particularly recommended to us by the deputies of the Six Nations when they parted from us last summer, we desire to accompany you. But we are afraid, notwithstanding the care of the governor, that this may prove like many former attempts. The people will be put off now, and next year come again; and if so, the Six Nations will no longer bear it, but do themselves justice. To prevent this, therefore, when you shall have turned the people off, we recommend it to the governor to place two or three faithful persons over the mountains who may be agreeable to him and us, with commissions empowering them immediately to remove every one who may presume after this to settle themselves, until the Six Nations shall agree to make sale of their land."

To enforce this they gave a string of wampum, and received one in return from the magistrates, with the strongest assurances that they would do their duty.

On Tuesday, the twenty-second of May, Matthew Dill, George Croghan, Benjamin Chambers, Thomas Wilson, John Finley, and James Galbreath, Esqrs., justices of the said county of Cumberland, attended by the under-sheriff, came to Big Juniata, situate at the distance of twenty miles from the mouth thereof, and about ten miles north from the Blue Hills—a place much esteemed by the Indians for some of their best hunting-ground; and there they found five cabins or log-houses; one possessed by William White, another by George Cahoon, another not quite yet finished, in possession of David Hiddleston, another possessed by George and William Galloway, and another by Andrew Lycon. Of these persons, William White and George and William Galloway, David Hiddleston, and George Cahoon, appeared before the magistrates, and, being asked by what right or authority they had possessed themselves of those lands and erected cabins thereon, they replied, by no right or authority, but that the land belonged to the proprietaries of Pennsylvania. They then were asked whether they did not know that they were acting against the law, and in contempt of frequent notices given them by the governor's proclamation? They said they had seen one such proclamation, and had nothing to say for themselves, but craved mercy. Hereupon the said William White, George and William Galloway, David Hiddleston, and George Cahoon, being convicted by said justices on their view, the under-sheriff was charged with them, and he took William White, David Hiddleston, and George Cahoon into custody; but George and William Galloway resisted, and having got at some distance from the under-sheriff, they called to us, "You may take our lands and houses, and do what you please with them; we deliver them to you with all our hearts, but we will not be carried to jail!"

The next morning, being Wednesday, the twenty-third of May, the said justices went to the log-house or cabin of Andrew Lycon, and finding none there but children, and hearing that the father and mother were expected soon, and William White and others offering to become security jointly and severally, and to enter into recognisance as well for Andrew's appearance at court and immediate removal as for their own, this proposal was accepted, and William White, David Hiddleston, and George Cahoon entered into a recognisance of one hundred pounds, and executed bonds to the proprietaries in the sum of five hundred pounds, reciting that they were trespassers, and had no manner of right, and had delivered possession to me for the proprietaries. When the magistrates went to the cabin or log-house of George and William Galloway, (which they had delivered up as aforesaid the day before, after they were convicted, and were flying from the sheriff,) all the goods belonging to the said George and William were taken out, and the cabin being quite empty, I took possession thereof for the proprietaries; and then a conference was held what should be done with the empty cabin; and after great deliberation, all agreed that if some cabins were not destroyed, they would tempt the trespassers to return again, or encourage others to come there should these trespassers go away; and so what was doing would signify nothing, since the possession of them was at such a distance from the inhabitants, could not be kept for the proprietaries; and Mr. Weiser also giving it as his opinion that, if all the cabins were left standing, the Indians would conceive such a contemptible opinion of the government that they would come themselves in the winter, murder the people, and set their houses on fire. On these considerations the cabin, by my order, was burnt by the under-sheriff and company.

Then the company went to the house possessed by David Hiddleston, who had entered into bond as aforesaid; and he having voluntarily taken out all the things which were in the cabin, and left me in possession, that empty and unfurnished cabin was likewise set on fire by the under-sheriff, by my order.

The next day, being the twenty-fourth of May, Mr. Weiser and Mr. Galbreath, with the under-sheriff and myself, on our way to the mouth of the Juniata called at Andrew Lycon's, with intent only to inform him that his neighbors were bound for his appearance and immediate removal, and to caution him not to bring him or them into trouble by a refusal; but he presented a loaded gun to the magistrates and sheriff; said he would shoot the first man that dared to come nigher. On this he was disarmed, convicted, and committed to the custody of the sheriff. This whole transaction happened in the sight of a tribe of Indians who had by accident in the night time fixed their tent on that plantation; and Lycon's behavior giving them great offence, the Shickcalamies insisted on our burning the cabin, or they would do it themselves. Whereupon every thing was taken out of it, (Andrew Lycon all the while assisting,) and, possession being delivered to me, the empty cabin was set on fire by the under-sheriff, and Lycon was carried to jail.

Mr. Benjamin Chambers and Mr. George Croghan had about an hour before separated from us; and on meeting them again in Cumberland county, they reported to me they had been at Sheerman's creek, or Little Juniata, situate about six miles over the Blue Mountain, and found there James Parker, Thomas Parker, Owen McKeib, John McClare, Richard Kirkpatrick, James Murray, John Scott, Henry Gass, John Cowan, Simon Girtee, and John Kilough, who had settled lands and erected cabins or log-houses thereon; and having convicted them of the trespass on their view, they had bound them, in recognisances of the penalty of one hundred pounds, to appear and answer for their trespasses on the first day of the next county court of Cumberland, to be held at Shippensburgh; and that the said trespassers had likewise entered into bonds to the proprietaries, in five hundred pounds penalty, to remove off immediately, with all their servants, cattle, and effects, and had delivered possession of their houses to Mr. George Stevenson for the proprietaries' use; and that Mr. Stevenson had ordered some of the meanest of those cabins to be set on fire, where the families were not large nor the improvements considerable.

On Monday, the twenty-eighth of May, we were met at Shippensburgh by Samuel Smith, William Maxwell, George Croghan, Benjamin Chambers, William Allison, William Trent, John Finley, John Miller, Hermanus Alricks, and James Galbreath, Esquires, justices of Cumberland county, who informed us that the people in the Tuscarora Path, in Big Cove, and at Aucquick, would submit. Mr. Weiser most earnestly pressed that he might be excused any further attendance, having abundance of necessary business to do at home; and the other magistrates, though with much reluctance, at last consenting, he left us.

On Wednesday, the thirtieth of May, the magistrates and company being detained two days by rain, proceeded over the

Kittochtinny Mountains and entered into the Tuscarora Path or Path Valley, through which the road to Alleghany lies. Many settlements were formed in this valley, and all the people were sent for, and the following persons appeared, viz.: Abraham Slach, James Blair, Moses Moore, Arthur Dunlap, Alexander McCartie, David Lewis, Adam McCartie, Felix Doyle, Andrew Dunlap, Robert Wilson, Jacob Pyatt, Jr., William Ramage, Reynolds Alexander, Robert Baker, John Armstrong, and John Potts ; who were all convicted by their own confession to the magistrates of the like trespasses with those at Sheerman's Creek, and were bound in the like recognisances to appear at court, and bonds to the proprietaries to remove with all their families, servants, cattle, and effects; and having voluntarily given possession of their houses to me, some ordinary log-houses, to the number of eleven, were burnt to the ground; the trespassers, most of them cheerfully, and a very few of them with reluctance, carrying out all their goods. Some had been deserted before, and lay waste.

At Aucquick, Peter Falconer, Nicholas De Long, Samuel Perry, and John Charleton, were convicted on the view of the magistrates, and having entered into like recognisances and executed the like bonds, Charleton's cabin was burnt, and fire set to another that was just begun, consisting only of a few logs piled and fastened to one another.

The like proceedings at Big Cove (now within Bedford county) against Andrew Donnaldson, John MacClelland, Charles Stewart, James Downy, John MacMean, Robert Kendell, Samuel Brown, William Shepperd, Roger Murphy, Robert Smith, William Dickey, William Millican, William MacConnell, James Campbell, William Carrell, John Martin, John Jamison, Hans Patter, John MacCollin, James Wilson, and John Wilson; who, coming before the magistrates, were convicted on their own confession of the like trespasses, as in former cases, and were all bound over in like recognisances and executed the like bond to the proprietaries. Three waste cabins of no value were burnt at the north end of the Cove by the persons who claimed a right to them.

The Little Cove (in Franklin county) and the Big and Little Conolloways being the only places remaining to be visited, as this was on the borders of Maryland, the magistrates declined going there, and departed for their homes.

About the year 1740 or 1741, one Frederick Star, a German, with two or three more of his countrymen, made some settlements at the place where we found William White, the Galloways, and Andrew Lycon, on Big Juniata, situate at the distance of twenty miles from the mouth thereof, and about ten miles north of the Blue Hills,—a place much esteemed by the Indians for some of their best hunting ground; which (German settlers) were discovered by the Delawares at Shamokin to the deputies of the Six Nations as they came down to Philadelphia in the year 1742, to hold a treaty with this government; and they were disturbed at, as to inquire with a peculiar warmth of Governor Thomas if these people had come there by the orders or with the privilege of the government; alleging that, if it was so, this was a breach of the treaties subsisting between the Six Nations and the proprietor, William Penn, who in the most solemn manner engaged to them not to suffer any of the people to settle lands till they had purchased from the Council of the Six Nations. The governor, as he might with great truth, disowned any knowledge of those persons' settlements; and on the Indians insisting that they should be immediately thrown over the mountains, he promised to issue his proclamation, and, if this had no effect, to put the laws in execution against them. The Indians, in the same treaty, publicly expressed very severe threats against the inhabitants of Maryland for settling lands for which they had received no satisfaction, and said that if they would not do them justice they would do justice to themselves, and would certainly have committed hostilities if a treaty had not been under foot between Maryland and the Six Nations, under the mediation of Governor Thomas; at which the Indians consented to sell lands and receive a valuable consideration for them, which put an end to the danger.

The proprietaries were then in England; but observing, on perusing the treaty, with what asperity they had expressed themselves against Maryland, and that the Indians had just cause to complain of the settlements at Juniata, so near Shamokin, they wrote to their governor, in very pressing terms, to cause those trespassers to be immediately removed; and both the proprietaries and governor laid these commands on me to see this done, which I accordingly did in June, 1743, the governor having first given them notice by a proclamation served on them.

At that time none had presumed to settle at a place called the Big Cove—having this name from its being enclosed in the form of a basin by the southernmost range of the Kittochtinny Hills and Tuscarora Hills; which last end here, and lose themselves in other hills. This Big Cove is about five miles north of the temporary line, and not far west of the place where the line terminated. Between the Big Cove and the temporary line lies the Little Cove,— so called from being likewise encircled with hills; and to the west of the Little Cove, toward Potowmec, lie two other places, called the Big and Little Conollaways, all of them situate on the temporary line, and all of them extended toward the Potowmec.

In the year 1741 or 1742 information was likewise given that people were beginning to settle in those places, some from Maryland and some from this province. But as the two governments were not then on very good terms, the governor did not think proper to take any other notice of these settlements than to send the sheriff to serve his proclamation on them, though they had ample occasion to lament the vast inconveniences which attend unsettled boundaries. After this the French war came on, and the people in those parts, taking advantage of the confusion of the times, by little and little stole into the Great Cove; so that at the end of the war it was said thirty families had settled there; not, however, without frequent prohibitions on the part of the government, and admonitions of the great danger they run of being cut off by the Indians, as these settlements were on lands not purchased of them. At the close of the war, Mr. Maxwell, one of the justices of Lancaster county, delivered a particular message from this government to them, ordering their removal, that they might not occasion a breach with the Indians, but it had no effect.

These were, to the best of my remembrance, all the places settled by Pennsylvanians in the unpurchased part of the province, till about three years ago, when some persons had the presumption to go into Path Valley or Tuscarora Gap, lying to the east of the Big Cove, and into a place called Aucquick, lying to the northward of it; and likewise into a place called Sheerman's creek, lying along the waters of Juniata, and is situate east of the Path Valley, through which the present road goes from Harris's Ferry to Alleghany; and lastly, they extended their settlements to Big Juniata; the Indians all this while repeatedly complaining that their hunting-ground was every day more and more taken from them; and that there must infallibly arise quarrels between their warriors and these settlers, which would in the end break the chain of friendship, and pressing in the most importunate terms their speedy removal. The government in 1748 sent the sheriff and three magistrates, with Mr. Weiser, into these places to warn the people; but they, notwithstanding, continued their settlements in opposition to all this; and, as if those people were prompted by a desire to make mischief, settled lands no better, nay not so good, as many vacant lands within the purchased parts of the province.

The bulk of these settlements were made during the administration of President Palmer; and it is well known to your honor, though then in England, that his attention to the safety of the city and the lower counties would not permit him to extend more care to places so remote.

Finding such a general submission, except the two Galloways and Andrew Lycon, and vainly believing the evil would be effectually taken away, there was no kindness in my power which I did not do for the offenders. I gave them money where they were poor, and telling them they might go directly on any part of the two millions of acres lately purchased of the Indians; and where the families were large, as I happened to have several of my own plantations vacant, I offered them to stay on them rent free, till they could provide for themselves: then I told them that if after all this lenity and good usage they would dare to stay after the time limited for their departure, no mercy would be shown them, but that they would feel the rigor of the law.

It may be proper to add that the cabins or log-houses which were burnt were of no considerable value; being such as the country people erect in a day or two, and cost only the charge of an entertainment.   RICHARD PETERS.

July 2, 1750.

From this summary proceeding originated the name of the place called the Burnt Cabins, the locality of which is pointed out to the traveller to this day.

That these ejected tenants *at will* did not remain permanently ejected from the fertile valley of the Juniata is evident from the fact that their descendants, or many of them, of the third and fourth generations, are now occupying the very lands they were driven from.

In July, 1750, the government was thrown into alarm by the rumor that a Mr. Delany had, while speaking of the removal of the trespassers on the unpurchased lands northwest of the Kittochtinny Hills, said, "that if the people of the Great and Little Coves would apply to Maryland they might have warrants for their lands; and if those of the Tuscarora Path Valley would apply to Virginia, he did not doubt but they might obtain rights there."

Petitions were sent to the Council from the residents of the Coves, in which it was set forth that they did not wish to be either in the province of Maryland or Virginia, and prayed permission to remain, until the boundary of the provinces was determined, on the lands purchased from the Indians.

This proposition was not accepted, and was only followed up by proclamations imposing severe penalties upon trespassers. This was deemed absolutely necessary by Governor Hamilton, for the French were assuming a menacing attitude along the frontier, and it was necessary, at all hazards, to preserve the alliance of the Indians.

The Provincial Government was strong enough to drive the settlers out of the valley, but immeasurably too weak to keep them out. This brought about the treaty at Albany in 1754, to which we have previously alluded. Thomas and Richard Penn, seeing the government unable to remove the squatters permanently, in consequence of the feelings of the people being with the latter, bought from the sachems the very considerable slice of land in which was included the Valley of the Juniata, for the trifling consideration of £400. This was supposed to act as a healing balm for the trespasses upon their hunting-grounds, and at the same time the Penns undoubtedly entertained the idea that they could realize a handsome profit in re-selling the lands at an advanced price to those who occupied them, as well as to European emigrants constantly arriving and anxious to purchase.

The Indian chiefs and sachems who were not present at this treaty were highly indignant, and pronounced the whole transaction a gross fraud; and those who were present at the treaty declared they were outwitted by misrepresentations, and grossly defrauded. Conrad Weiser, the Indian interpreter, in his journal of a conference at Aughwick, stated that the dissatisfaction with the purchase of 1754 was general. The Indians said they did not understand the points of the compass, and if the line was so run as to include the west branch of Susquehanna, they would never agree to it. According to Smith's Laws, vol. xxi., p. 120, "the land where the Shawnee and Ohio Indians lived, and the hunting-grounds of the Delawares, the Nanticokes, and the Tutelos, were all included."

So decided and general was the dissatisfaction of the Indians, that, in order to keep what few remained from being alienated, the proprietors found it necessary to cede back to them, at a treaty held in Easton, in October, 1758, all the land lying north and west of the Alleghany Mountains within the province. The restoration, however, came too late to effect much good.

But even the lands west of the Alleghany Mountains were not sacred to the Indians, mountainous as they were and unfertile as they were deemed; for westward the squatter went, gradually encroaching upon the red men's last reserve, until he finally settled in their midst. These aggressions were followed by the usual proclamations from the government, but they had little or no effect in preventing the bold adventurers from crossing the Alleghany Mountains and staking out farms in the valley of the Conemaugh. This continued for a number of years, until the government, wearied by unavailing efforts to keep settlers from Indian lands, caused a stringent law to be passed by Council in February, 1768, when it was enacted " that if any person settled upon the unpurchased lands neglected or refused to remove from the same within thirty days after they were required so to do by persons to be appointed for that purpose by the governor or by his proclamation, or, having so removed, should return to such settlement, or the settlement of any other person, with or without a family, to remain and settle on such lands, or if any person after such notice resided and settled on such lands, every such person so neglecting or refusing to remove, or returning to settle as aforesaid, or that should settle after the requisition or notice aforesaid, being legally convicted, *was to be punished with death without the benefit of clergy.*"

There is no evidence on record that the provision of this act was ever enforced, although it was openly violated. It was succeeded by laws a little more lenient, making fine and imprisonment the punishment in lieu of the death-penalty "without the benefit of clergy."

Neither does the record say that the coffers of the provincial treasury ever became plethoric with the collection of fines paid by trespassers.

During the Indian wars of 1762–63, many of the inhabitants of the valley fled to the more densely populated districts for safety. Up to this time few forts were built for defence, and the settlers dreaded the merciless warfare of the savages. The restoration of peace in the latter year brought a considerable degree of repose to the long harassed colonies. The turbulent Indians of the Ohio buried the hatchet in October, 1764, on the plains of Muskingum, which enabled the husbandman to reassume his labors and to extend his cultivation and improvements. The prosperity of Pennsylvania increased rapidly; and those who were compelled by Indian warfare to abandon their settlements rapidly returned to them. The Juniata Valley, and especially the lower part of it, gained a considerable accession of inhabitants in the shape of sturdy tillers of the soil and well-disposed Christian people.

For a time the Scotch-Irish Presbyterians maintained rule in religion; but, about 1767, German Lutherans, Irish Catholics, and some few Dunkards and other denominations, found their way to the valley. Meeting-houses were built, stockade forts erected, and communities of neighbors formed for mutual protection, without regard to religious distinctions.

The first settlements of the upper portion of the valley were not effected until between 1765 and 1770. True, there was here and there an isolated family, but the danger of being so near the Kittaning Path was deemed too hazardous. It was in the upper part of the valley, too, that most of the massacres took place between 1776 and 1782, as the lower end of it was too thickly populated and too well prepared for the marauders to permit them to make incursions or commit depredations.

CHAPTER III.

JUNIATA ISLAND — AN INDIAN PARADISE — REV. DAVID BRAINERD
AMONG THE SAVAGES — THE EARLY SETTLERS, HULINGS, WATTS,
AND BASKINS — INDIAN BATTLES — REMARKABLE ESCAPE OF MRS.
HULINGS, ETC.

JUNIATA ISLAND — now called Duncan's Island, in consequence of the Duncan family being the proprietors for
many years — is formed by the confluence of the Juniata
and Susquehanna. Stretching northward, it presents a
lovely and fertile plain, surrounded by gorgeous and
romantic scenery, surpassed by few places in the State.
This must have been a very paradise for the sons of the
forest. Facing to the west, before them lay their beautiful hunting-grounds; facing to the south, the eye rested
upon the "long crooked river," over whose rippling bosom
danced the light bark canoe, and whose waters were filled
with the choicest of fish. With such blessings within
their reach, the inhabitants of the Juniata Island should
have been superlatively happy, and probably would,
had it not been for the internal feuds which existed
among the tribes. Although the wigwams of two distinct
tribes dotted the island on the arrival of the white man,
social intercourse and the most friendly terms of intimacy
existed between them. They were the Shawnees and the

Conoys. Then, too, it betokened a peaceable spot, and yet it had been a famous Indian battle-ground in its day. The traditions speak of a battle fought many years ago, between the Delawares and the Cayugas, on this island, when the gullies ran red with blood of mighty warriors, and the bones of a thousand of them were entombed in one common grave upon the battle-field. Both tribes suffered severely. The Delawares, although they lost the most braves, and were ultimately driven from the field, fought with the most savage desperation; but the Cayugas had the advantage in point of numbers, and some of them used fire-arms, then totally unknown to the Delawares.

The first adventurers who went up the Susquehanna were Indian traders, who took up articles for traffic in canoes. Fascinated by the beautiful scenery of the country, and impressed with the idea that corn and fruits grew upon the island spontaneously, these traders did not fail to give it a name and reputation; and curiosity soon prompted others to visit the " Big Island," as they called it. Some of them soon went so far as to contemplate a settlement upon it. This, however, the Indians would not permit; they were willing to trade at all times with them, but the island was a kind of reservation, and on no condition would they permit the pale-faces to share it with them. Even had they suffered white men to settle among them, none would have repented the act, as a rash step, more bitterly than the white men themselves; for the Shawnees were a treacherous nation, and exceedingly jealous of any innovations upon their rights or the customs of their fathers.

Still, the island became settled at an early day. The

roving Shawnees pushed their way westward, and the prejudices of those who took their place were probably overcome by presents of guns, ammunition, tobacco, and *fire-water*.

The Rev. David Brainerd, a devout and pious missionary, visited the island in 1745, in the spring while going up the river, and in the fall while returning. His object was to convert the Indians, which he found quite as hopeless a task as did Heckwelder and Loskiel, who preceded him with the same object in view. During his peregrinations Brainerd kept a journal, which, together with his life, was published by the American Tract Society. From this journal we extract the following, in order to give his views of savage life, as well as an interesting account of what he saw and heard at the island:—

Sept. 20.—Visited the Indians again at Juneauta Island, and found them almost universally very busy in making preparations for a great sacrifice and dance. Had no opportunity to get them together in order to discourse with them about Christianity, by reason of their being so much engaged about their sacrifice. My spirits were much sunk with a prospect so very discouraging, and specially seeing I had this day no interpreter but a pagan, who was as much attached to idolatry as any of them, and who could neither speak nor understand the language of these Indians; so that I was under the greatest disadvantages imaginable. However, I attempted to discourse privately with some of them, but without any appearance of success; notwithstanding, I still tarried with them.

The valuable interpreter was probably a Delaware Indian, who was a visitor to take part in the dance and sacrifice, while the inhabitants of the island were Shawnees, who originally came from the south, and their languages were entirely dissimilar. Brainerd calls them "pagans" and "idolaters." This is a charge the Indians used to combat most vehemently. They most unquestionably had small images carved out of wood to represent the Deity; yet they repudiated the idea of worshipping the wood, or the wooden image, merely using it as a symbol through which to worship the Unseen Spirit. If such was the fact, they could not well be called pagans in the common acceptation of the term. The journal goes on to say :—

In the evening they met together, nearly one hundred of them, and danced around a large fire, having prepared ten fat deer for the sacrifice. The fat of the inwards they burnt in the fire while they were dancing, which sometimes raised the flame to a prodigious height, at the same time yelling and shouting in such a manner that they might easily have been heard two miles or more. They continued their sacred dance nearly all night; after which they ate the flesh of the sacrifice, and so retired each one to his own lodging.

Making a burnt-offering of the deer-fat to illuminate the dance, and to make a meat-offering to the insatiate Indian appetite, after undergoing such fatigues, of the roasted venison, had not much idolatry in it. Unconnected with any religious ceremony, such a proceeding might have been considered rational, and coming altogether within the meaning of the Masonic principle which recognises "refreshment after labor." Mr. Brainerd continues :—

Lord's-day, Sep. 21.—Spent the day with the Indians on the island. As soon as they were well up in the morning, I attempted to instruct them, and labored for that purpose to get them together, but soon found they had something else to do; for near noon they gathered together all their powaws, or conjurors, and set about half a dozen of them playing their juggling tricks and acting their frantic, distracted postures, in order to find out why they were then so sickly upon the island, numbers of them being at that time disordered with a fever and bloody flux.   In this exercise they were engaged for several hours, making all the wild, ridiculous, and distracted motions imaginable; sometimes singing, sometimes howling, sometimes extending their hands to the utmost stretch and spreading all their fingers: they seemed to push with them as if they designed to push something away, or at least to keep it off at arm's-end; sometimes stroking their faces with their hands, then spouting water as fine as mist; sometimes sitting flat on the earth, then bowing down their faces to the ground; then wringing their sides as if in pain and anguish, twisting their faces, turning up their eyes, grunting, puffing, &c.

This looks more like idolatry than sacrificing ten fat deer and dancing by the light of their burning fat.   Yet, if curing disease by powwowing, incantation, or the utterance of charms, can be considered idolatry, we are not without it even at this late day.   We need not go out of the Juniata Valley to find professing Christians who believe as much in cures wrought by charms as they do in Holy Writ itself.

"Their monstrous actions tended to excite ideas of horror, and seemed to have something in them, as I thought, peculiarly suited to raise the devil, if he could be raised by any thing odd, ridiculous, and frightful.   Some of them, I could observe, were much more fervent and devout in the business than others, and seemed to chant, whoop, and mutter, with a degree of warmth and vigor as if determined to awaken and engage the powers below.   I sat at a small distance, not more than thirty feet from them, though undiscovered, with my Bible in my hand, resolving, if possible, to spoil their sport and prevent their receiving any answers from the infernal world, and there viewed the whole scene.   They continued their hideous charms and incantations for more than three hours, until they had all wearied themselves out, although they had in that space of time taken several intervals of rest; and at length broke up, I apprehend, without receiving any answer at all."

Very likely they did not; but is it not most singular that a man with the reputation for piety and learning that Brainerd left behind him should arm himself with a Bible to spoil the spirit of the Indians, in case their incantations should raise the demon of darkness, which, it would really appear, he apprehended? In speaking of the Shawnee Indians, or "Shawanose," as they were then called, he stigmatizes them as "drunken, vicious, and profane." What their profanity consisted of he does not say. According to all Indian historians, the Indians had nothing in their language that represented an oath. Brainerd goes on to say of the Shawnees:—

Their customs, in various other respects, differ from those of the other Indians upon this river. They do not bury their dead in a common form, but let their flesh consume above the ground, in close cribs made for that purpose. At the end of a year, or sometimes a longer space of time, they take the bones, when the flesh is all consumed, and wash and scrape them, and afterward bury them with some ceremony. Their method of charming or conjuring over the sick seems somewhat different from that of the other Indians, though in substance the same. The whole of it, among these and others, perhaps, is an imitation of what seems, by Naaman's expression, (2 Kings v. 11,) to have been the custom of the ancient heathen. It seems chiefly to consist of their "striking their hands over the deceased," repeatedly stroking them, "and calling upon their God," except the spurting of water like a mist, and some other frantic ceremonies common to the other conjurations which I have already mentioned.

In order to give Mr. Brainerd's impression of their customs, as well as an interesting account of a "medicine-man" who possessed rather singular religious opinions, we shall close with his journal, with another paragraph:—

When I was in this region in May last, I had an opportunity of learning many of the notions and customs of the Indians, as well as observing many of their practices. I then travelled more than one hundred and thirty miles upon the river, above the English settlements, and in that journey met with individuals of seven or eight distinct tribes, speaking as many different languages. But of all the sights I ever saw among them, or indeed anywhere else, none appeared so frightful or so near akin to what is usually imagined of *infernal powers*, none ever excited such images of terror in my mind, as the appearance of one who was a devout and zealous reformer, or rather restorer of what he supposed was the ancient religion of the Indians. He made his appearance in his *pontifical garb*, which was a coat of *bear-skins*, dried with the hair on, and hanging down to his toes; a pair of bear-skin stockings, and a great *wooden* face, painted, the one half black, the other half tawny, about the color of an Indian's skin, with an extravagant mouth, but very much awry; the face fastened to a bear-skin cap, which was drawn over his head. He advanced toward me with the instrument in his hand which he used for music in his idolatrous worship, which was a dry tortoise-shell with some corn in it, and the neck of it drawn on to a piece of wood, which made a very convenient handle. As he came forward, he beat his tune with the rattle, and danced with all his might, but did not suffer any part of his body, not so much as his fingers, to be seen. No one would have imagined, from his appearance or actions, that he could have been a human creature, if they had not had some intimation of it otherwise. When he came near me, I could not but shrink away from him, although it was then noonday, and I knew who it was, his appearance and gestures were so prodigiously frightful. He had a house consecrated to religious uses, with divers images cut upon the several parts of it. I went in, and found the ground beaten almost as hard as a rock with their frequent dancing upon it. I discoursed with him about Christianity. Some of my discourse he seemed to like, but some of it he disliked extremely. He told me that God had taught him his religion, and that he never would turn from it, but wanted to find some who would join heartily with him in it; for the Indians, he said, were grown very degenerate and corrupt. He had thoughts, he said, of leaving all his friends, and travelling abroad, in order to find some who would join with him; for he believed that God had some good people somewhere, who felt as he did.

He had not always, he said, felt as he now did; but had formerly been like the rest of the Indians, until about four or five years before that time. Then, he said, his heart was very much distressed, so that he could not live among the Indians, but got away into the woods, and lived alone for some months. At length, he said, God comforted his heart, and showed him what he should do; and since that time he had known God and tried to serve him, and loved all men, be they who they would, so as he never did before. He treated me with uncommon courtesy, and seemed to be hearty in it. I was told by the Indians that he opposed their drinking strong liquor with all his power; and that if at any time he could not dissuade them from it by all he could say, he would leave them, and go crying into the woods. It was manifest that he had a set of religious notions, which he had examined for himself and not taken for granted upon bare tradition; and he relished or disrelished whatever was spoken of a religious nature, as it either agreed or disagreed with *his standard*. While I was discoursing, he would sometimes say, "Now that I like; so God has taught me," &c.; and some of his sentiments seemed very just. Yet he utterly denied the existence of a devil, and declared there was no such creature known among the Indians of old times, whose religion he supposed he was attempting to revive. He likewise told me that departed souls went *southward*, and that the difference between the good and bad was this: that the former were admitted into a beautiful town with spiritual walls, and that the latter would forever hover around these walls in vain attempts to get in. He seemed to be sincere, honest, and conscientious, in his own way, and according to his own religious notions, which was more than ever I saw in any other pagan. I perceived that he was looked upon and derided among most of the Indians as a *precise zealot*, who made a needless noise about religious matters; but I must say that there was something in his temper and disposition which looked more like true religion than any thing I ever observed among other heathens.

If Brainerd was not grossly imposed upon, the Indian was a remarkable man, and his code of ethics might be used with profit by a great many persons now treading the paths of civilization and refinement. But it is more than probable that he had based the groundwork of his religion on what he had learned from the Moravian missionaries. In the ensuing summer Brainerd again ascended the Susquehanna, where he contracted disease by exposure, and died in the fall.

The earliest permanent white settler upon the island was a gentleman named Hulings, who located near the mouth of the Juniata, over which, in after years, he established a ferry; and, after travel increased and the traders took their goods up the rivers on pack-horses, he built a sort of causeway, or bridge, for the passage of horses, at the upper end of the island. He settled on the island in 1746. He was followed by another adventurer, named Watts, who staked out a small patch of land, with the view of farming it. It was already cleared, and he purchased it from the Indians. The children of these families intermarried, and their descendants to this day own the greater portion of the island. A few years after the settlement of Watts and Hulings, a gentleman named Baskin came from below, and settled near the point of the island. He was an enterprising man, and had no sooner erected himself a temporary shelter than he established a ferry across the Susquehanna. The ferry became profitable, and Baskin realized a fortune out of it. It was a sort of heirloom in the family for several generations, until the State improvements were built, when a bridge was erected. Baskin's Ferry was known far and wide; and there are still some descendants of the name residing, or who did reside a few years ago, where the ferry crossed.

Shortly after Braddock's defeat, the country was greatly

alarmed by rumors that the French and Indians were coming down the Susquehanna in great numbers, with the avowed intention of slaughtering the British colonists and laying waste all their habitations. Nor was this rumor without foundation; for the massacres already committed up the Susquehanna seemed fully to justify the apprehension. Travel along the river was suspended, and a portion of the settlers fled to Paxton. Hulings abandoned his ferry, and, with a convoy of friendly Delaware Indians, he went to Fort Duquesne, where he immediately purchased land, with the view of settling permanently. There, however, he found little more peace and quiet than he enjoyed at the island. The country was rife with alarms of Indian depredations, and the settlers were in constant dread of an attack which they could not repel. Hulings became dissatisfied, because the exchange had disappointed all his reasonable expectations, and he determined to return. To this end he disposed of his land for £200—land which now composes the heart of the city of Pittsburg, and could not be purchased for £2,000,000. In company with another party of friendly Indians on their way to the east, he returned to the island, re-established his ferry, built himself a house at the bridge, and for some years lived in security.

About 1761, accounts of Indian depredations above again alarmed the lower settlements; but Mr. Hulings paid no attention to them, until a large number of them were seen but a short distance above the island, encamped upon a piece of table-land. In great haste he packed up a few of his most valuable articles, and, putting his wife and child upon a large black horse, took them to the

5

Point, so as to be ready to fly the moment the savages made their appearance. At this place there was a half-fallen tree, from the branches of which an excellent view of his house, as well as of the path beyond it, could be obtained. Here Hulings watched for some time, hoping that if the Indians did come down, and find his house abandoned, they would go up the Juniata. Suddenly it occurred to Hulings that in his haste he had left some valuable keepsakes, and he returned forthwith alone. After reconnoitering for some time, he entered the house, and was somewhat surprised to find an Indian tinkering at his gun-lock. The savage was unable to shoot, and, as Hulings was a man of powerful frame, he feared to make a personal attack upon him. Both appeared to be ready to act upon the defensive, but neither was willing to risk an attack.

In the mean time, the reconnoitering and parleying of Hulings had taken up so much time that Mrs. Hulings became alarmed, and concluded that her husand had been murdered. Without a thought of the danger, she took her child upon the horse before her, plunged him into the Susquehanna, and the noble charger carried them safely to the other shore—a distance of nearly a mile, and at a time, too, when the river was unusually high! Such an achievement in modern times would make a woman a heroine, whose daring would be extolled from one end of the land to the other.

Soon after this extraordinary feat, Mr. Hulings arrived, and he, in turn, became alarmed at the absence of his wife; but he soon saw her making a signal on the other side, and, immediately unmooring a canoe at the mouth of the

Juniata, he got into it and paddled it over. It was the only canoe in the neighborhood,—an old one left by Baskin when he fled. Hulings had scarcely rejoined his wife before he saw the flames shooting up from the old log ferry-house, and the savages dancing around it, brandishing their weapons; but they were out of harm's way, and succeeded in reaching Paxton the same day. In a year or so they returned, and ended their days on the island.

Reference is made by historians to a battle fought between the whites and Indians on the island in 1760. The old inhabitants, too, spoke of one, but we could ascertain nothing definite on the subject. No mention whatever is made of it in the Colonial Records.

After this period but few of the roving bands or war-parties ever came down either the Susquehanna or the Juniata as far as the island. The massacre of the Conestoga Indians inspired the up-country savages with so much terror that they deemed it certain death to go near the settlement of the Paxton boys.

By the time the Revolution commenced, the neighborhood of the mouth of the Juniata was thickly populated, and the inhabitants had within their reach ample means of defence; so that the savages in the employ of the British prudently confined their operations to the thickly-settled frontier.

CHAPTER IV.

INDIAN TOWNS ALONG THE JUNIATA — LOST CREEK VALLEY DISCO-
VERED—MEXICO FIRST SETTLED BY CAPTAIN JAMES PATTERSON IN
1751—INDIAN ATTACK UPON SETTLERS AT THE HOUSE OF WILLIAM
WHITE — MASSACRE OF WHITE — CAPTURE OF A LAD NAMED JOHN
RIDDLE — HIS RELEASE FROM CAPTIVITY, ETC.

[FOR the facts on which the two chapters following are based we are
indebted to a gentleman named ANDREW BANKS, an old resident of Lost
Creek Valley, Juniata county. He was born near York, and settled near
his late place of residence in 1773, and was nearly eighty-nine years of
age when we called upon him early in December, 1855. We found him
enjoying the evening of a long and well-spent life, with his sense of hearing
somewhat impaired, but his intellect and memory both good. He was a
man of considerable intelligence, and we found him quite willing to give
all he knew of the past worthy of record. He died about the last of the
same month.]

THE river, from the island to Newport, is hemmed in
by mountains; and while it afforded excellent territory
for hunting, fishing, and trapping, it held out no inducements for the Indians to erect their lodges along it. The
first Indian village above the mouth of the river was
located on the flat, a short distance above where the town
of Newport now is. Another was located at the mouth
of a ravine a little west of Millerstown. At the former
place the Cahoons, Hiddlestons, and others were settled,

who were ejected, and had their cabins burnt by Secretary Peters. After the purchase of these lands at Albany, in 1754, both these towns were destroyed, and the Indians went to Ohio.

Lost Creek Valley, unquestionably one of the most beautiful valleys in the Juniata region, was entered by some Indian traders as early as 1740. They found it occupied by two or three Indian settlements, and they made a successful barter with the aborigines. The next year they essayed to revisit the place, but were unable to find it. The following summer they found it again; hence arose the name of the *lost* creek. There is no record of any massacres by the Indians in this valley, and the impression is that they left it about 1754, some going toward the frontier, and others to the head of Tuscarora Valley.

The first settlement on the river, in what now constitutes Juniata county, was made in 1751, by an adventurous Scotch-Irishman known as Captain James Patterson. He came across the country from Cumberland county, accompanied by some five or six others, most of whom settled very near to where Mexico now stands. Patterson was a bold and fearless man; and he had not long resided in his new location before the Indians of the neighborhood both hated and feared him. He and his companions cleared the land on both sides of the river, built two large log-houses, and pierced them with loopholes, so that they might defend themselves from any attacks the savages might make. Patterson soon became aware of the fact that his reckless daring, especially in braving the proclamations of the proprietors in settling upon unpurchased Indian lands, had

inspired the Indians with fear; hence he did not condescend to make an effort to purchase from the Indians, or
even build a fort for the protection of his little colony.
In addition to his recklessness, he possessed a good share
of cunning, that on many occasions served his purpose.
For instance, he used to keep a target, the centre of which
was riddled with bullets, leaning against a tree. Whenever he found a party of friendly Indians approaching, he
used to stand under his door and blaze away at the target,
but always stop when the Indians were near the house.
The Indians would invariably examine the target, measure the distance—about four hundred feet—with the
eye, and conclude among themselves that Patterson would
be an exceedingly tough customer in a fight! His reputation for shooting obtained for him among the Delawares
the name of "Big Shot."

Patterson was a very bold squatter, and staked off for
himself a large body of land, declaring that Providence
had designed it for the use of Christian people to raise
food upon, and not for Indian war-dances. But, with all
his fancied security and his contemptuous opinion of the
"cowardly red-skins," they put him to his trumps at last.
In the year 1755 they no longer visited his settlement on
the friendly mission of bartering furs and venison for rum
and tobacco, but they commenced prowling about in small
parties, painted for war, armed with the rifle—the use of
which they had already acquired—and exceedingly danger-
ous-looking knives and tomahawks. Patterson became
alarmed, and, actuated by a settled conviction that "dis-
cretion" was the better part of valor, himself and his companions crossed the Tuscarora Mountain and took refuge

in Sherman's Valley. A few years after he returned, but he found his land parcelled, and occupied by others, who held deeds of purchase for it from the proprietory government. Nothing daunted, however, he took possession of another piece of land, and commenced cultivating it, without going through the land-office formula of obtaining a legal title for it. He was a man of some intelligence, and held in supreme contempt the Penn family and their treaties with the Indians. He declared that the Albany treaty did not give them a shadow of right to the land; and, as it was not considered morally wrong for the Penns to wheedle the Indians out of millions of acres of land for the paltry sum of £400, he did not see any wrong in his cheating the Penn family out of a farm.

For some years peace and quiet reigned in the neighborhood; but in the spring of 1763 the red man again lifted the hatchet, and the settlers were thrown into awe and consternation. Constant rumors were afloat of their de-predations, and at length a scouting party returned with the unwelcome intelligence that a body of Shawnees were encamped in Tuscarora Valley. As speedily as possible, all the movable effects were placed upon pack-horses, and the settlers, by extremely cautious manœuvering, succeeded in escaping safely, and again took up their residence in Sherman's Valley.

The spring having been exceedingly favorable, the grain crop was ready to cut early in July, and a party was formed by the settlers, and some few others, to go back and assist each other in getting in their harvest. On their arrival they set vigorously to work; and, no traces of savages being perceptible, in their anxiety to get in the grain they appeared to forget them, notwithstanding each man carried with him his trusty rifle wheresoever he went. On Sunday, while resting from their labors, some ten or twelve Shawnee Indians approached the house of William White, where all the settlers were spending the Sabbath. They crawled up to the house unperceived, and fired a volley through the open door, killing Mr. White and wounding some of his family. The wildest consternation seized upon the party within, and, in the great confusion which followed, all escaped by the back-door except William Riddle. Some swam the river; others escaped in different directions. Riddle did not see a son of his, aged about twelve years, escape; and, without probably being conscious of what he was doing, walked toward the front-door, where a savage fired at him. The muzzle of the gun was so near Riddle's face that the discharge literally filled it with gunpowder. The ball grazed, but did not injure him. At the moment the savage discharged his rifle, Riddle was tripped by something upon the floor, and fell. The Indians took it for granted that both were killed, and set up a loud shout of victory. While holding a consultation about their future movements, Riddle jumped up suddenly and ran. Several Indians fired, and for a short distance pursued him; but he soon distanced the fleetest runner among them. The marauders then returned, and, after scalping Mr. White, plundered the house of all the ammunition they could find, some few other trifling articles, and then set fire to it.

On taking their departure from the place, from a high bluff near the house they discovered Riddle's son, who was trying to conceal himself in a rye-field. They captured him and took him along with them. In order to give an account of his captivity, we shall be compelled to defer an account of the further depredations of the same band until the next chapter.

Some years after peace was restored—the precise year not known, but supposed to have been in 1767,—Riddle started for the frontier in search of his son. This was a time of almost profound peace, which followed the numerous massacres of the few preceding years, and a time, too, when the Indians had been taught some severe lessons, and were disposed to act friendly toward the whites. Riddle travelled on horseback, and passed numerous Indian villages, but could hear no tidings of his son until he came upon an encampment of Shawnee Indians near Lake Erie. As he neared the village, he saw the warriors returning from the chase, and among them a youthful-looking brave with an eagle-feather waving on his cap, and all the paraphernalia of a young chief decorating his person. His bearing erect, his step firm, he trod the path with a proud and haughty air. But a single glance sufficed for Riddle to recognise in the youthful warrior his son John. Dismounting from his horse, he sprang forward and attempted to throw himself into his arms; but, strange to say, his *advances were repulsed!* Even when the lad was convinced that he was Riddle's offspring, he refused to go with him, but declared his determination to remain with the tribe.

During the few years that he had been among the sons of the forest, he had most thoroughly imbibed their habits and a strong love for their wild and romantic life. The chase, the woods, the council-fires and the wigwams, the canoe and the dance of the squaws, were enchantment to him, in the enjoyment of which he lost all recollections of home or his parents; and when his father declared that he would use a parent's prerogative to force him to accompany him, young Riddle, almost frantic with despair, called upon his warrior friends to interfere in his behalf. But the Indians, fearful of the consequences that might result from any interference of the kind, acknowledged Riddle's right to reclaim his son, since the red man and the white man had smoked the pipe of peace. It was, therefore, with great reluctance that John Riddle prepared to depart immediately. He took a hasty farewell of his warrior companions, and, mounting behind his father, they turned their faces toward the valley of the Juniata. Mr. Riddle, with commendable zeal and a great deal of prudence, put as much ground between him and the Shawnee village, before nightfall, as possible. He pitched his tent for the night on the edge of a thicket, and partook of some provisions which he had in his saddle-bag; and, after talking for an hour or two, they stretched themselves before the fire to sleep. Young Riddle appeared resigned, and had even conversed gayly and cheerfully with his father; but the old man had his misgivings, and he feared that treachery was hidden beneath this semblance of cheerfulness. The consequence was that he lay awake for hours; but at length the fatigues of the day overcame him, and he sank into a deep sleep, from which he did not awake until the sun was up, and then only to find that his son had fled! The emotions of a father under such circumstances may be imagined, but certainly they cannot well be described. A man of less energy would have given up the object of his mission as hopeless, and returned home.

Not so, however, with Riddle, for he hastened back to the Indian village, and asked the Indians sternly for his son. Unused or unwilling to dissemble, they frankly told him that he was in the council-house, and demanded their protection; that he had eaten, drank, and smoked, with the red man, and that he was unwilling to acknowledge a pale-face as a father or a brother. This highly incensed Riddle, and he declared that if his son were not delivered up to him, he would bring the forces from the nearest fort and exterminate them; and, further, that, if any injury befell him, his friends, who knew his mission, would follow and avenge him. A council was immediately called, and the subject debated. The young warriors of the village were determined that young Riddle should remain among them at all hazards; but the counsel of the older chiefs, who evidently foresaw what would follow, prevailed, and young Riddle was again placed in charge of his father. The old man, profiting by experience, took his son to a frontier fort, and from thence home, reasoning with him all the way on the folly of adopting the life of a savage.

Riddle grew to manhood, and reared a large family in Walker township, all of whom many years ago went to the West. He is represented by Mr. Banks as having been a quiet and inoffensive man, except when he accidentally indulged in the too free use of "*fire-water.*" It was then that all the characteristics of the red man manifested themselves. "On such occasions his eye flashed, and all his actions betokened the wily savage."

CHAPTER V.

THE neighborhood of the mouth of Licking Creek was
settled about 1750. The first settler was Hugh Hardy,
a Scotch-Irishman, who located about a mile from the
mouth of the creek. He was followed by families named
Castner, Wilson, Law, Scott, Grimes, and Sterrit, all
Scotch-Irish, and the last two traders in Indian goods.

At the time of their advent at Licking Creek, the Indians were exceedingly friendly, and pointed out to them
a famous battle-ground near the creek. The oral tradition of the battle preserved by them was as follows:—On
the one side of the creek was a village of the Delawares,
on the other a village of the Tuscaroras. Both tribes
lived in harmony—hunted on the same grounds, seated
themselves around the same council-fires, and smoked in
common the pipe of peace, and danced the green-corn
dance together beneath the pale rays of the mellow harvest-
moon. These amicable relations might have existed for
years, had not a trivial incident brought about a sad rup-

ture. Some Indian children at play on the bank of the creek commenced quarrelling about a grasshopper. High words led to blows. The women of the respective tribes took up their children's quarrel, and in turn the wives' quarrel was taken up by the men. A bloody and most sanguinary battle was the result. The struggle was long and fierce, and hundreds of warriors, women, and children, fell beneath the deadly tomahawk or by the unerring arrow. To this day, relics, such as arrow-heads, pipes, and human bones, are found upon the spot where tradition says the battle occurred. The "grasshopper war" was long held up by the sachems as a terrible warning to any tribe about to embroil itself in a bootless war.

Some historians assert that there was once a fort at the mouth of Licking Creek, called Fort Campbell, all traces of which are now obliterated. Such was not the case. Robert Campbell owned the largest house in the settlement, which was pierced with loopholes for defence similar to that belonging to Patterson. The settlers had also been driven away, and had returned to reap their harvest. On the Sabbath referred to in the preceding chapter, while the harvesters were gathered in the house of Campbell, and immediately after the massacre at Patterson's, the same band of Indians stealthily approached the house of Campbell and fired a volley at the inmates. Several persons were wounded, but there is no authentic record of any one being killed.

James Campbell was shot through the wrist, and taken prisoner. He was taken to the frontier, probably to Lake Erie, and returned in a year or eighteen months afterward. But the particulars attending his captivity were never published, neither could we find any person who knew any thing about the matter further than that he was captured, and returned again to his home.

Immediately after the Indians had discharged their rifles, one of them sprang into the house, and with uplifted tomahawk approached a bed on which a man named George Dodds was resting. Fortunately for Dodds, his rifle was within reach, which he immediately grasped and fired at the savage, wounding him in the groin. The Indian retreated, and Dodds made his way up-stairs, and through an opening in the roof he escaped, went direct to Sherman's Valley, and spread the alarm.

This same band of marauders proceeded up Tuscarora Valley, laying waste the country as they went. In the dusk of the evening, they came to the house of William Anderson. They shot down the old man, who was seated by the table with the open Bible upon his lap, and also killed and scalped his son and a young woman — an adopted daughter of Mr. Anderson. Two brothers named Christy, and a man named Graham, neighbors of Mr. Anderson, hearing the guns firing, conjectured that the Indians had attacked him; and, their own means of defence being inadequate, they fled, and reached Sherman's Valley about midnight. Their arrival spread new terror, and a volunteer force of twelve men was soon raised to go over to the valley to succor the settlers. This force consisted of three brothers named Robinson, John Graham, Charles Elliot, William and James Christy, Daniel Miller, John Elliot, Edward McConnel, William McCallister, and John Nicholson.

Fearing that the savages would murder men engaged

in harvesting farther up the valley, they endeavored to intercept them by crossing through Bigham's Gap early on Monday morning. They had no sooner entered the valley than they discovered traces of the enemy. Houses were pillaged, and some razed to the ground. At one place they had killed four hogs and a number of fowls, which they had roasted by a fire, fared sumptuously and dined leisurely. At Graham's there were unmistakable signs that they had been joined by another party, and that the entire force must number at least twenty-five Indians. From their tracks, too, it was evident that they had crossed the Tuscarora Mountain by way of Run Gap. The dread to encounter such a force would have deterred almost any small body of men; but the Robinsons, who appeared to be leaders of the party, were bold, resolute backwoodsmen, inured to hardship, toil, and danger, and, without taking time to reflect, or even debate, upon the probability of being attacked by the enemy from ambuscade, they pushed forward rapidly to overtake the savages.

At the cross-roads, near Buffalo Creek, the savages fired upon the party from an ambuscade of brush, and killed five. William Robinson was shot in the abdomen with buckshot; still he managed to follow Buffalo Creek for half a mile. John Elliot, a mere lad of seventeen, discharged his rifle at an Indian, and then ran. The Indian pursued him, but, fearing the boy would get off, he dropped his rifle, and followed with tomahawk alone. Elliot, perceiving this, threw some powder into his rifle at random, inserted a ball in the muzzle, and pushed it in as far as he could with his finger; then, suddenly turning around, he shot the Indian in the breast. The Indian gave a prolonged scream, and returned in the direction of his band. There is little doubt but that the Indian was killed; but, agreeably to their custom, his companions either concealed the body or took it with them.

Elliot went but a short distance before he overtook William Robinson, who was weltering in his blood upon the ground, and evidently in the agonies of death. He begged Elliot to carry him off, as he had a great horror of being scalped. Elliot told him it was utterly impossible for him to lift him off the ground, much less carry him. Robinson then said—

"Take my gun, and save yourself. And if ever you have an opportunity to shoot an Indian with it, *in war or peace*, do so, for my sake."

There is no record of the fact that he obeyed the dying injunction of his friend; but he did with the rifle what was more glorious than killing ignorant savages; he carried it for five years in the Continental army, and battled with it for the freedom of his country. How many of his Majesty's red-coats it riddled before the flag of freedom floated over the land, is only known to the God of battles. The body of Robinson was not found by the Indians.

During the action Thomas Robinson stood still, sheltered by a tree, until all his companions had fled. He fired a third time, in the act of which two or three Indians fired, and a bullet shattered his right arm. He then attempted to escape, but was hotly pursued by the Indians, one of whom shot him through the side while in the act of stooping to pass a log. He was found scalped and most shockingly mutilated. John Graham died while sitting upon a log, a short distance from the scene of action. Charles Elliot and McConnel escaped, and crossed Buffalo Creek, but they were overtaken and shot just as they were in the act of ascending the bank. Their bodies were found in the creek.

These bloody murders caused the greatest alarm in the neighborhood. The Indians, flushed with success, manifested no disposition to leave; and the inhabitants of the sparsely-settled country fled toward the lower end of Sherman's Valley, leaving all behind them. A party of forty men, armed and organized and well-disciplined, marched in the direction of the Juniata for the purpose of burying the dead and slaying the Indians; but when they came to Buffalo Creek, they were so terrified at the sight of the slaughtered whites and probably exaggerated stories of the strength of the enemy, that the commander ordered a return. He called it *prudent* to retire ; some of his men called it *cowardly*. The name of the valiant captain could not be ascertained.

Captain Dunning went up the valley from Carlisle with a posse, determined to overtake and punish the savages if possible. Before his arrival, however, some five or six men conceived the rash idea of giving the Indians battle, and attacked them while in a barn. The attack was an exceedingly ill-judged affair, for but few Indians were wounded, and none killed. They bounded out with great fury, and shot the entire party but one, who managed to escape. Those who were killed were Alexander Logan and his son John, Charles Coyle, and William Hamilton. Bartholomew Davis made his escape, and at Logan's house overtook Captain Dunning and his command. Judging that the Indians would visit Logan's for plunder, Captain

Dunning ambuscaded his men, and in a very short time the savages came, boldly, and entirely unconscious of impending danger. They were greeted by a volley from Dunning's men, and but a short engagement followed. Three or four Indians fell at the first fire; and the rest, dismayed, fled in consternation toward the mountain, and were not pursued.

Thus it will be perceived that a large number of most cruel and cold-blooded murders were committed by these marauders before they were checked, simply because in treachery and cunning the white men could not cope with them.

CHAPTER VI.

TUSCARORA VALLEY — ITS EARLY SETTLERS — ITS MOUNDS AND ITS
FORTS — MASSACRES, ETC.

TUSCARORA PATH VALLEY, as it was formerly called, is one of the most fertile and beautiful within the Juniata range. It embraces an extent of probably thirty miles in length, beginning in Franklin county, and ending at the river at Perrysville, in Juniata county. The name of "Path" was given to it in consequence of the old western Indian path running through it nearly its entire length.

Tuscarora, in its day, must have been a famous place for the Indians. Its great natural advantages, and the abundance of game it contained, must alone have rendered it an attractive place, independent of the fact that it was the regular highway between the East and the West, where the warrior, the politician, and the loafer, could lie in the

"Umbrageous grots and caves of cool recess,"

before the wigwam door, and hear from travellers all the news astir worthy of their profound attention.

Tradition, however, speaks of battles among them; for they would fight among themselves, and that, too, with all the relentless fury that characterized their warfare with the whites. But of these battles said to be fought in the valley the tradition is so vague and unsatisfactory that we omit any further mention of them.

There are two mounds in the valley,—one of them near its head, the other some twelve or fourteen miles from its mouth, at or near a place, we believe, now called Academia. Some persons who examined this mound about twenty years ago tried to make it appear that it had been enclosed in a fortification, as they averred that they had discovered fragments of a wall. This was probably a wrong conclusion, as a burial-place would not likely be within a fortification. If the mound was once enclosed within a wall for protection, it was an act that stands without a parallel in Indian history.

Near the lower mound is an academy; and during the last ten years the students used their leisure hours in exhuming the bones and searching for relics, so that by this time, probably, but a mere visible trace of it is left.

The first settlers in Tuscarora were Samuel Bigham, Robert Hagg, and James and John Grey,— all Scotch. They came from Cumberland county about the year 1749, or probably 1750. They were in search of a location for permanent settlement. The valley pleased them so well that they immediately staked out farms; and, notwithstanding the Indians of the valley treated them with apparent hospitality, they took the precaution to build themselves a fort for defence, which was named Bigham's Fort. By the year 1754 several other persons had settled in Tuscarora, among them George Woods and a man named Innis.

Some time in the spring of 1756, John Grey and Innis went to Carlisle with pack-horses, for the purpose of procuring groceries. On their return, while descending the mountain, in a very narrow defile, Grey's horse, frightened at a bear which crossed the road, became unmanageable and threw him off. Innis, anxious to see his wife and family, went on; but Grey was detained for nearly two hours in righting his pack. As far as his own personal safety was concerned, the detention was a providential one, for he just reached the fort in time to see the last of it consumed. Every person in it had either been massacred or taken prisoners by the Indians. He examined the charred remains of the bodies inside of the fort, but he could find none that he could bring himself to believe were those of his family. It subsequently appeared that his wife and his only daughter, three years of age, George Woods, Innis's wife and three children, and a number of others, had been carried into captivity. They were taken across the Alleghany to the old Indian town of Kittaning, and from thence to Fort Duquesne, where they were delivered over to the French.

Woods was a remarkable man, and lived to a good old age, and figured somewhat extensively afterward in the history of both Bedford and Alleghany counties. He took his captivity very little to heart, and even went so far as to propose marriage to Mrs. Grey while they were both prisoners in the fort.

The French commander, in apportioning out the prisoners, gave Woods to an old Indian named John Hutson, who removed him to his own wigwam. But George proving neither useful nor ornamental to Hutson's establishment, and as there was no probability of any of his friends paying a ransom for him—inasmuch as he had neither kith nor kin,—he opened negotiations with George to let him off. The conditions made and entered into between the two were that the aforesaid George Woods should give to the aforesaid John Hutson an annuity of ten pounds of tobacco, until death should terminate the existence of either of the parties named. This contract was fulfilled until the massacre of the Bedford scout, when Harry Woods, a lieutenant of the scout, and son of George Woods, recognised among the most active of the savages the son of John Hutson, who used to accompany his father to Bedford, where Harry Woods had often seen him. It is hardly necessary to add that old Hutson never called upon Woods after that for his ransom annuity.

Woods was a surveyor by profession, and assisted in laying out the city of Pittsburg, one of the principal streets of which bears his name, or, at least, was named after him, notwithstanding it is called "Wood" instead of Woods street.

Mr. Woods, after he removed to Bedford, became a useful and influential citizen. He followed his profession, and most of the original surveys in the upper end of the Juniata Valley were made by him. He reared a large family, and his descendants are still living. One of his daughters was married to Ross, who was once a candidate for the office of governor of the State. He lived to a good old age, and died amid the deep regrets of a most extended circle of acquaintances.

Mrs. Grey and her daughter were given to some Indians, who took them to Canada. In the ensuing fall

John Grey joined Colonel Armstrong's expedition against Kittaning, in hopes of recapturing, or at least gaining some intelligence of, his family. Failing to do this, he returned home, broken in health and spirits, made his will, and died. The will divided the farm between his wife and daughter, in case they returned from captivity. If the daughter did not return, a sister was to have her half.

About a year after the fort was burnt, Mrs. Grey, through the connivance of some traders, managed to escape from bondage, and reached her home in safety, but, unfortunately, was compelled to leave her daughter behind her. She proved her husband's will and took charge of the property. The treaty of 1764 brought a large number of captive children to Philadelphia to be recognised and claimed by their friends. Mrs. Grey attended, in hopes of finding her child; but she was unsuccessful. There remained one child unclaimed, about the same age as Mrs. Grey's; and some person, who evidently knew the provisions of the will, hinted to her the propriety of taking the child to save the property. She did so, and in the year 1789, the heirs of the sister, having received some information as to the identity of the child, brought suit for the land. The trial was a novel one, and lasted from 1789 to 1834, a period of forty-five years, when it was decided in favor of the heirs and against the captive.

Innis remained among the Indians until the treaty. His wife escaped a short time previous. Two of her children she recovered in Philadelphia, but a third had been drowned by the savages on their way to some place in Canada. By the exposure it became sick and very weak, and, to rid themselves of any further trouble with it, they put it under the ice. When the captive children were at Philadelphia, some person had taken one of Innis's, and he had considerable difficulty to recover it. Had it not been for a private mark by which he proved it, the person who had it in charge would probably never have surrendered it.

The Indians of Tuscarora, before the French war, were on terms of great intimacy with the whites. They used to meet at the fort, and shoot mark, and, when out of lead, would go to the mouth of the valley, and return with lead ore, almost pure. Lead was a valuable article, and difficult to transport; hence the settlers were anxious to discover the location of the mine. Many a warrior was feasted and liquored until he was blind drunk, under a promise of divulging the precise whereabouts of the lead mine. Its discovery, if it contained any quantity of ore, would have realized any man a speedy fortune in those days; but, in spite of Indian promises and the most thorough search for years, the lead mines of Tuscarora were never found, and probably never will be until it is occupied by another race of cunning Indians.

The fort burnt down in 1756 was rebuilt some four years afterward, through the exertions of Ralph Sterrit, an old Indian trader. His son William was born in Bigham's Fort, and was the first white child born in Tuscarora Valley. At the time of burning the first fort, Sterrit was absent with his family.

It is related of Ralph Sterrit, that, one day, while sitting outside of the second fort, a wayworn Indian came along, who was hungry, thirsty, and fatigued. Sterrit was a humane man, and called the savage in, gave him bread and meat, a drink of rum, and some tobacco, and sent him on his way rejoicing.

The circumstance had entirely passed out of Sterrit's mind, when, one night in the spring of 1763, when the Indians had again commenced hostilities, the inmates of the fort were alarmed by a noise at the gate. Sterrit looked out, and by the light of the moon discovered that it was an Indian. The alarm was spread, and some of the more impetuous were for shooting him down as a spy. Sterrit, more cool than the others, demanded of the Indian his business. The Indian, in few words, reminded him of the circumstance above narrated, and for the hospitality extended to him he had come to warn the white man of impending danger. He said that the Indians were as "plenty as pigeons in the woods," and that even then they had entered the valley, and, before another moon, would be at the fort, carrying with them the firm determination to murder, scalp, and burn, all the whites in their path. The alarm was sounded, and it was soon determined, in consequence of the weakness of the fort, to abandon it. Nearly all the settlers of the valley were in it; but the number stated by the savage completely overawed them, so that they set to work immediately packing upon horses their most valuable effects, and long before daylight were on their way to Cumberland county.

The Indians came next night, and, after reconnoitering for a long time, approached the fort, which, much to their astonishment, they found evacuated. However, to show the settlers that they had been there, they burnt down the fort, and, on a cleared piece of ground in front of it, they

laid across the path a war-club painted red—a declaration
of war to the death against the whites.

The benevolent act of Sterrit, in relieving the weary
and hungry Indian, was the means of saving the lives of
eighty persons.

CHAPTER VII.

FORT GRANVILLE—OLD INDIAN TOWN—THE EARLY SETTLERS—CAP-
TAIN JACOBS—ASSAULT ON AND CAPTURE OF THE FORT.

PREVIOUS to the settlement by the whites, the flat on
which the eastern part of Lewistown now stands was an
Indian town of considerable importance. It was the outlet of a large and fertile valley, through which ran a northwestern Indian path, and in which dwelt five or six tribes,
who found this the natural outlet to the Juniata. The
council-house stood upon the east side of the creek, near its
mouth, and the line of wigwams stretched toward the north.

The first white settlers in this neighborhood came from
the Conecocheague, by way of Aughwick. They consisted of Arthur Buchanan and his two sons, and three
other families, all Scotch-Irish. Buchanan was a man of
great energy, and very fond of roving in the woods, far
from the haunts of men. He was the master-spirit of the
party, and with great self-reliance pitched his tent opposite
the Indian village, on the west bank of the creek. He
then called upon the Indians, and signified his intention
to purchase land. They were at first unwilling to sell;
but Captain Jacobs, (as Buchanan christened the chief, in
consequence of his close resemblance to a burly German in
Cumberland county,) who was the head chief, having been

liberally plied with liquor, decided that Buchanan should have the much-coveted land.   What was paid for it never transpired, but it is more than probable that the remainder of the contents of Buchanan's rum-keg, a few trinkets, and some tobacco, made him owner of the soil. This was in 1754.

Captain Jacobs had always professed great friendship toward the British colonists; but he was among the very first won over by the French.   He became very much dissatisfied with Buchanan, more especially as the latter had induced a number of his friends and acquaintances to come there and settle.   By this means the lands of Jacobs were encroached upon, which greatly roused his temper; and one day, without deigning to give an explanation of any kind, the Indians destroyed their town and left.   This was a movement the settlers did not understand; neither did they like it, for it seemed to forebode no good.   After a very brief consultation among them, they resolved forthwith to build a fort for protection.   They had for a time noticed a growing coldness on the part of Jacobs and his warriors, and, fearful that they might come down the valley, joined by other bands, and massacre the people, Fort Granville was erected with as much despatch as possible.   It was located about a mile above Lewistown, in order to be near a large spring.   Contrary to expectations, the Indians did not come, and things generally prospered about Fort Granville settlement during the summer and winter of 1755.   In the spring of 1756 the Indians made their appearance in Kishicoquillas Valley, in considerable numbers; and parties of roving tribes in search of scalps and plunder, emboldened by the success of the French and Indians the year previous, sometimes came down to the mouth of the creek, but, unable to ascertain the power of resistance concentrated within the fort, they never made an attack upon it. These incursions, however, became so frequent, that in the summer of 1756 the settlers only left the fort when necessity demanded it. Finally, succor reached them in July. The government despatched Lieutenant Armstrong from Cumberland county with a militia force to protect them while engaged in taking in their harvest, and, directly after his arrival, hearing of the exposed condition of the people in Tuscarora, Armstrong sent a portion of his command, with Lieutenant Faulkner, in order to guard them while reaping their grain.

In the absence of the latter, on or about the 22d of July, (the Indians having ascertained the strength of the garrison,) some sixty or seventy warriors, painted and equipped for battle, appeared before the fort and insolently challenged the settlers to combat. The commander pretended to treat the challange with contempt, though in truth he was considerably alarmed at the prospect of an attack. The Indians fired at one man, and wounded him. He happened to be outside, but got into the fort without sustaining any serious injury. The Indians divided themselves into small parties and started off in different directions. One of these parties killed a man named Baskins, a short distance from the river, burnt his house, and carried his wife and children into captivity. Another party took Hugh Carrol and his family prisoners.

On the 30th of July, Captain Edward Ward had command of Fort Granville, with a company regularly en-

listed and in the pay of the province. He went, with all
of his men but twenty-four, to Sherman's Valley, to protect the settlers while harvesting. The enemy soon
ascertained this, and on the first of August, according to
the affidavit of John Hogan, then and there taken
prisoner, (Colonial Records, vol. vii. p. 561,) one hundred
Indians and fifty Frenchmen made an attack upon the
fort. They assaulted the works during the entire afternoon and part of the night without gaining any advantage. About midnight the enemy got below the bank of
the river, and by a deep ravine they approached close
enough to the fort to set fire to it before they were
observed. The fire soon spread, and through an aperture made the Indians shot Lieutenant Armstrong, and
wounded some two or three others who were endeavor-
ing to put out the fire. The French commander ordered
a suspension of hostilities, and offered quarter to all who
would surrender, on several occasions; but Armstrong
would not surrender on any condition. He was certainly
a brave man, and held out nobly almost against hope.
Peter Walker, who was in the fort at the time and taken
prisoner, after his escape from Kittaning gave an account
of the capture of the fort to General John Armstrong.
He said that "of the enemy not less than one hundred
and twenty returned, all in health, except one Frenchman,
shot through the shoulder by Lieutenant Armstrong, a
little before his death, as the Frenchman was erecting his
body out of the hollow to throw pine-knots on the fire
made against the fort; and of this number there were
about a dozen of French, who had for their interpreter
one McDowell, a Scotchman."

There appears to be a discrepancy between the statements of Hogan and Walker in regard to the number engaged in the assault, but it is quite likely that the latter's estimate is correct.

General Armstrong, in his letter to Robert Hunter Morris, goes on to say:—

This McDowell told Walker they designed very soon to attack Fort Shirley with four hundred men. Captain Jacobs said he could take any fort that would catch fire, and would make peace with the English when they had learned him to make gunpowder. McDowell told Walker they had two Indians killed in the engagement; but Captains Armstrong and Ward, whom I ordered on their march to Fort Shirley to examine every thing at Granville and send a list of what remained among the ruins, assure me that they found some parts of eight of the enemy burnt, in two different places, the joints of them being scarcely separated; and part of their shirts found, through which there were bullet-holes. To secrete these from the prisoners was doubtless the reason why the French officer marched our people some distance from the fort before he gave orders to burn the barracks, &c. Walker says that some of the Germans flagged very much on the second day, and that the lieutenant behaved with the greatest bravery to the last, despising all the terrors and threats of the enemy whereby they often urged him to surrender. Though he had been near two days without water, but little ammunition left, the fort on fire, and the enemy situate within twelve or fourteen yards of the fort, under the natural bank, he was as far from yielding as when at first attacked. A Frenchman in our service, fearful of being burned up, asked leave of the lieutenant to treat with his countrymen in the French language. The lieutenant answered, " The first word of French you speak in this engagement, I'll blow your brains out!" telling his men to hold out bravely, for the flame was falling, and he would soon have it extinguished; but he soon after received the fatal ball. Col. Rec., vol. vii. p. 232.

Directly after Armstrong fell, a man named Turner

opened the gates and admitted the enemy. A soldier named Brandon, who had been shot through the knee, approached the French, told them he was a Roman Catholic, and would go with them. His faith, however, availed him little; for, as soon as it was discovered that he was not in marching condition, one of the Indians clove his skull with a tomahawk.

The soldiers, who loved their lieutenant, asked permission to bury him; but the inhuman French officer refused, although they offered to do it in a very few minutes where they had raised clay to stay the progress of the flames.

The Indians were under the command of Captain Jacobs and Shingas, but the name of the gallant French officer has not been preserved.

The prisoners taken were twenty-two soldiers, three women, and several children. For fear of being overtaken by the provincial forces, they made forced marches to Kittaning. When they arrived there, they pitched upon Turner to make a terrible example of. In front of the council-house they planted a stake painted black, and to this they tied him; and, after having heated several old gun-barrels red-hot, they danced around him, and, every minute or two, seared and burned his flesh. Without knowing but what such might be their own fate, the prisoners were compelled to look at the heart-rending sight, and listen to the shrieks and groans of the victim, without daring to utter a word. After tormenting him almost to death, the Indians scalped him, and then held up an Indian lad, who ended his sufferings by laying open his skull with a hatchet.

Some of the prisoners made their escape, and others were restored to their friends; but some few of the soldiers were never heard of again, having probably shared the fate of Turner.

One of the prisoners, named Girty, returned in a wounded condition. When he escaped, he was followed by two Indians to the head-waters of Blacklick, where they attempted to re-capture him; but in the fight that followed he slew one of the Indians, and the other ran. He scalped the one he killed, and took his scalp to Aughwick. The women and children were recovered, by the first exchange of prisoners that took place, in 1757.

7

CHAPTER VIII.

ORGANIZATION OF MIFFLIN COUNTY — DISPUTE WITH HUNTINGDON
COUNTY ABOUT THE BOUNDARY LINE—RIOT IN LEWISTOWN, ETC.

[NOTE.—It was not the author's original intention to publish any thing
of modern occurrence in the Juniata Valley, but to confine himself exclu-
sively to its early history; but several friends in Lewistown made a particular request that we should insert an account of the dispute arising
from the boundary question, and the riot of 1791. The latter has been
repeatedly published. Still, as it occurred sixty-four years ago, and few, if
any, living witnesses of the occurrence are to be found, it may be as well
to preserve the record.]

SHORTLY after Mifflin county was formed, in 1789, an
attempt was made to run the boundary line,— a proceeding which gave rise to great excitement and came very
near ending in riot and bloodshed. The bone of contention was a strip of disputed territory claimed by both
Huntingdon and Mifflin counties; and we are under the
impression that a majority of those residing in the territory in dispute favored the Mifflin county cause. They
were mostly Irish; and, since the wars were over and no
enemy to fight, were ever ready, with true Irish *hospitality*, to take a brush with their neighbors. Accordingly,
when the sheriff of Huntingdon came into the disputed
territory to serve a process upon a man, a party congre-

SCENE ON THE RIVER BELOW M'VEYTOWN.

gated at an Irish tavern, and, lying in wait for the sheriff, arrested and carried him to Lewistown and committed him to jail. He sued out a *habeas corpus*, and the judge discharged him. Filled with wrath, the sheriff went home swearing vengeance. He soon summoned a posse in Huntingdon, for the avowed purpose of taking his man at all hazards, and proceeded to the disputed territory. The people, aware of his coming, fired signal guns, and soon met in great numbers. The sheriff and his posse fortunately took a different route, which alone prevented riot and bloodshed. The boundary question was soon after settled amicably.

The riot of 1791, however, was a more serious affair. It will be remembered that in those days the military spirit in the Juniata Valley ran very high, though we are free to acknowledge that it has sadly degenerated since then. A gentleman named Bryson had been appointed an Associate Judge by the governor. Previous to his appointment, he held the office of Brigade Inspector; and, in his official capacity, refused to commission two colonels elected by their regiments, but in their stead commissioned two men of his own selection. This he had a right to do under the existing militia law; nevertheless, the men composing the regiments looked upon it as a most unwarrantable assumption of power in thus setting at defiance the expressed will of the majority, and they resolved that Judge Bryson should not enjoy his office. The following copy of a letter published in a paper in York, Pennsylvania, from the district attorney, is a full history of the case:

On Monday, the 12th of September, 1791, the Hon. W. Brown, James Bryson, and James Armstrong, Esquires, met in the forenoon, in order to open the court and proceed to business; but Thomas Beale, Esq., one of the associate judges, not having arrived, their honors waited until three o'clock in the afternoon; at which time he arrived, and was requested to proceed with them and the officers of the court to the court-house. He declined going, and the procession moved on to the court-house, where the judges' commissions were read, the court opened, and the officers and the attorneys of the court sworn in, and the court adjourned till ten o'clock next morning.

About nine o'clock, while preparing business to lay before the grand-jury, I received information that a large body of men were assembled below the Long Narrows, at David Jordan's tavern, on the Juniata, and were armed with guns, swords, and pistols, with an avowed intention to proceed to Lewistown and seize Judge Bryson on the bench, and drag him from his seat, and march him off before them, and otherwise ill-treat him. This information was instantly communicated to Messrs. Brown, Bryson, and Armstrong, the judges, who agreed with me that Samuel Edminton, Esq., the prothonotary, Judge Beale, —— Stewart, Esq., —— Bell, Esq., should, with George Wilson, Esq., the sheriff of Mifflin county, proceed and meet the riotors. And the sheriff was commanded to inquire of them their object and intention; and, if hostile, to order them to disperse, and tell them that the court was not alarmed at their proceedings.

Two hours after this the court opened, and a grand-jury was impanelled. A fife was heard playing, and some guns fired, and immediately the mob appeared, marching toward the court-house, with three men on horseback in front, having the gentlemen that had been sent to meet them under guard in the rear; all of whom, on their arrival at Lewistown, they permitted to go at large, except the sheriff, whom four of their number kept a guard over. The court ordered me, as the representative of the commonwealth, to go and meet them, remonstrate against their proceedings, and warn them of their danger; which order was obeyed. But all endeavors were in vain, the mob crying out, "March on! march on! draw your sword on him! ride over him!" I seized the reins of the bridle that the principal commander held, viz., —— Wilson, Esq., brother of the sheriff aforesaid, who was well mounted and well dressed, with a sword, and, I think, two pistols belted around him; a cocked-hat, and one or two feathers in it. He said he would not desist, but at all events proceed and take Judge Bryson off the bench, and march him down to the Narrows, to the judge's farm, and make him sign a written paper that he would never sit there as a judge again.

The mob still crying out, "March on! march on!" he drew his sword, and told me he must hurt me unless I would let go the reins. The crowd pushed forward and nearly pressed me down; one of them, as I learned afterward, a nephew of Judge Beale, presented his pistol at my breast, with a full determination to shoot me. I let the reins go, and walked before them until I arrived at the stairs on the outside of the court-house, when Judge Armstrong met me, and said, "Since nothing else will do, let us defend the stairs." We instantly ascended, and Mr. Hamilton, and the gentlemen of the bar, and many citizens; and the rioters, headed by William Wilson, Colonel Walker, and Colonel Holt, came forward, and the general cry was, "March on, damn you; proceed and take him!" Judge Armstrong replied, "You damned rascals, come on; we will defend the court and ourselves; and before you shall take Judge Bryson you shall kill me and many others, which seems to be your intention, and which you may do!" At this awful moment, one Holt seized Judge Armstrong by the arm with intent to pull him down the stairs, but he extricated himself. Holt's brother then got a drawn sword and put it into his hands, and damned him to run the rascal through; and Wilson drew his sword on me with great rage, and young Beale his sword, and cocked his pistol, and presented it. I told them they might kill me, but the judge they could not, nor should they take him; and the words "fire away!" shouted through the mob. I put my hand on his shoulder, and begged him to consider where he was, who I was, and reflect but for a moment. I told him to withdraw the men, and appoint any two or three of the most respectable of his people to meet me in half an hour and try to settle the dispute. He agreed, and with difficulty got them away from the court-house. Mr. Hamilton then went with me to Mr. Alexander's tavern, and in Wilson and Walker came, and also Sterrett; who I soon discovered to be their chief counsellor.

Proposals were made by me that they should return home, offer no insult to Judge Bryson or the court, and prefer to the governor a decent petition, stating their grievances, (if they had any,) that might be laid before the legislature; and that, in the mean time, the judge should not sit on the bench of this court. They seemed agreed, and our mutual honor to be pledged; but Sterrett, who pretended not to be concerned, stated that great delay would take place, that injuries had been received which demanded instant redress, and objected to the power of the governor as to certain points proposed. At this moment young Beale and Holt came up, the former with arms, and insisted on Wilson's joining them, and broke up the conference. I followed, and on the field, among the rioters, told Wilson, "Your object is that Judge Bryson leave the bench and not sit on it this court." He and Walker said "Yes." "Will you promise to disperse and go home, and offer him no insult?" He said, "Yes;" and our mutual honor was then pledged for the performance of this agreement.

Mr. Hamilton proceeded to the court, told the judge, and he left his seat and retired. I scarce had arrived until the fife began to play, and the whole of the rioters came on to the court-house, then headed by Wilson. I met them at the foot of the stairs, and told them the judge was gone, in pursuance of the agreement, and charged them with a breach of the word and forfeiture of honor; and Walker said it was so, but he could not prevail on them. Wilson said he would have the judge, and attempted going up the stairs. I prevented him, and told him he should not, unless he took off his military accoutrements. He said he had an address to present, and complied with my request, and presented it, signed "The People." Young Beale, at the moment I was contending with Wilson, cocked and presented his pistol at my breast, and insisted that Wilson and all of them should go; but on my offering to decide it by combat with him, he declined it; and by this means they went off swearing, and said that they were out-generalled.

The next day, Colonel M'Farland, with his regiment, came down and offered to defend the court, and addressed it; the court answered, and stated that there was no occasion, and thanked him.

Judge Bryson read a paper, stating the ill-treatment he received, and mentioned that no fear of danger prevented him from taking and keeping his seat; but that he understood an engagement had been entered into by his friends that he should not, and on that account only he was prevented. The court adjourned until two o'clock that day, and were proceeding to open it, with the sheriff, coroner, and constable in front, when they observed that Judge Beale was at the house of one Con. They halted, and requested the sheriff to wait on him and request him to walk with them. He returned, and said the judge would not walk or sit with Bryson, and addressed Judge Bryson with warmth, who replied to it in a becoming manner. The sheriff struck at him, and kicked also. Judge Armstrong seized the sheriff, and commanded the peace, and took the sheriff's rod from him; the coroner took his place, and the sheriff was brought up before the court. I moved he might be committed to gaol; and his mittimus being writen and signed, the court ordered the coroner and gaoler to take him, and he submitted. The court adjourned. After night the drum beat, and Holt collected about seventy men, who repeatedly huzzaed, crying out "liberty or death;" and he offered to rescue the sheriff, but the sheriff refused. At ten o'clock at night I was informed expresses were sent down the Narrows, to collect men to rescue the sheriff, and Major Edmiston informed me he was sorry for his conduct, and offered to beg the court's pardon and to enter into recognisance. I communicated this to the Judges Brown and Armstrong, and requested they would write to the gaoler to permit him to come down. They did, and the sheriff came with Major Edmiston, begged pardon of every member of the court but Judge Bryson, who was not present, and entered into recognisance to appear at next sessions.

The next day near three hundred were assembled below the Narrows, and I prevailed on some gentlemen to go down and disperse them; and upon being assured the sheriff was out of gaol, they returned to their respective homes, and the court have finished all business. Nothing further requiring the attendance of the grand-jury, the court dismissed them and broke up. I must not omit to inform that Judge Beale had declared, during the riot, in court, that he would not sit on the bench with Judge Bryson, and that both he and said Stewart appeared to countenance the rioters, and are deeply concerned.

I must now close the narrative with saying that, owing to the spirit and firmness of Judge Armstrong and the whole of the bar, I was enabled to avert the dreadful blow aimed at Judge Bryson, and to keep order and subordination in court; and unless the most vigorous measures are exerted soon, it will be impossible ever to support the laws of the State in that county, or punish those who dare transgress.

The excise law is execrated by the banditti; and, from every information, I expect the collection of the revenue will be opposed.

I am happy to add, the dispute, which originated by a mistake, between Huntingdon and Mifflin counties, is happily closed in the most amicable manner, without any prosecution in Mifflin.

I am, sir, your most obedient,

JOHN CLARK, Dy. St. Attorney.

To THOMAS SMITH, *Esq., President of the Court of Mifflin county.*

The following is another account of the affair, and evidently written by a friend of the offending judge:—

Carlisle, September 21.

At a period when the general voice of the people proclaims the excellence of the Federal Government, and the State of Pennsylvania in particular is anticipating every blessing from a Constitution so conformable to it, an alarming sedition, together with a most daring turbulent temper, has unhappily manifested itself in the county of Mifflin.

The Governor has lately appointed Samuel Bryson, Esquire, second Associate Judge of the Court of Common Pleas of that county. This gentleman, having been Lieutenant of the county of Mifflin, had excited the determined enmity of two men who were ambitious of being colonels of militia, and against the commissioning of whom (as unfit persons) Mr. Bryson, as County Lieutenant, had made representations. Enraged at the promotion of Judge Bryson, and unhappily yielding to the impulse of the most unjustifiable passions, one William Wilson, brother to the sheriff of Mifflin county, and one David Walker, levied a considerable force, and marched at the head of about forty armed men, with a fife playing, to Lewistown, with the avowed determination to seize upon the person of Judge Bryson whilst on the bench, drag him from thence, oblige him to resign his commission, and compel him to march many miles along the rugged Narrows of Juniata River.

Secresy marked this unexampled treasonable riot. It was not known at Lewistown until about an hour before the insurgents appeared. Justice Stuart, who had been lately commissioned, and who is a very worthy man, had been imprisoned in the morning by four men who belonged to the party of the rioters. They attempted to make him engage his word that he would not give information; but he refused. Ignorant of the private movers of this daring and turbulent procedure, it was agreed by Judges Brown and Armstrong, and other gentlemen, to request the sheriff of the county and Judge Beale, who were presumed to have influence over them, together with the prothonotary of the county, to represent the illegality and imprudence of their conduct, and prevail on them if possible, to return. No advantage has been derived from this step. Mr. Edmiston, the prothonotary, was insulted; the sheriff was taken into a mock imprisonment; and Judge Beale soon after adopted a part which evinced that little real exertion could have been expected from him in quieting this disturbance.

The court was sitting when this armed force, levying war against the State, with a fife playing, marched resolutely forward. At this juncture Judge Bryson asked Judge Beale if it was not likely they would stop; to which the other replied that they never would whilst such a rascal sat upon the bench.

Mr. Clark and Mr. Hamilton, two attorneys of the court, at the desire of some of the judges, remonstrated with Mr. Wilson, who was on horseback and within a few paces of the court-house, at the head of the troops, respecting his conduct. Mr. Wilson was dressed in a military style, with a cockade in his hat, and was armed with a horseman's sword and pistols. He declared his intention was to oblige Mr. Bryson to resign his commission and go down the Narrows with him and his men. He was warned by the gentlemen of the danger of the attempt; he observed that nothing would divert him from his purpose, and immediately drew his sword and marched to storm the court-room, where Judge Armstrong and others were stationed at the door. The two gentlemen who had addressed Wilson ran to the steps in front of the force, where they found a number of persons on the stairs. The rioters followed, with a cry of "Liberty or Death!" Mr. Armstrong halloed out repeatedly, "Villains, come on, but you shall first march over my dead body before you enter." This resolution, seconded by the circumstance of the gentlemen above mentioned, and a number of other persons, keeping their ground on the stairs, (although once or twice some called to the rioters to fire,) seemed to stagger the resolution of

Wilson. At this moment a gentleman proposed to him that if he would disarm, he might have admittance into the court-room. To this he seemed immediately to accede. The troops were filed off to a short distance. It was then agreed that a meeting should take place in half an hour with the leaders of the party. Messrs. Clark and Hamilton, with the assent of some members of the court, met Messrs. William Wilson, David Walker, and William Sterrett, who appeared on behalf of the rioters. Entertaining hopes of preserving the person of Mr. Bryson from injury, it was thought prudent to promise, if the party would disperse, that Mr. Bryson would not sit during that week on the bench. During this conference, Mr. Wilson offered no other charge against Mr. Bryson but what respected the militia commissions for him and Mr. Walker; but it was not until after much discourse that the leaders of the troops could be convinced that an extorted resignation would not avail. When they saw the futility of this idea, it was long insisted that Mr. Bryson should go with them down the Narrows.

Mr. Wilson, in contravention of the agreement, marched the troops to the court-house. In the meantime, Judge Bryson had sent for a horse and effected his escape. It was then Mr. William Sterrett exclaimed, with an oath, " We are out-generalled !"

An address was presented by Mr. Wilson to the court, who went in unarmed, signed "The People." It was in the handwriting, as is supposed, of Mr. Sterrett. It congratulated the other judges upon their appointments, but mentioned and avowed their design in coming armed to the court to force the dismission of Judge Bryson. Mr. Beale, one of the most active of the rioters, armed with a sword and pistols slung around him, wished to force his way into the court-room, but was prevented by Mr. Clark. Four armed men surrounded the person of the sheriff. Under this delusive imprisonment, all intercourse of conversation with him was prohibited. In the evening, the rioters departed in a turbulent, straggling manner, generally intoxicated. At night, one Corran, who had been very active in raising men, was drowned, together with his horse, in a mill-dam, about one mile and a half from the town.

About twelve or one o'clock the next day, Judge Bryson returned. Soon afterward, Col. James McFarland, with about seventy militia on horseback, appeared in support of the court and the laws. At three o'clock, Judges Brown, Bryson, and Armstrong, preceded by the sheriff, prepared to open the court. The sheriff was sent with a message to Judge Beale, informing him that the judges waited for him to join them in proceeding to the courthouse. His reply was that he would not go whilst Mr. Bryson was with them. The judges had not walked more than a few paces, followed by the attorneys and citizens, when the sheriff, with his rod of office in his hand, suddenly stopped, and demanded of Mr. Bryson if he had said any thing injurious of him. Mr. Bryson made a very moderate reply; notwithstanding, he was immediately assaulted by the sheriff, and received a kick in the same leg which had been shattered by a ball at the battle of Germantown. The sheriff was immediately taken into custody. The coroner received the sheriff's rod, and undertook to go before the judges to court. There the sheriff refused to give any recognisance for his appearance at the next court, and was therefore committed to jail.

Colonel McFarland presented an address to the judges on behalf of himself and the militia under his command, mentioning his abhorrence of the proceedings which had taken place, and offering, at the hazard of their lives, to protect the court. To which the following answer was returned:—

"The judges of the Court of Common Pleas of the county of Mifflin are very sensible of the laudable zeal of Colonel McFarland and the militia now under arms, subject to his command, in support of the laws and government of Pennsylvania, and particularly for the purpose of protecting this court from injury and insult. They trust that the daring mob who, being armed, assembled yesterday and assaulted the court, threatening the lives of the members, are now too conscious of the magnitude of their offence and the spirit of the citizens of this county to repeat their attack. Measures are preparing to vindicate the dignity of our insulted laws, and to bring to a just punishment the atrocious offenders and their abettors, who have brought disgrace upon the county and trampled upon the most sacred rights of the community. The court, therefore, sir, return you thanks for the support which you and the militia under your command have with so much alacrity brought to the aid of the administration of justice in this county; but being of opinion that all danger from these infatuated men has ceased, we do not think it necessary that your attendance should be longer continued."

After which Judge Bryson, standing at the bar, spoke the following words :—

"Fellow-citizens :—It is not my intention to resume my seat on the bench during this term. I do not decline it from any apprehension of the mob who yesterday assaulted the court and marked me for their vengeance. Supported by my country, by every virtuous citizen, and a consciousness of my integrity, I have nothing to fear; but understanding that some gentlemen, anxious for my personal safety, entered into an engagement with the leaders of the banditti that I should not sit as judge during this court, my respect for these gentlemen is my sole and only motive for making this declaration."

Colonel McFarland, after this, thanked the militia in the following terms :—

"Colonel McFarland returns his thanks to the militia of his regiments who now attend in support of the laws of their country. He is particularly indebted to Captain Robert Johnston and Captain John Brown, for their extraordinary vigilance in collecting the men of their respective companies upon a notice given to them so late as last night after twelve o'clock. He has no doubt but that the same zeal which has distinguished the militia under his command upon this occasion will always be as honorably manifested, should this county ever be so unhappy as to be disgraced by a similar necessity."

Soon after which, the militia, having been discharged by the court, returned home.

The evening of the day was replete with alarms. One Holt, who thought he had cause of complaint respecting a militia commission, assembled a body of men to the amount of about forty. They paraded a considerable time with sound of drum. At length, at eight o'clock, they appeared before the prison-door, with an intention to break it and enlarge the sheriff. Mr. Sterrett then appeared, and informed them that the sheriff thanked his friends for their intention to serve him, but this is not a proper period; or words to that effect.

About nine o'clock, several persons, having long applied to the sheriff without success, prevailed on him at length to give a recognisance to appear at the next court to answer for the assault and battery on Judge Bryson. Happily, the sheriff, in this instance, relinquished a system which was collecting new horrors and threatened to involve in new scenes of guilt a number of the inhabitants. Great numbers in Tuscarora Valley and its vicinity prepared the following day to march and liberate the sheriff, and probably to demolish the court-house and prison. The news of his release arrived in time to stop the progress of those infatuated men, who appear to have lost sight of the social compact, and whose felicity seems to lie in scenes of tumult, disorder, and licentiousness. It is to be hoped, however, that government, when it comes to enforce the laws, will contemplate the ignorance and delusion of these unfortunate men, and that mercy will so far temper the prosecution as that it will not be extended to a capital charge ; yet it is indispensably necessary that they be taught that genuine liberty consists in the power of doing every thing which is not prohibited by the laws, and that the exercise of an unbounded licentiousness which threatens the dissolution of society itself must receive a punishment in some degree commensurate to the greatness of the offence.

How far Mr. Bryson's representations to the governor against Messrs. Wilson, Walker, and Holt, have been founded in a just estimate of the characters of these men, cannot be elucidated here; but it would appear to afford the highest evidence of its propriety that they were the principals in this most unexampled riot.

CHAPTER IX.

KISHICOQUILLAS VALLEY—THE SHAWNEE CHIEF KISHICOKELAS—THE
MINGO CHIEF LOGAN.

AMONG the many valleys composing the Juniata Valley, or, indeed, among all the fine and productive valleys of the State, few, if any, can surpass Kishicoquillas. Its outlet is at Lewistown, from whence it stretches west a distance of nearly thirty miles, varying in breadth from two to four miles.

After the treaty of Fort Stanwix, the whites returned to the neighborhood of Granville, and some of them commenced exploring the valley. The land was then included in what was termed the new purchase, and was in the market. The land-office was opened in 1769, and the first actual settler in the valley was Judge Brown.

Old Kishicokelas was a Shawnee chief, on terms of friendship with the whites. With the Buchanans he was very intimate, and gave them early intimation of the impending danger, which enabled them to escape. While the Delawares and most of his own tribe went over to the French in a body, Kishicokelas remained loyal to the proprietary government; and, although they made him splendid offers at the time they corrupted Jacobs, he re-jected them all, and declared that no earthly consideration could induce him to lift the hatchet against the sons of Onas.

It is to be regretted that historians never made mention of Kishicokelas, except incidentally. He was the fast friend of the old chief Shickalemy, who resided at Fort Augusta, and it is probable that he was converted by some of the Moravian missionaries. He died in 1756, as appears by a letter directed to his sons, as follows:—

"Philadelphia, June 13, 1756.

"I am obliged to you for your letter by our good friend, John Shickcalamy. Your father's letter and present were received by the late Governor Hamilton, who acquainted me with it; and I intended, at a time when less engaged by public business, to have sent you my acknowledgments and answer.

"I heartily condole with you on the loss of your aged father, and mingle my tears with yours, which however I would now have you wipe away with the handkerchief herewith sent.

"As a testimony of love the proprietors and this government retain for the family of Kishycoquillas, you will be pleased to accept of the present which is delivered to John Shickcalamy for your use.

"May the Great Spirit confer on you health and every other blessing. Continue your affection for the English and the good people of this province, and you will always find them grateful.

"I am your assured friend,

"ROBERT H. MORRIS."

Soon after the treaty at Albany,—probably in 1755,— settlers, who had heard of the beauty and fertility of Kishicoquillas Valley, flocked thither for the purpose of locating lands. Few locations, however, were effected, for the Indians of the valley, with the exception of the chief Kishicokelas and his immediate followers, were opposed to it, and threw every obstacle, short of downright murder, in

the way of the new-comers.   There is no positive evidence
that any murders were committed in Kishicoquillas at
that period, but the savages certainly did every thing in
their power to menace and harass the settlers, in order to
induce them to relinquish the design of settling upon what
they still considered their lands.   The following letter
from Colonel Armstrong to Governor Morris gives some
information of the trials these early settlers were subjected to:—

"*Carlisle, May* 26, 1755.

"This day I received a letter from my brother, who is laying out
lands for the settlers in the new purchase, giving an account of
three Indians, very much painted, who last week robbed and drove
off several settlers from the Valley of Kishicoquillas.   One of the
Indians, by his skulking position, seemed as if he designed secretly
to have shot, but, the white man discovering him, escaped.   They
took three horses, three or four guns, and some cash.   'Tis said
they robbed another man up Juniata.

"To-morrow I am to set out for Kishicoquillas, there to decide
some controversies, and thence to proceed to Susquehanna, near
Shamokin, where I expect to meet Conrad Weiser.   If he is there,
he may, by the assistance of the Shickcalamies, be of use in regard
to those robberies.   I am, sir, yours, &c.,

"JOHN ARMSTRONG."

Colonel Armstrong did go to Shamokin, where he met
Shickalemy, and induced him to use his influence in behalf
of the settlers in the new purchase; but Shickalemy's
labors were lost, for he could effect nothing among the
savages of Kishicoquillas, and the settlers were forced to fly
for protection to Fort Granville; nor did they or any other
whites venture into the valley until some time in 1765.

Shickalemy, or Shickellimus, as he was sometimes
called, was a Cayuga chief, of the Six Nations, and for
many years resided at Fort Augusta, on the Susquehanna,

where Sunbury now stands. He was converted to Christianity by the Moravian missionaries about 1742, and was, to the day of his death, the firm and steadfast friend of the English colonists. To his exertions, in a great measure, may be traced the cause why none of the Six Nations on the Susquehanna joined the French, and why a portion of the Delawares spurned the most tempting offers of the French agents and remained loyal to the colonists.

Shickalemy attended numerous treaties in Philadelphia, during which he was kindly entertained by James Logan, the secretary of the province. The chief esteemed him so highly that he named his second son after him, on his return from one of these treaties, and immediately had him, as well as two other sons, baptized with Christian rites by the Moravians.

In 1755, Shickalemy paid a visit to the old chief Kishicokelas, for the purpose of adopting some conciliatory measures to prevent the Indians of the valley from committing depredations upon the settlers. On this occasion he was accompanied by his sons, John and James Logan. The latter, probably charmed with the beauty of the valley, soon after the demise of Kishicokelas settled in the valley which bore the name of his father's friend. He built himself a cabin (not a wigwam) by the side of a fine limestone spring, whose pure waters gushed out of a small hill-side in the very heart of the valley, where his sole pursuit was hunting. This was Logan, the Mingo chief, whose name is perpetuated by counties, towns, townships, valleys, paths, mountains, and even hotels, and which will live in history, probably, to the end of time.

There is no evidence that he had a family at the time

8

he resided in Kishicoquillas; neither was he a chief at that time, for he lived away from his tribe, and what little intercourse he held with his fellow-men was with the whites, to whom he bartered venison and deer-skins for such articles as he stood in need of. He maintained himself solely by hunting, and was passionately fond of it. A gentleman who saw Logan at Standing Stone, in 1771 or 1772, described him to Mr. Maguire as "a fine-looking, muscular fellow, apparently about twenty-eight years of age. He weighed about two hundred pounds, had a full chest, and prominent and expansive features. His complexion was not so dark as that of the Juniata Indians, and his whole actions showed that he had had some intercourse with the whites." This noble specimen of the red men, unfortunately, had the failing common to his kind: he would indulge in intoxicating liquors to excess on nearly every occasion that offered. When sober, he was dignified and reserved, but frank and honest; when intoxicated, he was vain, boastful, and extremely foolish.

Judge Brown, a short time previous to his death, in the course of a conversation with R. P. Maclay, Esq., about Logan, said:—

"The first time I ever saw that spring, (Logan's,) my brother, James Reed, and myself, had wandered out of the valley in search of land, and, finding it very good, we were looking about for springs. About a mile from this we started a bear, and separated to get a shot at him. I was travelling along, looking about on the rising ground for the bear, when I came suddenly upon the spring; and, being dry, and more rejoiced to find so fine a spring than to have killed a dozen bears, I set my rifle against a bush, and rushed down the bank, and laid down to drink. Upon putting my head down, I saw reflected in the water, on the opposite side, the shadow of a tall Indian. I sprang to my rifle, when the Indian gave a yell, whether for peace or war I was not just then sufficiently master of my faculties to determine; but upon my seizing my rifle and facing him, he knocked up the pan of his gun, threw out the priming, and extended his open palm toward me in token of friendship. After putting down our guns, we again met at the spring, and shook hands. This was Logan—the best specimen of humanity I ever met with, either *white* or *red*. He could speak a little English, and told me there was another white hunter a little way down the stream, and offered to guide me to his camp. There I first met your father, (Samuel Maclay.) We remained together in the valley for a week, looking for springs and selecting lands, and laid the foundation of a friendship which never has had the slightest interruption.

"We visited Logan at his camp, at Logan's Spring, and your father and he shot at a mark, for a dollar a shot. Logan lost four or five rounds, and acknowledged himself beaten. When we were about to leave him, he went into his hut and brought out as many deer-skins as he had lost dollars, and handed them to Mr. Maclay, who refused to take them, alleging that he had been his guest, and did not come to rob him; that the shooting had only been a trial of skill, and the bet merely nominal. Logan drew himself up with great dignity, and said, 'Me bet to make you shoot your best; me gentleman, and me take your dollar if me beat.' So he was obliged to take the skins, or affront our friend, whose nice sense of honor would not permit him to receive even a horn of powder in return.

"The next year," said Judge Brown, "I brought my wife up, and camped under a big walnut-tree on the bank of Tea Creek, until I had built a cabin near where the mill now stands, and I have lived in the valley ever since. Poor Logan" (and the tears chased each other down his cheeks) "soon after went into the Alleghany, and I never saw him again."

Many other characteristic anecdotes are given of Logan, the publication of which in these pages would answer no very desirable end.

In looking over the few pages of manuscripts left by the

late Edward Bell, Esq., we find mention made of "Captain Logan, an Indian friendly to the whites." This confirmed us in the belief that there were two Logans. "Logan, the Mingo chief," left Kishicoquillas Valley in 1771; while Captain Logan resided in the upper end of Huntingdon county at that time, and a few years afterward in Logan's Valley, in Blair county. When the Revolution broke out, he moved toward the mountain, in the neighborhood of Chickalacamoose, near what is now Clearfield. He served as a spy for the settlers, and rendered them valuable service. He was an Iroquois or Mingo Indian, too, and a chief; whereas Logan, the Mingo, was no chief until he removed to Ohio after his relatives were murdered and he took up the hatchet against the whites. This explanation is necessary, because many people of Huntingdon and Blair counties are under the impression that the Captain Logan who resided in Tuckahoe as late as 1785, and Logan, the Mingo chief, were one and the same person.

Logan, in consequence of Kishicoquillas becoming too thickly populated, and the game becoming proportionately scarce, emigrated to Ohio, where he settled at the mouth of Yellow Creek, thirty miles above Wheeling. There he was joined by his surviving relatives and some Cayugas from Fort Augusta, and a small Indian village of log-huts was built up.

Heckwelder, who must have seen him previous to settling at Yellow Creek, speaks of him as follows:—

About the year 1772, Logan was introduced to me by an Indian friend, as son of the late reputable chief Shikelemus, and as a friend to the white people. In the course of conversation, I thought him a man of superior talents than Indians generally were. The subject turning on vice and immorality, he confessed his too great share of this, especially his fondness for liquor. He exclaimed against the white people for imposing liquors upon the Indians. He otherwise admired their ingenuity; spoke of gentlemen, but observed the Indians unfortunately had but few of these neighbors, &c. He spoke of his friendship to the white people, wished always to be a neighbor to them, intended to settle on the Ohio, below Big Beaver; was (to the best of my recollection) then encamped at the mouth of this river, (Beaver;) urged me to pay him a visit. I was then living at the Moravian town on this river, in the neighborhood of Cuskuskee. In April, 1773, while on my passage down the Ohio for Muskingum, I called at Logan's settlement, where I received every civility I could expect from such of the family as were at home.

Indian reports concerning Logan, after the death of his family, ran to this: that he exerted himself during the Shawnees war (then so called) to take all the revenge he could, declaring he had lost all confidence in the white people. At the time of the negotiation, he declared his reluctance to lay down the hatchet, not having (in his opinion) yet taken ample satisfaction; yet, for the sake of the nation, he would do it. His expression, from time to time, denoted a deep melancholy. Life, said he, had become a torment to him; he knew no more what pleasure was; he thought it had been better if he had never existed. Report further states that he became in some measure delirious; declared he would kill himself; went to Detroit, and, on his way between that place and Miami, was murdered. In October, 1781, while a prisoner, on my way to Detroit, I was shown the spot where this was said to have happened.

That Logan's temper should have soured on the murder of his relatives and friends, after the friendship he had always extended to the whites, is not at all strange. These murders changed his nature from a peaceable Indian to a most cruel and bloodthirsty savage. Revenge stimulated him to the most daring deeds; and

how many innocent. white men, women, and children,
he ushered into eternity to appease his wrath, is only
known to Him "whose eye seeth all things."

His people—some say his family, but it never was
ascertained that he had any—were murdered in May,
1774. Some roving Indians had committed depredations
in the neighborhood, and the settlers, highly incensed,
determined to drive them out of the neighborhood. To
this end, about thirty men, completely armed, and under
the command of Daniel Greathouse, without knowing the
character and disposition of Logan and his friends, made
a descent upon the village and destroyed it, and killed
twelve and wounded six or eight of the Indians. Among
the former was Logan's sister and a son of Kishicokelas.
Logan was absent, at the time of the occurrence, on a
hunting expedition. On his return, as soon as he saw
the extent of the injury done him, he buried the dead,
cared for the wounded, and, with the remnant of his
band, went into Ohio, joined the Shawnees, and fought
during their war against the whites with the most bitter
and relentless fury.

In the autumn of 1774, the Indians, getting some very
rough usage, and fearing that the powerful army of Lord
Dunmore would march upon and exterminate them, sued
for peace. Lord Dunmore sent a belt of wampum to all
the principal chiefs, and, among the rest, one to Logan,
inviting them to a treaty. Logan refused to attend the
council, but sent the following speech by an interpreter,
in a belt of wampum. The treaty was held under an
oak-tree, near Circleville, Ohio, and it was there that the
eloquent and purely Indian speech which rendered Logan's

name immortal was read, and brought tears to the eyes of
many of the sturdy pioneers assembled:—

"I appeal," says Logan, "to any white man to say if he ever
entered Logan's cabin hungry, and he gave him not meat; if he
came naked and cold, and I clothed him not.   During the last long
and bloody war, Logan remained idle in his cabin, an advocate of
peace.   Such was my love for the whites that my countrymen, as
they passed, said, 'Logan is the friend of the whites.'   I had
thought of living among you, but for the injuries of one man.
Captain Cressap, last spring, in cold blood, and unprovoked,
murdered all the relations of Logan, not sparing even my women
and children.   There runs not one drop of my blood in any living
creature.   This called on me for revenge.   I have sought it; I have
killed many; I have fully glutted my vengeance.   For my country,
I rejoice in the beams of peace.   But do not harbor the thought
that mine is the joy of fear.   Logan never felt fear.   He will not
turn on his heel to save his life.   Who is there to mourn for
Logan?   Not one!"

The authorship of this speech was attributed to Thomas
Jefferson, but he most emphatically denied it, as did others
who were present at the treaty.

With respect to Captain Cressap, Logan was doubtless
misinformed.   It is true Captain Cressap was a daring
frontier-man, who considered it an obligation imposed
upon him by the Creator to slay Indians, but he was
altogether innocent of the charge made against him by
Logan.   The massacre in question, when the facts were
known after Dunmore's treaty, was deeply deplored, and
the wanton butchery of Cressap execrated.   Cressap's
friends, however, would not suffer the stigma of an inhuman act, of which he was not guilty, to be fixed upon
him; so they procured all the evidence to be had in the
case, and fixed the disreputable deed upon Daniel Great-

house and his followers. A number of affidavits to that effect were made by men who accompanied Greathouse, and published a year or two after the treaty; others in 1799, when the subject was revived and freely discussed.

Seeing the great disadvantages the Indians labored under in trying to cope with well-armed and disciplined troops, and believing that his revenge was far from being satiated, it is quite likely that Logan became partially insane, as Heckwelder avers; but it is quite certain that he became a misanthrope, and for a long time refused to mingle with human beings. At length he plunged into deep excesses, and all he could earn, by the most skilful use of the rifle, went to gratify his inordinate thirst for strong drink. The once proud and noble Mingo chief gradually descended the scale of dignified manhood, outlived his greatness, and was killed in a drunken brawl. Sorry are we to say this, in the face of the *romance* of history; nevertheless it is true. We had the statement from an old Ohio pioneer, nearly twenty years ago.

CHAPTER X.

COL. JOHN ARMSTRONG'S EXPEDITION AGAINST KITTANING — LIST OF
THE KILLED AND WOUNDED — DELAWARE CHIEFS, CAPTAIN JACOBS
AND SHINGAS.

THE following account of the famous expedition against
the Indian town of Kittaning we deem worthy of being
recorded, not only because the companies of Captains
Potter and Steel belonged to the Juniata Valley, but on
account of its being an interesting detail of an important
event in the early settlement of the country.

The expedition was planned and carried out with great
secresy, for the sole purpose of punishing the Indians engaged in the Juniata Valley massacres, and who it was
known had their head-quarters at Kittaning, where the
chief instigators of all the mischief, Shingas and Captain
Jacobs, lived. The command was intrusted to Colonel
John Armstrong, a brave and prudent officer, and the
forces consisted of seven companies. He left Fort Shirley
(Aughwick, Huntingdon county) on the 30th of August,
1756, and on the 3d of September came up with the advanced party at "Beaver Dams, a few miles from Frankstown, on the north branch of the Juniata." This junction
of the forces occurred on the flat where Gaysport now

stands, where the little army struck the celebrated trail
known as the Kittaning Path.   In his official account of
the expedition, dated at Fort Littleton, September 14,
1756, Colonel Armstrong says:—

We were there [at the Beaver Dams] informed that some of
our men, having been out upon a scout, had discovered the tracks
of two Indians about three miles this side of the Alleghany Mountain and but a few miles from the camp.   From the freshness of
the tracks, their killing of a cub bear, and the marks of their fires,
it seemed evident they were not twenty-four hours before us, which
might be looked upon as a particular providence in our favor that
we were not discovered.   Next morning we decamped, and in two
days came within fifty miles of the Kittaning.   It was then ad-
judged necessary to send some persons to reconnoitre the town,
and to get the best intelligence they could concerning the situation
and position of the enemy; whereupon an officer, with one of the
pilots and two soldiers, were sent off for that purpose.   The day
following we met them on their return, and they informed us that
the roads were entirely clear of the enemy, and that they had the
greatest reason to believe they were not discovered; but from the
rest of the intelligence they gave it appeared they had not been
nigh enough the town, either to perceive the true situation of it,
the number of the enemy, or in what way it might most advantageously be attacked.   We continued our march, in order to get as
near the town as possible that night, so as to be able to attack it
next morning about daylight; but, to our great dissatisfaction, about
nine or ten o'clock at night one of our guides came and told us
that he perceived a fire by the road-side, at which he saw two or
three Indians, a few perches distant from our front; whereupon,
with all possible silence, I ordered the rear to retreat about one
hundred perches, in order to make way for the front, that we might
consult how we could best proceed without being discovered by the
enemy.   Soon after, the pilot returned a second time, and assured
us, from the best observations he could make, there were not above
three or four Indians at the fire, on which it was proposed that we
should immediately surround and cut them off; but this was thought
too hazardous, for, if but one of the enemy had escaped, it would

have been the means of discovering the whole design; and the light of the moon, on which depended our advantageously posting our men and attacking the town, would not admit of our staying until the Indians fell asleep; on which it was agreed to leave Lieutenant Hogg, with twelve men and the person who first discovered the fire, with orders to watch the enemy, but not to attack them, till break of day, and then, if possible, to cut them off. It was also agreed (we believing ourselves to be but about six miles from the town) to leave the horses, many of them being tired, with what blankets and other baggage we then had, and to take a circuit off the road, which was very rough and incommodious on account of the stones and fallen timber, in order to prevent our being heard by the enemy at the fire place. This interruption much retarded our march, but a still greater loss arose from the ignorance of our pilot, who neither knew the true situation of the town nor the best paths that led thereto; by which means, after crossing a number of hills and valleys, our front reached the river Ohio [Alleghany] about one hundred perches below the main body of the town, a little before the setting of the moon, to which place, rather than by the pilot, we were guided by the beating of the drum and the whooping of the warriors at their dance. It then became us to make the best use of the remaining moonlight; but, ere we were aware, an Indian whistled in a very singular manner, about thirty perches from our front, in the foot of a corn-field; upon which we immediately sat down, and, after passing silence to the rear, I asked one Baker, a soldier, who was our best assistant, whether that was not a signal to the warriors of our approach. He answered "No," and said it was the manner of a young fellow's calling a squaw after he had done his dance, who accordingly kindled a fire, cleaned his gun, and shot it off before he went to sleep. All this time we were obliged to lie quiet and lurk, till the moon was fairly set. Immediately after, a number of fires appeared in different places in the corn-field, by which Baker said the Indians lay, the night being warm, and that these fires would immediately be out, as they were only designed to disperse the gnats. By this time it was break of day, and the men, having marched thirty miles, were mostly asleep. The time being long, the three companies of the rear were not yet brought over the last precipice. For these some proper hands were immediately despatched; and the weary soldiers being

roused to their feet, a proper number, under sundry officers, were
ordered to take the end of the hill at which we then lay, and march
along the top of the said hill at least one hundred perches, and so
much farther (it then being daylight) as would carry them opposite
the upper part, or at least the body, of the town. For the lower
part thereof and the corn-field, presuming the warriors were there,
I kept rather the larger number of men, promising to postpone the
attack in that part for eighteen or twenty minutes, until the detachment along the hill should have time to advance to the place
assigned them—in doing of which they were a little unfortunate.
The time being elapsed, the attack was begun in the corn-field,
and the men, with all expedition possible, despatched through the
several parts thereof, a party being also despatched to the houses,
which were then discovered by the light of the day. Captain
Jacobs immediately then gave the war-whoop, and, with sundry
other Indians, as the English prisoners afterward told, cried the
white men were at last come, they would then have scalps enough;
but, at the same time, ordered their squaws and children to flee to
the woods. Our men, with great eagerness, passed through and
fired in the corn-field, where they had several returns from the
enemy, as they also had from the opposite side of the river. Presently after, a brisk fire began among the houses, which from the
house of Captain Jacobs was returned with a great deal of resolution, to which place I immediately repaired, and found that from
the advantage of the house and portholes sundry of our people
were wounded and some killed; and, finding that returning the fire
upon the house was ineffectual, I ordered the contiguous houses to
be set on fire, which was performed by sundry of the officers and
soldiers with a great deal of activity, the Indians always firing
whenever an object presented itself, and seldom missing of wounding or killing some of our people—from which house, in moving
about to give the necessary orders and directions, I received a
wound with a large musket-ball in the shoulders. Sundry persons,
during the action, were ordered to tell the Indians to surrender
themselves prisoners, but one of the Indians in particular answered
and said he was a man, and would not be a prisoner; upon which
he was told, in Indian, he would be burnt. To this he answered he
did not care, for he would kill four or five before he died; and, had
we not desisted from exposing ourselves, they would have killed a

great many more, they having a number of loaded guns by them. As the fire began to approach and the smoke grew thick, one of the Indian fellows, to show his manhood, began to sing. A squaw in the same house, and at the same time, was heard to cry and make a noise, but for so doing was severely rebuked by the man; but by-and-by, the fire being too hot for them, two Indian fellows and a squaw sprang out and made for the corn-field, who were immediately shot down by our people then surrounding the houses. It was thought Captain Jacobs tumbled himself out at a garret or cockloft window at which he was shot—our prisoners offering to be qualified to the powder-horn and pouch there taken off him, which they say he had lately got from a French officer in exchange for Lieutenant Armstrong's boots, which he carried from Fort Granville, where the lieutenant was killed. The same prisoners say they are perfectly assured of his scalp, as no other Indians there wore their hair in the same manner. They also say they know his squaw's scalp by a particular *bob*, and also know the scalp of a young Indian called the King's Son. Before this time, Captain Hugh Mercer, who, early in the action, was wounded in the arm, had been taken to the top of a hill above the town,—to whom a number of the men and some of the officers were gathered, from whence they had discovered some Indians pass the river and take the hill, with an intention, as they thought, to surround us and cut off our retreat, from whom I had sundry pressing messages to leave the houses and retreat to the hills, or we should all be cut off. But to this I would by no means consent until all the houses were set on fire. Though our spreading upon the hills appeared very necessary, yet did it prevent our researches of the corn-field and river-side, by which means sundry scalps were left behind, and doubtless some squaws, children, and English prisoners, that otherwise might have been got. During the burning of the houses, which were near thirty in number, we were agreeably entertained with a quick succession of charged guns gradually firing off as reached by the fire, but much more so with the vast explosion of sundry bags and large kegs of gunpowder, wherewith almost every house abounded; the prisoners afterward informing us that the Indians had frequently said they had a sufficient stock of ammunition for ten years' war with the English. With the roof of Captain Jacobs's house, when the powder blew up, was thrown the leg and thigh of an Indian, with a child of three or four years old, to such a height that they appeared as nothing, and fell in an adjoining corn-field. There was also a great quantity of goods burnt, which the Indians had received in a present but ten days before from the French. By this time I had proceeded to the hill, to have my wound tied up and the blood stopped, where the prisoners which in the morning had come to our people informed me that that very day two bateaux of Frenchmen, with a large party of Delaware and French Indians, were to join Captain Jacobs at the Kittaning, and to set out early the next morning to take Fort Shirley, or, as they called it, George Crogan's Fort; and that twenty-four warriors, who had lately come to the town, were set out the evening before, for what purpose they did not know,—whether to prepare meat, to spy the fort, or to make an attack on some of our back inhabitants. Soon after, upon a little reflection, we were convinced these warriors were all at the fire we had discovered but the night before, and began to doubt the fate of Lieutenant Hogg and his party. From this intelligence of the prisoners,—our provisions being scaffolded some thirty miles back, except what were in the men's haversacks, which were left, with the horses and blankets, with Lieutenant Hogg and his party,—and having a number of wounded people then on hand, by the advice of the officers it was thought imprudent then to wait for the cutting down the corn-field, (which was before designed,) but immediately to collect our wounded and force our march back in the best manner we could; which we did, by collecting a few Indian horses to carry off our wounded. From the apprehension of being waylaid and surrounded, (especially by some of the woodsmen,) it was difficult to keep the men together, our march, for sundry miles, not exceeding two miles an hour; which apprehensions were heightened by the attempt of a few Indians, who, for some time after the march, fired upon each wing and immediately ran off; from whom we received no other damage but one of our men being wounded through both legs. Captain Mercer—being wounded, was induced, as we have every reason to believe, by some of his men, to leave the main body, with his ensign, John Scott, and ten or twelve men, they being heard to tell him that we were in great danger, and that they could take him into the road a nigh way—is probably lost, there being yet no account of him, and the most of the men come in. A detachment was sent back to bring

him, but could not find him; and upon the return of the detachment it was generally reported he was seen, with the above number of men, to take a different road. Upon our return to the place
where the Indian fire had been discovered the night before, we met
with a sergeant of Captain Mercer's company, and two or three
other of his men, who had deserted us that morning, immediately after the action at the Kittaning. These men, on running away, had met with Lieutenant Hogg, who lay wounded in
two different parts of his body by the road-side. He there told
them of the fatal mistake of the pilot, who had assured us there
were but three Indians, at the most, at the fire place; but when
he came to attack them that morning, according to orders, he
found a number considerably superior to his, and believes they
killed or mortally wounded three of them the first fire, after
which a warm engagement began, and continued for above an
hour, when three of his best men were killed and himself twice
wounded. The residue fleeing off, he was obliged to squat in a
thicket, where he might have lain securely until the main body
had come up, if this cowardly sergeant and others that fled with
him had not taken him away.

They had marched but a short space when four Indians appeared, on which these deserters began to flee. The lieutenant
then, notwithstanding his wounds, as a brave soldier, urged and
commanded them to stand and fight, which they all refused. The
Indians pursued, killing one man and wounding the lieutenant a
third time, through the belly, of which he died in a few hours,
but, having some time before been put on horseback, rode some miles
from the place of action. This last attack of the Indians upon
Lieutenant Hogg and the deserters was by the before-mentioned
sergeant represented to us quite in a different light, he telling us
that there was a far larger number of the Indians there than appeared to them, and that he and the men with him had fought five
rounds; that he had there seen the lieutenant and sundry others
killed and scalped, and had also discovered a number of Indians
throwing themselves before us, and insinuated a great deal of such
stuff as threw us into much confusion; so that the officers had a
great deal to do to keep the men together, but could not prevail
upon them to collect what horses and other baggage the Indians
had left after the conquest of Lieutenant Hogg and the party

under his command in the morning, except a few of the horses,
which some of the bravest of the men were prevailed on to collect; so
that from the mistake of the pilot who spied the Indians at the fire,
and the cowardice of the said sergeant and other deserters, we here
sustained a considerable loss of our horses and baggage.   It is impossible to ascertain the exact number of the enemy killed in the
action, as some were destroyed by fire, and others in different parts
of the corn-field; but, upon a moderate computation, it is generally
believed there cannot be less than thirty or forty killed and mortally wounded, as much blood was found in sundry parts of the
corn-field, and Indians seen in several places crawl into the woods
on hands and feet,—whom the soldiers in pursuit of others then overlooked, expecting to find and scalp them afterward,—and also several
killed and wounded in crossing the river.   On beginning our march
back, we had about a dozen of scalps and eleven English prisoners;
but now we find that four or five of the scalps are missing, part
of which were lost on the road, and part in possession of those
men who, with Captain Mercer, separated from the main body, with
whom went also four of the prisoners, the other seven being now
at this place, where we arrived on Sunday night, not being separated or attacked through our whole march by the enemy, though
we expected it every day.   Upon the whole, had our pilots understood the true situation of the town and the paths leading to it, so
as to have posted us at a convenient place where the disposition of
the men and the duty assigned to them could have been performed
with greater advantage, we had, by divine assistance, destroyed a
much greater number of the enemy, recovered more prisoners, and
sustained less damage, than what we at present have.   But though
the advantage gained over this our common enemy is far from
being satisfactory to us, yet we must not despise the smallest de-
grees of success that God is pleased to give, especially at a time
of such general calamity, when the attempts of our enemies have
been so prevalent and successful.   I am sure there was the greatest
inclination to do more, had it been in our power, as the officers
and most of the soldiers, throughout the whole action, exerted
themselves with as much activity and resolution as could be expected.   Our prisoners inform us the Indians have for some time
past talked of fortifying at the Kittaning and other towns.

The following is a list of the killed and wounded, returned in Colonel Armstrong's official report of the expedition:—

LIEUTENANT-COLONEL JOHN ARMSTRONG'S COMPANY.— *Killed*—Thomas Power, John M'Cormick. *Wounded*— Lieutenant-Colonel Armstrong, James Caruthers, James Strickland, Thomas Foster.

CAPTAIN HAMILTON'S COMPANY.—*Killed*—John Kelly.

CAPTAIN MERCER'S COMPANY.—*Killed*—John Baker, John McCartney, Patrick Mullen, Cornelius McGinnis, Theophilus Thompson, Dennis Kilpatrick, Bryan Carrigan. *Wounded*—Richard Fitzgibbons. *Missing*—Captain Hugh Mercer, Ensign John Scott, Emanuel Minskey, John Taylor, John Francis Phillips, Robert Morrow, Thomas Burk, Philip Pendergrass.

CAPTAIN ARMSTRONG'S COMPANY.—*Killed*—Lieutenant James Hogg, James Anderson, Holdcraft Stringer, Edward Obrians, James Higgins, John Lasson. *Wounded*— William Findley, Robert Robinson, John Ferrol, Thomas Camplin, Charles O'Neal. *Missing*—John Lewis, William Hunter, William Barker, George Appleby, Anthony Grissy, Thomas Swan.

CAPTAIN WARD'S COMPANY.— *Killed*—William Welch. *Wounded*—Ephraim Bratton. *Missing*—Patrick Myers, Lawrence Donnahow, Samuel Chambers.

CAPTAIN POTTER'S COMPANY.—*Wounded*—Ensign James Potter, Andrew Douglass.

CAPTAIN STEEL'S COMPANY.—*Missing*—Terence Cannaherry.

Total killed, 17; wounded, 13; missing, 19. All the

missing, with one or two exceptions, reached their homes, and nearly all of the wounded recovered.

The loss on the part of the colonists was severe, when we consider that they had three hundred and fifty men engaged in the action, while the Indian force did not consist of over one hundred warriors. The ignorance of the pilot, and the great error of some of the officers in persisting in trying to dislodge the enemy from the houses by discharge of fire-arms, was no doubt the direct cause of the death of many of the brave men; for all must admit that the expedition was well planned, and admirably carried out, as far as circumstances would permit.

In speaking of the horrible Indian massacres which followed the defeat of Braddock, Drake, in his Indian history, says :—

Shingas and Captain Jacobs were supposed to have been the principal instigators of them, and a reward of seven hundred dollars was offered for their heads. It was at this period that the dead bodies of some of the murdered and mangled were sent from the frontiers to Philadelphia, and hauled about the streets, to inflame the people against the Indians, and also against the Quakers, to whose mild forbearance was attributed a laxity in sending out troops. The mob surrounded the House of Assembly, having placed the dead bodies at its entrance, and demanded immediate succor. At this time, the above reward was offered.

King Shingas, as he was called by the whites, (who is noticed in the preceding paragraph,) but whose proper name was *Shingask*, which is interpreted *Bog-meadow*, was the greatest Delaware warrior at that time. Heckwelder, who knew him personally, says, "Were his war exploits all on record, they would form an interesting document, though a shocking one." Conococheague, Big Cove, Sherman's Valley, and other settlements along the frontier, felt his strong arm sufficiently to attest that he was a " bloody warrior,"—cruel his treatment, relentless his fury. His person was small, but in point of courage, activity, and savage prowess, he was said to have never been exceeded by any one. In 1753, when Washington was on his expedition to fight the French on the Ohio, (Alleghany,) Shingas had his house at Kittaning.

King Shingas was at Fort Duquesne when Lieutenant Armstrong destroyed Kittaning; but there is no doubt whatever that Captain Jacobs fell in the engagement, notwithstanding Hans Hamilton, in a letter to the council, dated at Fort Lyttleton, April 4, 1756, said, " Indian Isaac hath brought in the scalp of Captain Jacobs." This Indian Isaac claimed, and we believe received, the reward offered for killing and scalping Captain Jacobs, and yet Captain Jacobs lived to do a great deal of mischief before his scalp fell into the hands of the English colonists.

Not only was Captain Jacobs a great warrior, but it would appear that all his family connections were Indians of note. In a letter from Colonel Stephen to Colonel Armstrong, it is stated, on the authority of a returned captive from Muskingum, that

A son of Captain Jacobs is killed, and a cousin of his, about seven foot high, called Young Jacob, at the destroying of Kittaning, and it is thought a noted warrior by the name of The Sunfish, as many of them were killed that we know nothing of.

There is no doubt that Armstrong's return did not embrace half the actual loss of the enemy, including women and children; but it was a mistake in Stephen or his informant to include the warrior Sunfish among the slain, for he was a hale old chief in 1781.

CHAPTER XI.

OLD INDIAN TOWN — INDIAN PATHS — AUGHWICK — MURDER OF JOHN
ARMSTRONG AND PARTY — CAPTAIN JACK, THE WILD HUNTER OF
THE JUNIATA — GEORGE CROGAN, ETC.

As we ascend the river, the nearer we approach the base of the Alleghany Mountains the fewer places we find even mentioned in quite early history. On the flat eight or nine miles west of Lewistown, near a large spring, stood an old Shawnee town. It is mentioned as early as 1731, in a report of the number of Indians accompanying the deposition of some traders. The town was called *Ohesson*, on the "Choniata," and supposed to be sixty miles distant from the Susquehanna. As this is Indian computation, some allowance must be made, for in the same connection we notice the Indian town of *Assunnepachla* set down as being distant one hundred miles from Ohesson by water and fifty miles by land. Assunnepachla was the Indian name of Frankstown; and no person, by following the most sinuous windings of the river, can make the distance to Lewistown over eighty miles.

These places were probably never visited by any but Indian traders previous to Braddock's defeat, and the consequence is that we are without any record of Ohesson, which was evidently destroyed and abandoned at an early day. Assunnepachla, however, stood for many years, but it lost its name before it became a place of importance to the whites.

Aughwick, it is said, had the honor of receiving the first white settlers, in 1749, that came within the present limits of Huntingdon county. Of course, they were in search of choice lands, and there is reason to believe they found them, too, notwithstanding the proprietors and their man Peters, in a year thereafter, ousted them by burning their cabins over their heads. Aughwick Valley is in the extreme southern part of Huntingdon county, and, if not a regular continuation of the Tuscarora Valley, is at least one of the chain of valleys through whose entire length ran the celebrated Indian path from Kittaning to Philadelphia,—the great western highway for footmen and pack-horses.

This path, traces of which can yet be plainly seen in various places, and especially in the wilds of the mountains, must have been a famous road in its day. It commenced at Kittaning, on the Alleghany River, and crossed the Alleghany Mountains in a southeastern direction, the descent on the eastern slope being through a gorge, the mouth of which is five or six miles west of Hollidaysburg, at what is well known as Kittaning Point. From this it diverged in a southern direction until it led to the flat immediately back of Hollidaysburg, from thence east, wound round the gorge back of the Presbyterian graveyard, and led into Frank's old town. From thence it went through what is now called

Scotch Valley, Canoe Valley, and struck the river at Water street. From thence it led to Alexandria, crossed the river, and went into Hartsog Valley; from thence to Woodcock Valley; from Woodcock Valley, across the Broadtop Mountain, into Aughwick; from thence into the Tuscarora Valley, and from thence into Sherman's Valley, by Sterritt's Gap.

At Kittaning Point, this path, although it is seldom that the foot of any one but an occasional hunter or fisher treads it, is still the same path it was when the last dusky warrior who visited the Juniata Valley turned his face to the west, and traversed it for the last time. True, it is filled up with weeds in summer-time, but the indentation made by the feet of thousands upon thousands of warriors and pack-horses which travelled it for an unknown number of years are still plainly visible. We have gone up the Kittaning gorge two or three miles, repeatedly, and looked upon the ruins of old huts, and the road, which evidently never received the impression of a wagon-wheel, and were forcibly struck with the idea that it must once have been traversed, without knowing at the time that it was the famous Kittaning trail. In some places, where the ground was marshy, close to the run, the path is at least twelve inches deep, and the very stones along the road bear the marks of the iron-shod horses of the Indian traders. Two years ago, we picked up, at the edge of the run, a mile up the gorge, two gun-flints,—now rated as relics of a past age. At the time we supposed that some modern Nimrod lost them. Now, however, we incline to the belief that they fell from the pocket of some weary soldier in Armstrong's battalion, who lay down upon the bank of the brook to slake his thirst, nearly a hundred years ago. The path can be traced in various other places, but nowhere so plain as in the Kittaning gorge. This is owing to the fact that one or two other paths led into it, and no improvement has been made in the gorge east of "Hart's Sleeping Place," along the line of the path.

Aughwick was an Indian town, located probably near where Shirleysburg now stands, and for a long time was an important frontier post. The name of the place figures extensively in the Colonial Records, first as a place where many conferences were held, and afterward as Fort Shirley.

Previous to actual settlers coming into the Juniata Valley, every inch of it was known to the traders—or, at least, every Indian town in it; and how long they trafficked with the red men before actual settlers came is unknown. Thus, for instance, six or seven years before the settlement of Aughwick, a trader named John Armstrong, and his two servant-men, were murdered at what is now Jack's Narrows, in Huntingdon county. As there are several narrows along the Juniata, we should have been at a loss to locate the scene of the murder, had we not accidentally noticed in the Archives a calculation of distances by John Harris, wherein he says—"From Aughwick to Jack Armstrong's Narrows—so called from his being there murdered,—eight miles." At the time of the massacre, the British colonists and the Indians were on the most friendly terms of intimacy, and Armstrong was a man of some standing and influence, so that the murder (the first one of so atrocious a nature in that region) created the most intense excitement. Along with Armstrong, his servant-men, James Smith and Woodward Arnold, were also murdered. The charge was laid to a Delaware Indian, named Musemeelin, and two companions. Seven white men and five Indians searched for the bodies, found and buried them. The Indian was arrested and taken to Lancaster, and from there removed to Philadelphia for trial, but whether convicted or not the record does not say. *Allumoppies*, King of the Delawares, Shickallemy, and a number of other Indians of standing and influence, were brought before the council in Philadelphia, when the friends of Armstrong produced the following affidavit of those who searched for the bodies:—

Paxton, April 19, 1744.

The deposition of the subscribers testifieth and saith, that the subscribers, having a suspicion that John Armstrong, trader, together with his men, James Smith and Woodward Arnold, were murdered by the Indians, they met at the house of Joseph Chambers, in Paxton, and there consulted to go to Shamokin, to consult with the Delaware king and Shickcalimy, and there council what they should do concerning the affair. Whereupon the king and council ordered eight of their men to go with the deponents to the house of James Berry, in order to go in quest of the murdered persons; but that night they came to the said Berry's house three of the eight Indians ran away; and the next morning these deponents, with the five Indians that remained, set out on their journey, peaceably, to the last supposed sleeping-place of the deceased; and upon their arrival, these deponents dispersed themselves, in order to find out the corpse of the deceased; and one of the deponents, named James Berry, a small distance from the aforesaid sleeping-place, came to a white-oak tree, which had three notches on it, and close by said tree he found a shoulder-bone, which the deponent does suppose to be John Armstrong's,—and that he himself was eaten by the Indians,—which he carried to the aforesaid sleeping-place, and showed it to his companions, one of whom handed it to the said five Indians to know what bone it was;

and they, after passing different sentiments upon it, handed it to a
Delaware Indian, who was suspected by the deponents; and they tes-
tify and say that as soon as the Indian took the bone in his hand
his nose gushed out with blood, and he directly handed it to another.
From whence these deponents steered along a path, about three or
four miles, to the Narrows of Juniata, where they suspected the
murder to have been committed; and where the Alleghany Road
crosses the creek these deponents sat down, in order to consult on
what measures to take to proceed on a discovery. Whereupon
most of the white men, these deponents, crossed the creek again,
and went down the creek, and crossed into an island, where these
deponents had intelligence the corpse had been thrown; and there
they met the rest of the white men and Indians who were in company, and there consulted to go farther down the creek in quest
of the corpse. And these deponents further say, they ordered the
Indians to go down the creek on the other side; but they all followed these deponents at a small distance, except one Indian, who
crossed the creek again; and soon after these deponents, seeing
some bald eagles and other fowls, suspected the corpse to be thereabouts, and then lost sight of the Indians, and immediately found
one of the corpses, which these deponents say was the corpse of
James Smith, one of said Armstrong's men; and directly upon
finding the corpse these deponents heard three shots of guns,
which they had great reason to think were the Indians their companions, who had deserted from them; and in order to let them
know that they had found the corpse these deponents fired three
guns, but to no purpose, for they never saw the Indians any more.
And about a quarter of a mile down the creek they saw more bald
eagles, whereupon they made down toward the place, where they
found another corpse (being the corpse of Woodworth Arnold, the
other servant of said Armstrong) lying on a rock, and then went
to the former sleeping-place, where they had appointed to meet
the Indians; but saw no Indians, only that the Indians had been
there, and cooked some victuals for themselves and had gone off.

And that night, the deponents further say, they had great reason
to suspect that the Indians were then thereabouts, and intended to
do them some damage; for a dog these deponents had with them
barked that night, which was remarkable, for the said dog had not
barked all the time they were out till that night, nor ever since,

which occasioned these deponents to stand upon their guard behind the trees, with their guns cocked, that night. Next morning these deponents went back to the corpses, which they found to be barbarously and inhumanly murdered by very gashed, deep cuts on their hands with a tomahawk, or such like weapon, which had sunk into their skulls and brains; and in one of the corpses there appeared a hole in his skull near the cut, which was supposed to be with a tomahawk, which hole these deponents do believe to be a bullet-hole. And these deponents, after taking as particular view of the corpses as their melancholy condition would admit, they buried them as decently as their circumstances would allow, and returned home to Paxton,—the Alleghany Road to John Harris's, thinking it dangerous to return the same way they went. And further these deponents say not.

These same deponents, being legally qualified before me, James Armstrong, one of his majesty's justices of the peace for the county of Lancaster, have hereunto set their hands in testimony thereof.

JAMES ARMSTRONG.

Alexander Armstrong, Thomas McKee, Francis Ellis, John Florster, William Baskins, James Berry, John Watt, James Armstrong, David Denny.

After the foregoing facts had been elicited, a regular Indian talk was had upon the matter, when Shickallemy gave the following as a true version of every thing connected with the massacre:—

BROTHER THE GOVERNOR:—

We have been all misinformed on both sides about the unhappy accident. Musemeelin has certainly murdered the three white men himself, and, upon the bare accusation of Neshaleeny's son, was seized and made a prisoner. Our cousins, the Delaware Indians, being then drunk, in particular Allumoppies, never examined things, but made an innocent person prisoner, which gave a great deal of disturbance among us. However, the two prisoners were sent, and by the way, in going down the river, they stopped at the house of James Berry. James told the young man, "I am sorry to see you in such a condition; I have known you from a boy, and always loved you." Then the young man seemed to be very much struck to the heart, and said, "I have said nothing yet, but I will tell all; let all the Indians come up, and the white people also; they shall hear it;" and then told Musemeelin, in the presence of the people, "Now I am going to die for your wickedness; you have killed all the three white men. I never did intend to kill any of them." Then Musemeelin, in anger, said, "It is true, I have killed them. I am a man, you are a coward. It is a great satisfaction to me to have killed them; I will die for joy for having killed a great rogue and his companions." Upon which the young man was set at liberty by the Indians.

We desire therefore our brother the governor will not insist to have either of the two young men in prison or condemned to die; it is not with Indians as with white people, to put people in prison on suspicion or trifles. Indians must first be found guilty of a cause; then judgment is given and immediately executed. We will give you faithfully all the particulars, and at the ensuing treaty entirely satisfy you; in the mean time, we desire that good friendship and harmony continue, and that we may live long together is the hearty desire of your brethren the Indians of the United Six Nations present at Shamokin.

The following is what Shickcalamy declared to be the truth of the story concerning the murder of John Armstrong, Woodworth Arnold, and James Smith, from the beginning to the end, to wit:—

That Musemeelin owing some skins to John Armstrong, the said Armstrong seized a horse of the said Musemeelin and a rifle-gun; the gun was taken by James Smith, deceased. Some time last winter Musemeelin met Armstrong on the river Juniata, and paid all but twenty shillings, for which he offered a neck-belt in pawn to Armstrong, and demanded his horse, and James Armstrong refused it, and would not deliver up the horse, but enlarged the debt, as his usual custom was; and after some quarrel the Indian went away in great anger, without his horse, to his hunting-cabin. Some time after this, Armstrong, with his two companions, on their way to Ohio, passed by the said Musemeelin's hunting-cabin; his wife only being at home, she demanded the horse of Armstrong, because he was her proper goods, but did not get him. Armstrong had by this time sold or lent the horse to James Berry. After

Musemeelin came from hunting, his wife told him that Armstrong was gone by, and that she had demanded the horse of him, but did not get him; and, as is thought, pressed him to pursue and take revenge of Armstrong. The third day, in the morning, after James Armstrong was gone by, Musemeelin said to the two young men that hunted with him, " Come, let us go toward the Great Hills to hunt bears;" accordingly they went all three in company. After they had gone a good way, Musemeelin, who was foremost, was told by the two young men that they were out of their course. " Come you along," said Musemeelin; and they accordingly followed him till they came to the path that leads to the Ohio. Then Musemeelin told them he had a good mind to go and fetch his horse back from Armstrong, and desired the two young men to come along. Accordingly they went. It was then almost night, and they travelled till next morning. Musemeelin said, "Now they are not far off. We will make ourselves black; then they will be frightened, and will deliver up the horse immediately; and I will tell Jack that if he don't give me the horse I will kill him;" and when he said so, he laughed. The young men thought he joked, as he used to do. They did not blacken themselves, but he did. When the sun was above the trees, or about an hour high, they all came to the fire, where they found James Smith sitting; and they also sat down. Musemeelin asked where Jack was. Smith told him that he was gone to clear the road a little. Musemeelin said he wanted to speak with him, and went that way, and after he had gone a little distance from the fire, he said something, and looked back laughing, but, he having a thick throat, and his speech being very bad, and their talking with Smith hindering them from un- derstanding what he said, they did not mind it. They being hungry, Smith told them to kill some turtles, of which there were plenty, and they would make some bread by-and-by, and would all eat together. While they were talking, they heard a gun go off not far off, at which time Woodworth Arnold was killed, as they learned afterward. Soon after, Musemeelin came back and said, " Why did you not kill that white man, according as I bid you? I have laid the other two down." At this they were surprised; and one of the young men, commonly called Jimmy, ran away to the river-side. Musemeelin said to the other, "How will you do to kill Catawbas, if you cannot kill white men? You cowards! I'll show you how you must do;" and then, taking up the English axe that lay there, he struck it three times into Smith's head before he died. Smith never stirred. Then he told the young Indian to call the other, but he was so terrified he could not call. Musemeelin then went and fetched him, and said that two of the white men were killed, he must now go and kill the third; then each of them would have killed one. But neither of them dared venture to talk any thing about it. Then he pressed them to go along with him; he went foremost. Then one of the young men told the other, as they went along, "My friend, don't you kill any of the white people, let him do what he will; I have not killed Smith; he has done it himself; we have no need to do such a barbarous thing." Musemeelin being then a good way before them, in a hurry, they soon saw John Armstrong sitting upon an old log. Musemeelin spoke to him and said, "Where is my horse?" Armstrong made answer and said, "He will come by-and-by; you shall have him." "I want him now," said Musemeelin. Armstrong answered, "You shall have him. Come, let us go to that fire," (which was at some distance from the place where Armstrong sat,) "and let us talk and smoke together." "Go along, then," said Musemeelin. "I am coming," said Armstrong, "do you go before, Musemeelin; do you go foremost." Armstrong looked then like a dead man, and went toward the fire, and was immediately shot in his back by Musemeelin, and fell. Musemeelin then took his hatchet and struck it into Armstrong's head, and said, "Give me my horse, I tell you." By this time one of the young men had fled again that had gone away before, but he returned in a short time. Musemeelin then told the young men they must not offer to discover or tell a word about what had been done, for their lives; but they must help him to bury Jack, and the other two were to be thrown into the river. After that was done, Musemeelin ordered them to load the horses and follow toward the hill, where they intended to hide the goods. Accordingly they did; and, as they were going, Musemeelin told them that, as there were a great many Indians hunting about that place, if they should happen to meet with any they must be killed to prevent betraying them. As they went along, Musemeelin going before, the two young men agreed to run away as soon as they could meet with any Indians, and not to hurt anybody. They came to the desired place; the horses were unloaded, and Musemeelin opened the bundles, and offered the two young men each a parcel of goods. They told him that as they had already sold their skins, and everybody knew they had nothing, they would certainly be charged with a black action were they to bring any goods to the town, and therefore would not accept of any, but promised nevertheless not to betray him. "Now," says Musemeelin, "I know what you were talking about when you stayed so far behind."

The two young men being in great danger of losing their lives —of which they had been much afraid all that day—accepted of what he offered to them, and the rest of the goods they put in a heap and covered them from the rain, and then went to their hunting-cabin. Musemeelin, unexpectedly finding two or three more Indians there, laid down his goods, and said he had killed Jack Armstrong and taken pay for his horse, and should any of them discover it, that person he would likewise kill, but otherwise they might all take a part of the goods. The young man called Jimmy went to Shamokin, after Musemeelin was gone to bury the goods, with three more Indians, with whom he had prevailed; one of them was Neshaleeny's son, whom he had ordered to kill James Smith; but these Indians would not have any of the goods. Some time after the young Indian had been in Shamokin, it was whispered about that some of the Delaware Indians had killed Armstrong and his men. A drunken Indian came to one of the Tudolous houses at night and told the man of the house that he could tell him a piece of bad news. "What is that?" said the other. The drunken man said, "Some of our Delaware Indians have killed Armstrong and his men, which if our chiefs should not resent, and take them up, I will kill them myself, to prevent a disturbance between us and the white people, our brethren." Next morning Shickcalamy and some other Indians of the Delawares were called to assist Allumoppies in council; when Shickcalamy and Allumoppies got one of the Tudolous Indians to write a letter to me, to desire me to come to Shamokin in all haste—that the Indians were very much dissatisfied in mind. This letter was brought to my house by four Delaware Indians, sent express; but I was then in Philadelphia, and when I came home and found all particulars mentioned in this letter, and that none of the Indians of the Six Nations had been down, I did not care to meddle with Delaware Indian affairs, and stayed at home till I received the

governor's orders to go, which was about two weeks after.   Allumoppies was advised by his council to employ a *conjuror*, or prophet,
as they call it, to find out the murderer.   Accordingly he did, and
the Indians met.   The *seer*, being busy all night, told them in the
morning to examine such and such a one that .was present when
Armstrong was killed, naming the two young men.   Musemeelin
was present.   Accordingly, Allumoppies, Quitheyquent, and Thomas
Green, an Indian, went to him that had fled first, and examined
him.   He told the whole story very freely.   Then they went to the
other, but he would not say a word, and they went away and left
him.   The three Indians returned to Shickcalamy and informed them
of what discovery they had made, when it was agreed to secure the
murderers and deliver them up to the white people.   Then a great
noise arose among the Delaware Indians, and some were afraid
of their lives and went into the woods.   Not one cared to meddle
with Musemeelin and the other that could not be prevailed on to
discover any thing, because of the resentment of their families;
but they being pressed by Shickcalamy's son to secure the
murderers, otherwise they would be cut off from the chain of
friendship, four or five of the Delawares made Musemeelin and
the other young man prisoners, and tied them both.   They lay
twenty-four hours, and none would venture to conduct them down,
because of the great division among the Delaware Indians; and
Allumoppies, in danger of being killed, fled to Shickcalamy and
begged his protection.   At last Shickcalamy's son, Jack, went to
the Delawares,—most of them being drunk, as they had been for
several days,—and told them to deliver the prisoners to Alexander
Armstrong, and they were afraid to do it; they might separate
their heads from their bodies and lay them in the canoe, and carry
them to Alexander to roast and eat them; that would satisfy his
revenge, as he wants to eat Indians.   They prevailed with the said
Jack to assist them; and accordingly he and his brother, and some
of the Delawares, went with two canoes and carried them off.

Conrad Weiser, in a letter to a friend, dated Heidelberg, 1746,
adverts to an interesting incident which occurred at the conclusion
of this interview at Shamokin.   He says, " Two years ago I was
sent by the governor to Shamokin, on account of the unhappy
death of John Armstrong, the Indian trader, (1744.)   After I had
performed my errand, there was a feast prepared, to which the

governor's messengers were invited. There were about one hundred persons present, to whom, after we had in great silence devoured a fat bear, the eldest of the chiefs made a speech, in which he said, that by a great misfortune three of the brethren, the white men, had been killed by an Indian; that, nevertheless, the sun was not set, (meaning there was no war;) it had only been somewhat darkened by a small cloud, which was now done away. He that had done evil was like to be punished, and the land remain in peace; therefore he exhorted his people to thankfulness to God; and thereupon he began to sing with an awful solemnity, but without expressing any words; the others accompanying him with great earnestness of fervor, spoke these words: 'Thanks, thanks be to thee, thou great Lord of the world, in that thou hast again caused the sun to shine, and hast dispersed the dark cloud! The Indians are thine.'"

Among the first settlers in Aughwick Valley was Captain Jack, certainly one of the most noted characters of his day. He flourished about Aughwick between 1750 and 1755, when, with two or three companions, he went to the Juniata and built himself a cabin near a beautiful spring. His sole pursuit, it would appear, was hunting and fishing; by which he procured the means of subsistence for his family. There was a mystery about him which no person ever succeeded in fathoming, and even his companions never learned his history or his real name.

He was a man of almost Herculean proportions, with extremely swarthy complexion. In fact, he was supposed by some to be a half-breed and by others a quadroon. Colonel Armstrong, in a letter to the governor, called him the "Half-Indian." The truth of it, however, is that he was a white man, possessing a more than ordinary share of intelligence for a backwoodsman, but his early history is altogether shrouded in mystery. It appears that in the summer of 1752 Captain Jack and his companions were on a fishing excursion.   Returning late in the evening, Jack found his cabin in ruins and his wife and two children murdered.   From that moment he became an altered man, quit the haunts of men, and roamed the woods alone, sleeping in caves, hollow logs, or wherever he could find a shelter.   The loss of his family, no doubt, crazed him for a time, as he did not appear among the settlers until the fall of 1753.   In the interim, however, he was frequently seen, and, we may add, frequently *felt*, by the savages, but he studiously avoided all intercourse with his fellow-men.   If we may judge of his subsequent career, there is every reason to believe that on the discovery of the wrongs done him by the savages he made a vow to devote the balance of his life to slaying Indians. If he did, right faithfully was his vow kept, for his fame spread far and wide among the red-skins, and many a one bit the dust by his trusty rifle and unerring aim.   The settlers about Aughwick, as well as those in Path Valley and along the river, frequently found dead savages, some in a state of partial decay, and others with their flesh stripped by the bald-eagles and their bones bleaching in the sun on the spot where Jack's rifle had laid them low.

On one occasion Captain Jack had concealed himself in the woods by the side of the Aughwick Path, where he lay in wait for a stray Indian.   Presently a painted warrior, with a red feather waving from his head and his body bedizened with gewgaws recently purchased from a trader, came down the path.   A crack from Captain Jack's rifle, and the savage bounded into the air and fell dead without a groan in the path. It appears that three others were in company, but had tarried at a spring, who, on hearing the discharge of the rifle, under the impression that their companion had shot a deer or bear, gave a loud " whoop." Captain Jack immediately loaded, and when the Indians came up to the dead body Jack again shot, and killed a second one. The Indians then rushed into the thicket, and one of them, getting a glimpse of Jack, shot at him, but missed him. The wild hunter, seeing that the chances were desperate, jumped out and engaged in a hand-to-hand encounter—the fourth savage being only armed with a tomahawk. He soon despatched the third one by beating his brains out with his rifle; but the fourth one, an athletic fellow, grappled, and a long and bloody fight with knives followed, and only ceased when both were exhausted by the loss of blood. The Indian managed to get away, and left the Black Hunter the victor on the field of battle. Weak and faint as Jack was, he scalped the three savages, fixed their scalps upon bushes overhanging the path, and then, without deigning to touch their gewgaws or their arms, he managed to work his way to the settlement, where his wounds, consisting of eight or ten stabs, were dressed. The settlers, then squatters, cared little about the loss of the Indians, since they deemed it right for Captain Jack to wreak his vengeance on any and every savage whom chance should throw in his way; and so little did they care about the proprietors knowing their whereabouts that no report of the case was ever made to the government of this combat.

It is said that one night the family of an Irishman named Moore, residing in Aughwick, was suddenly

awakened by the report of a gun. This unusual circumstance at such a late hour in the night caused them to
get up to discover the cause; and on opening the door
they found a dead Indian lying upon the very threshold.
By the feeble light which shone through the door they
discovered the dim outline of the wild hunter, who merely
said "I have saved your lives," and then plunged into the
dark ravine and disappeared.

With an eye like the eagle, an aim that was unerring,
daring intrepidity, and a constitution that could brave the
heat of summer as well as the frosts of winter, he roamed
the valley like an uncaged tiger, the most formidable foe
that ever crossed the red man's path. Various were the
plans and stratagems resorted to by the Indians to capture
him, but they all proved unavailing. He fought them
upon their own ground, with their own weapons, and
against them adopted their own merciless and savage
mode of warfare. In stratagem he was an adept, and in
the skilful use of the rifle his superior probably did not
exist in his day and generation.

These qualifications not only made him a terror to the
Indians, but made him famous among the settlers, who
for their own protection formed a scout, or company of
rangers, and tendered to Captain Jack the command,
which he accepted. This company was uniformed like
Indians, with hunting-shirts, leather leggings, and moc-
casins, and, as they were not acting under sanction of
government, styled themselves "Captain Jack's Hunters."
All the *hunting* done, however, after securing game to
supply their wants, was probably confined to *hunting* for
scalps of Indians; and, as it was a penal offence then to

occupy the hunting-grounds of the Juniata Valley, much more so to shed the blood of any of the savages, it is not likely that the *hunters* ever furnished the Quaker proprietors with an official list of the " killed and wounded." These exploits gave Captain Jack a number of names or sobriquets in the absence of his real name ; he was known as the " Black Rifle," " Black Hunter," " Wild Hunter of the Juniata," &c. On one occasion, with his band, he followed a party of marauding Indians to the Conococheague, and put them to rout. This act reached the authorities in Philadelphia, and Governor Hamilton granted him a sort of irregular roving commission to hold in check the unfriendly Indians of the frontier. With this authority he routed the savages from the Cove and several other places, and the general fear he inspired among them no doubt prevented a deal of mischief in the Juniata Valley.

Early in June, Captain Jack offered the services of himself and his band of hunters to government to accompany Braddock on his expedition against Fort Duquesne. His merits were explained to Braddock by George Crogan, who said, " They are well armed, and are equally regardless of heat or cold. They require no shelter for the night, *and ask no pay.*" This generous offer on the part of Captain Jack was not accepted by Braddock, because, as he alleged, "the proffered services were coupled with certain stipulations to which he could not consent." What these stipulations were was not mentioned. It is presumed, however, that Captain Jack wished his company to go as a volunteer force, free from the restraints of a camp life which a rigid disciplinarian like Braddock would be likely to adopt. Braddock had already accepted the services of a company of Indians under George Crogan, and, as he wished to gain laurels for himself and his troops by achieving a victory over the French and Indians by open European fighting, his own selfishness probably prompted him to refuse the assistance of any more who adopted the skulking Indian mode of warfare. He did not live, however, to discover his error. Hazzard, in his Pennsylvania Register, in speaking of the non-acceptance of Captain Jack's offer, says, "It was a great misfortune for Braddock that he neglected to secure the services of such an auxiliary." Very true; for such men as Jack's Hunters would never have suffered themselves to be fired upon by an ambuscaded enemy or an enemy hid away in a ravine. They would not have marched over the hill with drums beating and colors flying, in pride and pomp, as if enjoying a victory not yet won; but they would have had their scouts out, the enemy and his position known, and the battle fought without any advantages on either side; and in such an event it is more than probable that victory would have crowned the expedition.

Of the final end of Captain Jack we have nothing definite. One account says he went to the West; another that he died an old man in 1772, having lived the life of a hermit after the end of the war of 1763. It is said that his bones rest near the spring, at the base of the mountain bearing his name; and this we are inclined to believe. The early settlers of the neighborhood believed that Captain Jack came down from the mountain every night at twelve o'clock to slake his thirst at his favorite spring; and half a century ago we might readily have produced the affidavits of twenty respectable men who had seen the

Black Hunter in the spirit roaming over the land that was his in the flesh. The present generation, however, knows little about the wild hunter. Still, though he' sleeps the sleep that knows no waking, and no human being who ever saw him is above the sod now, the towering mountain, a hundred miles in length, bearing his name, will stand as an indestructable monument to his memory until time shall be no more.

George Crogan figured extensively about Aughwick for many years, both before and after Fort Shirley was built. He was an Irishman by birth, and came to the colony probably as early as 1742, and soon after took up the business of an Indian trader. At first he located at Harris's trading-house, on the Susquehanna, and from thence moved over the river into Cumberland county, some eight miles from his first place of abode. From there he made excursions to Path Valley and Aughwick, and finally to the Ohio River by way of the old Bedford trail. His long residence among the Indians not only enabled him to study Indian character thoroughly, but he acquired the language of both the Delaware and Shawnee tribes, and was of great use to the proprietary government; but we incline to the opinion that his services were illy requited.

His first letter, published in the Colonial Records, is dated "May yᵉ 26th, 1747," and is directed to Richard Peters. It was accompanied by a letter from the Six Nations, some wampum, and a French scalp, taken somewhere on Lake Erie.

In a letter from Governor Hamilton to Governor Hardy, dated 5th July, 1756, in speaking of Crogan, who was at one time suspected of being a spy in the pay of the

French, Hamilton says:—"There were many Indian traders with Braddock—Crogan among others, who acted as a captain of the Indians under a warrant from General Braddock, and I never heard of any objections to his conduct in that capacity. For many years he had been very largely concerned in the Ohio trade, was upon that river frequently, and had a considerable influence among the Indians, speaking the language of several nations, and being very liberal, or rather profuse, in his gifts to them, which, with the losses he sustained by the French, who seized great quantities of his goods, and by not getting the debts due to him from the Indians, he became bankrupt, and since has lived at a place called Aughwick, in the back parts of this province, where he generally had a number of Indians with him, for the maintenance of whom the province allowed him sums of money from time to time, but not to his satisfaction. After this he went, by my order, with these Indians, and joined General Braddock, who gave the warrant I have mentioned. Since Braddock's defeat, he returned to Aughwick, where he remained till an act of assembly was passed here granting him a freedom from arrest for ten years. This was done that the province might have the benefit of his knowledge of the woods and his influence among the Indians; and immediately thereupon, while I was last at York, a captain's commission was given to him, and he was ordered to raise men for the defence of the western frontier, which he did in a very expeditious manner, but not so frugally as the commissioners for disposing of the public money thought he might have done. He continued in the command of one of the companies he had raised, and of Fort Shirley, on the western frontier, about three months; during which time he sent, by my direction, Indian messengers to the Ohio for intelligence, but never produced me any that was very material; and, having a dispute with the commissioners about some accounts between them, in which he thought himself ill-used, he resigned his commission, and about a month ago informed me that he had not received pay upon General Braddock's warrant, and desired my recommendation to General Shirley; which I gave him, and he set off directly for Albany; and I hear he is now at Onondago with Sir William Johnston."

Crogan settled permanently in Aughwick in 1754, and built a stockade fort, and must have been some kind of an agent among the Indians, disbursing presents to them for the government. In December of that year he wrote to Secretary Peters, stating the wants of his Indians, and at the same time wrote to Governor Morris as follows :—

"*May it please your honor :—*

"I am Oblig^d to advertize the Inhabitance of Cumberland county in y^r honour's Name, nott to barter or Sell Spiretus Liquers to the Indians or any person to bring amongst them, to prevent ye Indians from Spending there Cloase, tho' I am oblig^d to give them a kag Now and then my self for a frolick, but that is Atended with no Expence to ye Government, nor no bad consequences to ye Indians as I do itt butt onst a Month. I hope your honour will approve of this Proceeding, as I have Don itt to Prevent ill consequences atending ye Indians if they should be Kept always Infleam^d with Liquors."

In September, 1754, notwithstanding the precautions taken by the government to conciliate the Indians by profuse presents, and immediately after Conrad Weiser, the

Indian interpreter, and Crogan, had held a conference at Aughwick, which it was supposed had terminated satisfactorily to all parties concerned, an Indian, named Israel, of the Six Nations, after leaving the conference, perpetrated a brutal murder in Tuscarora Valley. The following is Crogan's report of it to government:—

Aughwick, September 17, 1754.

May it please Your Honor:—

Since Mr. Weiser left this, an Indian of the Six Nations, named Israel, killed one Joseph Cample, an Indian trader, at the house of one Anthony Thompson, at the foot of the Tuscarora Valley, near Parnall's Knob. As soon as I heard it I went down to Thompson's, and took several of the chiefs of the Indians with me, when I met William Maxwell, Esq. The Indian made his escape before I got there. I took the qualification of the persons who were present at the murder, and delivered them to Mr. Maxwell, to be sent to your honor, with the speech made by the chiefs of the Indians on that occasion, which I suppose your honor has received.

I have heard many accounts from Ohio since Mr. Weiser left this, all of which agree that the French have received a reinforcement of men and provision from Canada to the fort. An Indian returned yesterday to this place whom I had sent to the fort for intelligence; he confirms the above accounts, and further says there were about sixty French Indians had come while he stayed there, and that they expected better than two hundred more every day. He says that the French design to send those Indians with some French, in several parties, to annoy the back settlements, which the French say will put a stop to any English forces marching out this fall to attack them. This Indian likewise says that the French will do their endeavor to have the half-king Scarrayooday, Captain Montour, and myself, killed this fall. This Indian, I think, is to be believed, if there can be any credit given to what an Indian says. He presses me strongly to leave this place, and not live in any of the back parts. The scheme of sending several parties to annoy the back settlements seems so much like French policy that I can't help thinking it true.

I hear from Colonel Innes that there certainly have been some French Indians at the camp at Wills's Creek, who fired on the sentry in the dead of the night. If the French prosecute this scheme, I don't know what will become of the back parts of Cumberland county, which is much exposed. The back parts of Virginia and Maryland are covered by the English camp, so that most of the inhabitants are safe.

I would have written to your honor before now on this head; I only waited the return of this Indian messenger, whose account I really think is to be depended on. The Indians here seem very uneasy at their long stay, as they have heard nothing from the Governor of Virginia nor of your honor since Mr. Weiser went away; nor do they see the English making any preparations to attack the French, which seems to give them a great deal of concern. I believe several of the Indians will soon go to the Six Nation country, and then, I suppose, the rest will be obliged to fall in with the French. If this happens, then all the back settlements will be left to the mercy of an outrageous enemy.

I beg your honor's pardon for mentioning the consequences which must certainly attend the slow motion of the English government, as they are well known to your honor, and I am sensible your honor had done all in your power for the security of those parts. I hope as soon as his honor, Governor Morris, is arrived, I shall hear what is to be done with those Indians. I assure your honor it will not be in my power to keep them together much longer.

I am your honor's most humble and most obedient servant,

GEO. CROGAN.

The Indian Israel was arrested, taken to Philadelphia, and tried, but, in consequence of the critical situation of affairs, the French having tampered with the Six Nations until they were wavering, he was let off, returned to his tribe, and the matter smoothed over as best it could under the circumstances.

The number of Indians under Crogan at Braddock's defeat was thirty; but what part they performed on that

eventful day was not recorded. That Crogan and his
Indians were of some service would appear from the fact
that the Assembly passed a law exempting him from
arrests — for debt, it is supposed — for ten years, and
commissioning him a captain in the colonial service.

The supposition that Crogan was a spy in the pay
of the French was based upon the idea that he was
a Roman Catholic, inasmuch as he was born in Dublin.
His loyalty was first brought into question by Governor
Sharpe, in December, 1753, who wrote to Governor
Hamilton, informing him that the French knew every
move for defence made in the colonies, and asked his
opinion of Crogan. In answer, Governor Hamilton
said :—

> I observe what you say of Mr. Crogan; and, though the several
> matters of which you have received information carry in them a
> good deal of suspicion, and it may be highly necessary to keep a
> watchful eye upon him, yet I hope they will not turn out to be any
> thing very material, or that will effect his faithfulness to the trust
> reposed in him, which, at this time, is of great importance and a
> very considerable one.   At present I have no one to inquire of as
> to the truth of the particulars mentioned in yours but Mr. Peters,
> who assures me that Mr. Crogan has never been deemed a Roman
> Catholic, nor does he believe that he is one, though he knows not
> his education, which was in Dublin, nor his religious profession.

Whatever Mr. Crogan's religious faith may have been,
he paid much less attention to it than he did to Indian
affairs; and that he was deeply devoted to the proprietary
government is evident from his subsequent career. To
keep the Indians loyal, he advanced many presents to
them, as appears by Governor Morris's letter to Governor
Hardy, for which he never was reimbursed; and the com-

pany of Indians he commanded was fitted out at his own expense; and it was the attempt to get what he advanced on that occasion that led to his quarrel with the commissioners and his resignation.

From Philadelphia he went to Onondago, in September, 1756, and soon after was appointed deputy-agent of Indian affairs by Sir William Johnston. On his arrival in Philadelphia, his appointment was announced to the council by Governor Denny.

"The council, knowing Mr. Crogan's circumstances, was not a little surprised at the appointment, and desired to see his credentials;" which he produced, and again took an active part in Indian affairs.

After the French had evacuated Fort Duquesne, in 1758, Crogan resided for a time in Fort Pitt. From there he went down the river, was taken prisoner by the French, and taken to Detroit. From thence he returned to New York, where he died in 1782.

On the 6th of October, 1754, the reigning chief of Aughwick, called *Tanacharrisan*, or Half-King, died at Paxton. In communicating his death to the governor, John Harris said:—

Those Indians that are here blame the French for his death, by bewitching him, as they had a conjurer to inquire into the cause a few days before he died; and it is his opinion, together with his relations, that the French have been the cause of their great man's death, by reason of his striking them lately; for which they seem to threaten immediate revenge, and desire me to let it be known.

The loss of the Half-King must have been a severe affliction to his tribe, for it appears by a letter of Cro-

gan's that he was compelled to "wipe away their tears
to the amount of thirty pounds fourteen shillings:"

Scarroyady* succeeded the Half-King in the administration of affairs at Aughwick. He was a brave and
powerful chief, and possessed the most unbounded influence among the Indians. Governor Morris, in a
speech, previously approved by council, made to Scarroyady and some Indians accompanying him, said:—

"Brethren:—For the encouragement of you and all who will
join you in the destruction of our enemies, I propose to give the
following bounties or rewards, viz.: for every male Indian prisoner
above twelve years old that shall be delivered at any of the government's forts or towns, one hundred and fifty dollars.

"For every female Indian prisoner or male prisoner of twelve
years old and under, delivered as above, one hundred and thirty
dollars.

"For the scalp of every male Indian of above twelve years old,
one hundred and thirty dollars.

"For the scalp of every Indian woman, fifty dollars."

Let this fixed price for scalps not stand upon the pages
of history as a stigma against the peaceable and non-
resistant Quakers of the province; for, at the time these
bounties were offered, John and Thomas Penn had abjured
the habits, customs, and religion of that people.

Fort Shirley was built in Aughwick Valley in the fall
of 1755, and the winter following Crogan resigned his
commission, after which the command was given to Captain Hugh Mercer.

---

* As the Indians could not pronounce the letter *r*, it is probable that the
names having such letters in were bestowed by the whites, or corrupted
by them.

Tradition says that one or two very serious battles were fought in Aughwick, after Fort Shirley was erected; but the accounts of them are so vague that we can give nothing like reliable information touching them.

In January, 1756, two Indians named Lackin, brothers, who professed to be friendly, came to what was then still called Crogan's Fort. The commander of the fort made them some few trifling presents, and plied them well with rum, when they promised to bring in a large number of prisoners and scalps. On leaving the fort, they fell in with a soldier, whom they invited to accompany them a short distance and they would give him some rum. To this the soldier assented, and, after getting out of sight of the fort, one of them suddenly turned and stabbed the soldier in the side with a scalping-knife. A man passing at the time of the occurrence immediately alarmed the garrison, and a posse of thirteen men sallied out; but when they came up near the Indians the latter suddenly turned and fired upon the soldiers, wounding one of them in the thigh. The savages were then surrounded, and one of them shot; the other they attempted to take to the fort alive, but he acted so outrageously that one of the soldiers beat his brains out with the stock of his musket. The Lackins were rather worthless fellows, and it required no wampum, or even coin, to dry up the tears of their friends.

Fort Shirley was abandoned for a while after the burning of Fort Granville, by order of Governor Morris, but the importance of the point prevented it from standing idle long. We hear of some few murders committed near the Three Springs of the valley at a later day, but no attack was made in the neighborhood during the second Indian war, as the entire valley was well protected by the friendly Indians of the Six Nations.

The Delawares and Shawnees, or at least a great portion of them, left the valley in 1754–55–56, and before 1761 all had disappeared. But to the friendly Indian the beautiful Aughwick was a favorite haunt until the Anglo-Saxon fairly ploughed and harrowed him out of his home and his hunting-grounds. The last of the Six Nations left Aughwick for Cattaraugus in 1771.

CHAPTER XII.

THE earliest settlement on the *Raystown* Branch of the
Juniata was made by a man named Ray, in 1751, who
built three cabins near where Bedford now stands. In
1755 the province agreed to open a wagon-road from
Fort Louden, in Cumberland county, to the forks of the
Youghiogheny River. For this purpose three hundred
men were sent up, but for some cause or other the project
was abandoned.

- This road was completed in 1758, when the allied forces
of Virginia, Maryland, and Pennsylvania marched against
Fort Duquesne, under General John Forbes. About the
same year the fort was built at Raystown, and called Fort
Bedford. Colonels Boquet and Washington first marched
to Bedford with the advance, and were followed by
General Forbes, who had been detained by illness at Carlisle. The successful troops that put to rout the French
without striking a blow, amounting to 7850 men, were

reviewed, where Bedford now stands, a little over *ninety-seven* years ago. Of the triumphant march and the bloodless victory of General Forbes and Colonels Boquet and Washington there is little use in speaking here, more than incidentally mentioning that, profiting by the dear-bought experience at Braddock's defeat, the suggestion of Washington to fight the savages after their own manner was adopted, and, after defeating them in several skirmishes, the Indians fled before them like chaff before the wind, and when they reached Fort Duquesne the name and the fort alone remained. The latter was preserved, but the former was speedily changed to Fort Pitt.

Colonel Armstrong, whose name has already frequently appeared, served as a captain in the expedition under General Forbes against Fort Duquesne. It may also be as well to remember that Colonel Washington, as well as the Virginians generally, jealous of the Pennsylvanians gaining a footing in the Monongahela country, violently opposed the cutting of the road from Raystown to the mouth of the Yough, and urged strongly upon Forbes the propriety of using the old Braddock trail. The decision of General Forbes procured for the people of Pennsylvania a wagon-road over the Alleghany at least twenty years before the inhabitants would have entertained the idea of so formidable an undertaking. Armstrong wrote to Richard Peters, under date of " Raystown, October 3, 1758," from whose letter we extract the following:—

Since our Quixotic expedition you will, no doubt, be greatly perplexed about our fate. God knows what it may be; but, I assure you, the better part of the troops are not at all dismayed. The general came here at a critical and seasonable juncture; he is weak, but his spirit is good and his head clear, firmly determined to proceed as far as force and provisions will admit, which, through divine favor, will be far enough. The road to be opened from our advanced post is not yet fully determined, and must be further reconnoitered: 'tis yet a query whether the artillery will be carried forward with the army when within fifteen or twenty miles of the fort or not. The order of march and line of battle is under consideration, and there are many different opinions respecting it. Upon this the general will have a conference with the commanders of the sundry corps. About four thousand five hundred are yet fit for duty, five or six hundred of which may be laid to the account of keeping of different posts, sickness, accidents, &c. We know not the number of the enemy, but they are greatly magnified, by report of sundry of the people with Major Grant, to what we formerly expected. The Virginians are much chagrined at the opening of the road through this government, and Colonel Washington has been a good deal sanguine and obstinate upon the occasion; but the presence of the general has been of great use on this as well as other accounts. We hear that three hundred wagons are on the road. If this month happens to be dry weather, it will be greatly in our favor. My people are in general healthy, and are to be collected together immediately, except such as are posted on the communication and in the artillery. Many of them will be naked by the end of the campaign, but I dare not enter upon clothing them, not knowing who or how many of the troops may be continued. Colonel B———t is a very sensible and useful man; notwithstanding, had not the general come up, the consequences would have been dangerous. Please to make my compliments to Mr. Allen, and, if you please, show him this letter, as I have not a moment longer to write. About the last of this month will be the critical hour. Every thing is vastly dear with us, and the money goes like old boots. The enemy are beginning to kill and carry off horses, and every now and then scalp a wandering person.

I leave this place to-day, as does Colonel Boquet and some pieces of the artillery.

In 1763, Fort Bedford was the principal depôt for military stores between Carlisle and Fort Pitt. In order to strengthen it, the command was given to Captain

Ourry, and the small stockades at the Juniata Crossing and Stony Creek were abandoned and the force concentrated at Bedford. By this means two volunteer companies were formed to guard the fort, which, besides being a refuge for the distressed families for ten or fifteen miles around, contained vast quantities of ammunition and other government stores.

In 1763, Colonel Boquet again passed up the Raystown Branch with two regiments of regulars and a large convoy of military stores, to relieve the beleaguered garrison at Fort Pitt. He found matters in a deplorable condition at Fort Bedford. The Indians, although they had never made an attack upon the fort, had for weeks been hovering around the frontier settlements, and had killed, scalped, or taken prisoner, no less than eighteen persons. This induced Colonel Boquet to leave two companies of his army at Bedford.

The names of the persons killed or taken prisoners at that time are not recorded, and, we regret to say, few of any of the particulars connected therewith have been preserved.

The town of Bedford was laid out by John Lukens, the surveyor-general, in 1766, and took its name (in honor of the Duke of Bedford) from the fort. The town for many years was the most prominent point between Carlisle and Pittsburg. The county was formed out of Cumberland, in 1771, and embraced a vast extent of territory, from which Huntingdon, Mifflin, Cambria, Somerset, Westmoreland, Fulton, and Indiana, were subsequently taken.

During the Revolutionary war, the town of Bedford

proper, as well as the surrounding country, was so well
settled that the Indians kept a respectful distance.   On
Yellow Creek, one of the tributaries of Raystown Branch,
settlements were made at an early day; also in the
Great Cove.   During the Revolution, Colonel John Piper,
of Yellow Creek, was the lieutenant-colonel of the
county, and George Ashman lieutenant, and James Martin, Edward Combs, and Robert Culbertson, were sub-
lieutenants.

Colonel James Smith, whose narrative has been published in several works, was taken by the Indians in 1755,
near Bedford.   He was taken to Fort Duquesne, and was
there when the victorious Frenchmen and savages returned
with the scalps and plunder taken from Braddock's van-
quished army.   After undergoing some severe trials, such
as running the gauntlet, &c., Smith was taken to Ohio,
and, after a ceremony of baptizing, painting, and hair-
pulling, he was adopted, as a warrior "in good standing,"
into the Conowaga tribe.   No other resort being left, as a
measure of self-defence he adopted the manners and customs of the tribe, and wandered over the West with them
until an opportunity offered to escape; which did not
occur until he reached Montreal, in 1760, when he obtained his freedom in the general exchange of prisoners
which took place.

In 1765, Smith figured conspicuously in Bedford
county, as the leader of the celebrated band of "*Black
Boys*," whose singular and summary administration of justice bore a marked affinity to the code sometimes adopted
by that worthy disseminator of criminal jurisprudence in

the West,—"Judge Lynch." Of the exploits of the
famous Black Boys Smith speaks as follows :—

Shortly after this (1764) the Indians stole horses and killed
some people on the frontiers. The king's proclamation was then
circulating, and set up in various public places, prohibiting any
person from trading with the Indians until further orders.

Notwithstanding all this, about the 1st of March, 1765, a number of wagons, loaded with Indian goods and warlike stores, were
sent from Philadelphia to Henry Pollens, Conococheague; and
from thence seventy pack-horses were loaded with these goods, in
order to carry them to Fort Pitt. This alarmed the country, and
Mr. William Duffield raised about fifty armed men, and met the
pack-horses at the place where Mercersburg now stands. Mr.
Duffield desired the employers to store up their goods and not proceed until further orders. They made light of this, and went over
the North Mountain, where they lodged in a small valley called the
Great Cove. Mr. Duffield and his party followed after, and came
to their lodging, and again urged them to store up their goods.
He reasoned with them on the impropriety of their proceedings
and the great danger the frontier inhabitants would be exposed to
if the Indians should now get a supply. He said as it was well
known that they had scarcely any ammunition, and were almost
naked, to supply them now would be a kind of murder, and would
be illegally trading at the expense of the blood and treasure of the
frontiers. Notwithstanding his powerful reasoning, these traders
made game of what he said, and would only answer him by ludi-
crous burlesque.

When I beheld this, and found that Mr. Duffield could not compel them to store up their goods, I collected ten of my old warriors
that I had formerly disciplined in the Indian way, went off privately
after night, and encamped in the woods. The next day, as usual,
we blacked and painted, and waylaid them near Sideling Hill. I
scattered my men about forty rods along the side of the road, and
ordered every two to take a tree, and about eight or ten rods
between each couple, with orders to keep a reserved fire—one not
to fire until his comrade had loaded his gun. By this means we
kept a constant slow fire upon them, from front to rear. We then
heard nothing of these traders' merriment or burlesque. When

they saw their pack-horses falling close by them, they called out, "Pray, gentlemen, what would you have us to do?" The reply was, "Collect all your loads to the front, and unload them in one place; take your private property, and immediately retire." When they were gone, we burnt what they left, which consisted of blankets, shirts, vermilion, lead, beads, wampum, tomahawks, scalping-knives, &c.

The traders went back to Fort Louden, and applied to the commanding officer there, and got a party of Highland soldiers, and went with them in quest of the robbers, as they called us; and, without applying to a magistrate or obtaining any civil authority, but purely upon suspicion, they took a number of creditable persons, (who were chiefly not anyway concerned in this action,) and confined them in the guard-house in Fort Louden. I then raised three hundred riflemen, marched to Fort Louden, and encamped on a hill in sight of the fort. We were not long there until we had more than double as many of the British troops prisoners in our camp as they had of our people in the guard-house. Captain Grant, a Highland officer who commanded Fort Louden, then sent a flag of truce to our camp, where we settled a cartel and gave them above two for one; which enabled us to redeem all our men from the guard-house without further difficulty.

This exploit of the *Black Boys* is supposed to have given Bloody Run its name. Soon after, some British officer wrote an account of the affair and transmitted it to London, where it was published, and from which the following is an extract. "The convoy of eighty horses, loaded with goods, chiefly on His Majesty's account, as presents to the Indians, and part on account of Indian traders, were surprised in a narrow and dangerous defile in the mountains by a body of armed men. A number of horses were killed, and the whole of the goods were carried away by the plunderers. *The rivulet was dyed with blood, and ran into the settlement below, carrying with it the stain of crime upon its surface.*"

Notwithstanding Smith's narrative may have been read by a majority of our readers, we cannot resist the temptation of transferring another graphic picture of frontier life from his work. He says :—

In the year 1769, the Indians again made incursions on the frontiers; yet the traders continued carrying goods and warlike stores to them. The frontiers took the alarm, and a number of persons collected, destroyed, and plundered, a quantity of their powder, lead, &c., in Bedford county. Shortly after this, some of these persons, with others, were apprehended and laid in irons in the guard-house in Fort Bedford, on suspicion of being the perpetrators of this crime.

Though I did not altogether approve of the conduct of this new club of Black Boys, yet I concluded that they should not lie in irons in the guard-house or remain in confinement by arbitrary or military power. I resolved, therefore, if possible, to release them, if they even should be tried by the civil law afterward. I collected eighteen of my old Black Boys that I had seen tried in the Indian war, &c. I did not desire a large party, lest they should be too much alarmed at Bedford, and accordingly be prepared for us. We marched along the public road in daylight, and made no secret of our design. We told those whom we met that we were going to take Fort Bedford, which appeared to them a very unlikely story. Before this, I made it known to one William Thompson, a man whom I could trust, and who lived there. Him I employed as a spy, and sent him along on horseback before, with orders to meet me at a certain place near Bedford one hour before day. The next day, a little before sunset, we encamped near the Crossings of Juniata, about fourteen miles from Bedford, and erected tents, as though we intended staying all night; and not a man in my company knew to the contrary save myself. Knowing that they would hear this in Bedford, and wishing it to be the case, I thought to surprise them by stealing a march.

As the moon rose about eleven o'clock, I ordered my boys to march, and we went on, at the rate of five miles an hour, until we met Thompson at the place appointed. He told us that the commanding officer had frequently heard of us by travellers, and had ordered thirty men upon guard. He said they knew our number, and only made game of the notion of eighteen men coming to rescue the prisoners; but they did not expect us until toward the middle of the day. I asked him if the gate was open. He said it was then shut, but he expected they would open it, as usual, at daylight, as they apprehended no danger. I then moved my men privately up under the banks of the Juniata, where we lay concealed about one hundred yards from the fort gate. I had ordered the men to keep a profound silence until we got into it. I then sent off Thompson again to spy. At daylight he returned and told us that the gate was open, and three sentinels were standing upon the wall; that the guards were taking a morning dram, and the arms standing together in one place. I then concluded to rush into the fort, and told Thompson to run before me to the arms. We ran with all our might; and, as it was a misty morning, the sentinels scarcely saw us until we were within the gate and took possession of the arms. Just as we were entering, two of them discharged their guns, though I do not believe they aimed at us. We then raised a shout, which surprised the town, though some of them were well pleased with the news. We compelled a blacksmith to take the irons off the prisoners, and then we left the place. This, I believe, was the first British fort in America that was taken by what they call American rebels.

For this exploit Smith was arrested, and, in the scuffle which attended the arrest—for he made a powerful resistance,—one of his captors was shot. He was taken to Carlisle and tried for murder; but, having the sympathies of the people with him, he was triumphantly acquitted. He afterward filled several important stations, and for a time served as a colonel in the Revolutionary army in New Jersey. In 1778 he moved to Kentucky, and joined McIntosh in his efforts against the savages. He had evidently imbibed the habits of frontier life so thoroughly that the strict routine of military discipline and its re straints were totally unsuited to his ideas of fighting.

After the year 1769, numerous robberies were committed near Bedford. The robbers taking the precaution to blacken their faces, all their crimes, as well as many others, were charged upon Smith's Black Boys, until they were looked upon as a band of outlaws. Under date of January 26, 1773, John Frazer and George Woods wrote from Bedford to Governor Penn, as follows:—

May it please Your Honor :—

The many robberies that have lately been committed in the eastern parts of this county oblige us to trouble you with this letter.

There are a number of people, who, we suspect, now reside at or near the Sideling Hill, that have been guilty of several highway-robberies, and have taken from different people—travelling on the public road between this place and Carlisle—considerable sums of money; in particular, a certain James McCashlan, of this place, hath made oath before us that he has been robbed of twenty-two pounds and a silver watch. We have already done our endeavor to apprehend the robbers, but have not succeeded, as there can be no positive proof made who they are, on account of their blacking themselves, which renders it impossible for any person robbed to discover or know who are the perpetrators.

We, therefore, pray your honor would take this matter into consideration, and grant us such relief as your honor may seem most reasonable for the safety of the public in general, and in particular for the inhabitants of this county.

These magistrates labored under the conviction that the highwaymen were none else than a portion of Smith's gang of Black Boys; or else why ask government for aid to disperse a few robbers, when men, arms, and ammunition, were plenty in Bedford?

The letter of Frazer and Woods was accompanied by an affidavit from McCashlan, setting forth that he was robbed, and that he had cause to suspect "a certain John

Gibson and William Paxton" of committing the robbery. These were two of Smith's Black Boys; but it subsequently appeared that a couple of independent footpads had relieved Mr. McCashlan of his pounds and watch, and not a party of the regular Black Boys, who, no doubt, had sins enough of their own to answer for, without having all the depredations committed in the county placed to their account.

Although we spared no effort to get some account of the Indian massacres near Bedford during the Revolution, we failed, and must content ourself—if we do not our readers—by giving the two following, which we copy from Mr. Day's " Historical Collections :"—

About December, 1777, a number of families came into the fort from the neighborhood of Johnstown. Among them were Samuel Adams, one Thornton, and Bridges. After the alarm had somewhat subsided, they agreed to return to their property. A party started with pack-horses, reached the place, and, not seeing any Indians, collected their property and commenced their return. After proceeding some distance, a dog belonging to one of the party showed signs of uneasiness and ran back. Bridges and Thornton desired the others to wait while they would go back for him. They went back, and had proceeded but two or three hundred yards when a body of Indians, who had been lying in wait on each side of the way, but who had been afraid to fire on account of the number of the whites, suddenly rose up and took them prisoners. The others, not knowing what detained their companions, went back after them. When they arrived near the spot the Indians fired on them, but without doing any injury. The whites instantly turned and fled, excepting Samuel Adams, who took a tree, and began to fight in the Indian style. In a few minutes, however, he was killed, but not without doing the same fearful service for his adversary. He and one of the Indians shot at and killed each other at the same moment. When the news reached the fort a party volunteered to visit the ground. When they reached it, although the snow had fallen ankle-deep, they readily found the bodies of Adams and the Indian, the face of the latter having been covered by his companions with Adams's hunting-shirt.

A singular circumstance also occurred about that time in the neighborhood of the Alleghany Mountain. A man named Wells had made a very considerable improvement, and was esteemed rather wealthy for that region. He, like others, had been forced with his family from his house, and had gone for protection to the fort. In the fall of the year, he concluded to return to his place and dig his crop of potatoes. For that purpose, he took with him six or seven men, an Irish servant girl to cook, and an old plough-horse. After they had finished their job, they made preparations to return to the fort the next day. During the night, Wells dreamed that on his way to his family he had been attacked and gored by a bull; and so strong an impression did the dream make that he mentioned it to his companions, and told them that he was sure some danger awaited them. He slept again, and dreamed that he was about to shoot a deer, and, when cocking his gun, the main-spring broke. In his dream he thought he heard distinctly the crack of the spring when it broke. He again awoke, and his fears were confirmed, and he immediately urged his friends to rise and get ready to start. Directly after he arose he went to his gun to examine it, and, in cocking it, the main-spring snapped off. This circumstance alarmed them, and they soon had breakfast, and were ready to leave. To prevent delay, the girl was put on the horse and started off, and, as soon as it was light enough, the rest followed. Before they had gone far, a young dog, belonging to Wells, manifested much alarm, and ran back to the house. Wells called him, but, after going a short distance, he invariably ran back.

Not wishing to leave him, as he was valuable, he went after him, but had gone only a short distance toward the house, when five Indians rose from behind a large tree that had fallen, and approached him with extended hands. The men who were with him fled instantly, and he would have followed, but the Indians were so close that he thought it useless. As they approached him, however, he fancied the looks of a very powerful Indian, who was nearest him, boded no good, and being a swift runner, and thinking it "neck or nothing" at any rate, determined to attempt an escape. As the Indian approached, he threw at him his useless rifle, and dashed off toward the woods in the direction his companions had gone. Instead of firing, the Indians commenced a pursuit, for the purpose of making him a prisoner, but he outran them. After running some distance, and when they thought he would escape, they all stopped and fired at once, and every bullet struck him, but without doing him much injury or retarding his flight. Soon after this he saw where his companions concealed themselves, and, as he passed, he begged them to fire on the Indians, and save him; but they were afraid, and kept quiet. He continued his flight, and, after a short time, overtook the girl with the horse. She quickly understood his danger, and dismounted instantly, urging him to take her place, while she would save herself by concealment. He mounted, but without a whip, and for want of one could not get the old horse out of a trot. This delay brought the Indians upon him again directly, and as soon as they were near enough they fired—and this time with more effect, as one of the balls struck him in the hip and lodged in his groin. But this saved his life; it frightened the horse into a gallop, and he escaped, although he suffered severely for several months afterward.

The Indians were afterward pursued, and surprised at their morning meal; and, when fired on, four of them were killed, but the other, though wounded, made his escape. Bridges, who was taken prisoner near Johnstown when Adams was murdered, saw him come to his people, and describes him as having been shot through the chest, with leaves stuffed in the bullet-holes to stop the bleeding.

The first white child born in Raystown was William Frazer. When the Revolution broke out, Bedford county furnished two companies, a greater portion of one of the companies being recruited in what now constitutes Huntingdon and Blair counties. Among these were a man named McDonald, another named Fee, from the mouth of Raystown Branch, and George Weston, a brother of the tory shot at Kittaning, and a man named Cluggage.

The town of Bedford was for a long time the residence of General A. St. Clair and a number of others who subsequently figured prominently in the affairs of the nation. For pure patriotism and a willingness to spend their blood and treasure for the cause of liberty, as well as the defence of their brethren on the confines of the county, few towns could excel Bedford, which reflected such credit upon them as will be remembered by the grateful descendants of the frontier-men when history fails to do them justice.

CHAPTER XIII.

RAYSTOWN BRANCH, CONTINUED—MURDER OF SANDERS AND HIS FAMILY —ENGLISHMAN AND WIFE TAKEN PRISONERS—FELIX SKELLY AND MRS. ELDER TAKEN CAPTIVES—THEIR RETURN, ETC.

THE country between the mouth of the Raystown Branch of the Juniata and what is called the Crossings was thinly settled prior to the Revolution. The land, and general appearance of things, did not strike settlers very favorably; hence it may be assumed that it was only taken up about 1772, when the new-comers from the eastern counties had already taken up the choice tracts lying contiguous to the river.

The first depredation committed on the Branch, near its mouth, by the savages, occurred in May, 1780. A band of roving Indians were known to be in the country, as several robberies had occurred in Hartslog Valley, at houses belonging to men who with their families were forted either at Lytle's or at Huntingdon. A scout had ranged the entire frontier in search of these depredators, but could not find them. They were seen in Woodcock Valley, and information immediately conveyed to the commander at the fort in Huntingdon. A scout was sent to Woodcock Valley, but got upon the wrong trail, as the

Indians had crossed the Terrace Mountain, where, it appears, they divided into two parties. One of them went to the house of one Sanders, on the Branch; and just as the family were seating themselves at the table to eat dinner, five of the savages bounded in, and killed Sanders, his wife, and three children. An Englishman and his wife, whose names are not recollected, were in the house at the time, both of whom begged for their lives, declared they were loyal to the king, and would accompany them. The Indians agreed to take them along as prisoners, notwithstanding at that period scalps commanded nearly as high a price as prisoners. The Englishman and his wife were taken to Montreal.

The day following the above massacre, the other party of savages, who it appears had taken the country nearer the Juniata to range through, made their appearance at the house of a Mrs. Skelly, who was sick in bed at the time, and her nearest neighbor, Mrs. Elder, being there on a visit. It was a beautiful May-day Sabbath afternoon, when Mrs. Elder prepared to go home, and Felix Skelly, the son, agreed to accompany her part of the way. They had gone probably a hundred rods through a meadow, when Mrs. Elder noticed a savage, partly concealed behind some elder-bushes. She stopped suddenly, and told Felix, who had got a little in advance, to return, as there were Indians about. Skelly said he thought not, and advised her to come on, or it would be night before he could return. Mrs. Elder stood still, however, and soon saw the figure of the Indian so plainly as not to be mistaken, when she screamed to Felix to run, and, when in the act of turning around, a savage sprang from behind an elder bush into the path, and seized her by the hair. Another seized Skelly, and in a moment the shout of victory went up, and three or four more Indians came from their places of concealment. Finding themselves captives, and unable to remedy matters, they submitted with a good grace.

Fortunately for them, the warrior who had command of the party could speak a little English, and was a little more humane than the generality of savages of the day. He gave Mrs. Elder positive assurance that no harm should befall her. He would not, however, give the same assurance to Skelly. They took up their line of march over the Terrace Mountain, crossed over to the base of the Alleghany, avoiding as much as possible the white settlements, and crossed the mountain by the Kittaning Path.

Skelly, although but seventeen years of age, was an atheletic fellow, well built, and weighed in the neighborhood of one hundred and eighty pounds. The Indians, noticing his apparent strength, and in order probably to tire him so that he would make no effort to escape, loaded him down with the plunder they had taken in Hartslog Valley. In addition to this, they found on the Alleghany Mountains some excellent wood for making bows and arrows, a quantity of which they cut and bound together, and compelled Skelly to carry. Mrs. Elder was obliged to carry a long-handled frying-pan, which had been brought all the way from Germany by a Dunkard family, and had, in all probability, done service to three or four generations. Of course, Mrs. Elder, burdened with this alone, made no complaint.

At length the party reached an Indian town on the Alleghany River, where it was determined that a halt

should take place in order to recruit.   One of the Indians
was sent forward to apprise the town of their coming;
and on their entering the town they found a large number of savages drawn up in two lines about six feet
apart, all armed with clubs or paddles.   Skelly was relieved of his load and informed that the performance
would open by his being compelled to run the gauntlet.
Skelly, like a man without money at one o'clock who has
a note to meet in bank before three, felt the importance
and value of *time;* so, walking leisurely between the
lines, he bounded off at a speed that would have done
credit to a greyhound, and reached the far end without
receiving more than one or two light blows.   He was
then exempt, as no prisoner was compelled to undergo
the same punishment twice.

The Indians, disappointed by the fleetness of Skelly,
expected to more than make up for it in pummelling Mrs.
Elder; but in this they reckoned without their host.   The
word was given for her to start, but the warrior who had
captured her demurred, and not from disinterested motives,
either, as will presently appear.   His objections were over-
ruled, and it was plainly intimated that she must conform to the custom.   Seeing no method of avoiding it,
Mrs. Elder, armed with the long-handled pan, walked
between the lines with a determined look.   The first
savage stooped to strike her, and in doing so his scant
dress exposed his person, which Mrs. Elder saw, and
anticipated his intention by dealing him a blow on the
exposed part which sent him sprawling upon all-fours.
The chiefs who were looking on laughed immoderately,
and the next four or five, intimidated by her heroism, did

not attempt to raise their clubs. Another of them, determined to have a little fun, raised his club; but no sooner had he it fairly poised than she struck him upon the head with the frying-pan in such a manner as in all likelihood made him see more stars than ever lit the "welkin dome." The Indians considered her an Amazon, and she passed through the lines without further molestation; but, as she afterward said, she "did it in a hurry."

The squaws, as soon as she was released, commenced pelting her with sand, pulling her hair, and offering her other indignities, which she would not put up with, and again had recourse to her formidable weapon—the long-handled pan. Lustily she plied it, right and left, until the squaws were right glad to get out of her reach.

In a day or two the line of march for Detroit was resumed, and for many weary days they plodded on their way. After the first day's journey, the warrior who had captured Mrs. Elder commenced making love to her. Her comely person had smitten him; her courage had absolutely fascinated him, and he commenced wooing her in the most gentle manner. She had good sense enough to appear to lend a willing ear to his plaintive outpourings, and even went so far as to intimate that she would become his squaw on their arrival at Detroit. This music was of that kind which in reality had "charms to soothe the savage," and matters progressed finely.

One night they encamped at a small Indian village on the bank of a stream in Ohio. Near the town was an old deserted mill, in the upper story of which Skelly and the rest of the male prisoners were placed and the door bolted. That evening the Indians had a grand dance and a drunken revel, which lasted until after midnight. When the revel ended, Skelly said to his comrades in captivity that he meant to escape if possible. He argued that if taken in the attempt he could only be killed, and he thought a cruel death by the savages would be his fate, at all events, at the end of the journey. They all commenced searching for some means of egress, but none offered, save a window. The sash was removed, when, on looking out into the clear moonlight, to their horror they discovered that they were immediately over a large body of water, which formed the mill-dam, the distance to it being not less than sixty feet. They all started back but Skelly. He, it appears, had set his heart upon a determined effort to escape, and he stood for a while gazing upon the water beneath him. Every thing was quiet; not a breath of air was stirring. The sheet of water lay like a large mirror, reflecting the pale rays of the moon. In a minute Skelly formed the desperate determination of jumping out of the mill-window.

"Boys," whispered he, "I am going to jump. The chances are against me; I may be killed by the fall, recaptured by the savages and killed, or starve before I reach a human habitation; but then I *may escape*, and, if I do, I will see my poor mother, if she is still alive, in less than ten days. With me, it is freedom from this captivity *now*, or death." So saying, he sprang from the window-sill, and, before the affrighted prisoners had time to shrink, they heard the heavy plunge of Skelly into the mill-dam. They hastened to the window, and in an instant saw him emerge from the water unharmed, shake himself like a spaniel, and disappear in the shadow of some tall trees. The wary savage sentinels, a few minutes after the plunge, came down to ascertain the noise, but Skelly had already escaped. They looked up at the window, concluded that the prisoners had amused themselves by throwing something out, and returned to their posts.

The sufferings of Skelly were probably among the most extraordinary ever endured by any mortal man. He supposed that he must have walked at least forty miles before he stopped to rest. He was in a dense forest, and without food. The morning was hazy, and the sun did not make its appearance until about ten o'clock, when, to his dismay, he found he was bearing nearly due south, which would lead him right into the heart of a hostile savage country. After resting a short time, he again started on his way, shaping his course by the sun northeast, avoiding all places which bore any resemblance to an Indian trail. That night was one that he vividly remembered the balance of his life. As soon as it was dark, the cowardly wolves that kept out of sight during the day commenced howling, and soon got upon his track. The fearful proximity of the ravenous beasts, and he without even so much as a knife to defend himself, drove him almost to despair, when he discovered a sort of cave formed by a projecting rock. This evidently was a wolf's den. The hole was quite small, but he forced his body through it, and closed the aperture by rolling a heavy stone against it. Soon the wolves came, and the hungry pack, like a grand chorus of demons, kept up their infernal noise all night. To add to the horrors of his situation, he began to feel the pangs of both hunger and thirst. With the break of day came relief, for his cowardly assailants fled at dawn. He ventured out of the den, and soon resolved to keep on the lowlands. After digging up some roots, which he ate, and refreshing himself at a rivulet, he travelled on until after nightfall, when he came upon the very edge of a precipice, took a step, and fell among five Indians sitting around the embers of a fire. Uninjured by the fall, he sprang to his feet, bounded off in the darkness before the Indians could recover from their surprise, and made good his escape.

In this way he travelled on, enduring the most excruciating pains from hunger and fatigue, until the fourth day, when he struck the Alleghany River in sight of Fort Pitt; at which place he recruited for a week, and then returned home by way of Bedford, in company with a body of troops marching east.

His return created unusual gladness and great rejoicing, for his immediate friends mourned him as one dead.

Mrs. Elder gave a very interesting narrative on her return, although she did not share in the sufferings of Skelly. She was taken to Detroit, where she lived in the British garrison in the capacity of a cook. From there she was taken to Montreal and exchanged, and reached home by way of Philadelphia.

Felix Skelly afterward moved to the neighborhood of Wilmore, in Cambria county, where he lived a long time, and died full of years and honors.

CHAPTER XIV.

STANDING STONE, ANCIENT AND MODERN — MURDER OF FELIX
DONNELLY AND HIS SON FRANCIS, ETC.

As an Indian post of ancient date, none is more universally known than "Standing Stone," where Huntingdon
now stands.   The very earliest traders could never ascertain by Indian tradition how long it had been a village,
but that it dated back to a very remote period may be
judged from the fact that the land on the flat between
Stone Creek and Huntingdon was under cultivation one
hundred and five years ago.   It was used as one extensive corn-field, with the exception of that portion lying
near the mouth of the creek, where the Indian town
stood, and where also was a public ground, used on great
occasions for councils or dances.

The Standing Stone—that is, the *original* stone—was,
according to John Harris, fourteen feet high and six
inches square.   It stood on the right bank of Stone
Creek, near its mouth, and in such a position as to
enable persons to see it at a considerable distance, either
from up or down the river.

About this self-same Standing Stone there still exist
contradictory opinions.   These we have endeavored to
ascertain; and, after weighing them carefully, we have
come to the conclusion that no person now living ever

saw part or parcel of the *original* stone, notwithstanding Dr. Henderson delivered what some are disposed to believe a portion of it to the Historical Society of Pennsylvania.

The original Standing Stone, we are induced to believe, in addition to serving a similar capacity to that of a guide-board at a cross-road, was the official record of the tribe. On it, no doubt, were engraved all the important epochs in its history,—its wars, its mighty deeds, its prowess in battle, and its skill in the chase. It might, too, have served as a sacred tablet to the memory of many a noble chief who fell by the arrow of an enemy. These things were, no doubt, in cabalistic characters; and, although each inscription may have been small, its meaning may have taken in almost an unbounded scope, as Indian brevity generally does.

This stone was once the cause of a war. The Tuscaroras, residing some thirty or forty miles down the river,— probably in Tuscarora Valley,—wished to declare war against the tribe at Standing Stone, for some real or fancied insult, and for this purpose sent them repeated war-messages, which the tribe at the Stone refused to give ear to, knowing as they did the strength and power of the enemy. Taking advantage of the absence of a large part of the tribe on a hunt, the Tuscaroras, in great force, came upon the village, captured the stone, and carried it off. Immediately after the return of the warriors, the entire available war-force was despatched after the depredators, who were soon overtaken. A bloody conflict ensued, and the trophy was recaptured and carried back in triumph.

Dr. Barton, it is said, discovered that the word *Oneida* meant "Standing Stone," in the language of the Southern Indians.* The *Oneida* tribe of the Iroquois had a tradition that their forefathers came from the South; consequently, the tribe at Standing Stone may have been part of the Oneida tribe instead of Delawares, as was generally supposed. The Tuscaroras, according to history, came from the South and became one of the Iroquois confederation in 1712. The language of the two tribes in question, although not identical, bore a strong affinity to each other. Hence we may surmise that the characters upon the stone were understood by the Tuscaroras, and that it possessed, in their eyes, sufficient value to move it some forty or fifty miles, under what we should call disadvantageous circumstances, especially when it is known that stones of a better finish could have been found anywhere along the Juniata River.

There is no doubt at all but what the original stone was removed by the Indians and taken with them in 1754 or 1755, for it is a well-ascertained fact that the Indians in the valley, with some few exceptions, (Aughwick, for instance,) joined the French in the above years.

The first survey of the land on which Huntingdon now stands was made by Mr. Lukens, in behalf of a claimant named Crawford, in 1756. It is therein named as "George Crogan's improvement." It is not improbable that Crogan may have claimed the improved fields and site of the deserted village, but that he ever made any improvement

* Morgan, in his "League of the Iroquois," gives it a different interpretation.

beyond probably erecting a trading-post there is a matter of some doubt. His whole history proves that he was no *improving* man.

On the second stone erected were found the names of John and Charles Lukens, Thomas Smith, and a number of others, with dates varying from 1768 to 1770, cut or chiselled. This stone was most unquestionably erected, by some of the men whose names it bore, on the same spot where the original stone stood, but was subsequently removed to or near where the old court-house in Huntingdon formerly stood. This position it occupied for many years, and might still stand as a monument of the past, had not some Vandal taken it into his head to destroy it. One piece of it still remains in a wall of the foundation of a house in Huntingdon.

The old Indian graveyard (and an extensive one it must have been) was on the high ground, near where the present Presbyterian church stands. To the credit of the Huntingdon folks be it said, they have never permitted a general exhumation of the bones of the Indians, to fill scientific cabinets, gratify the morbid appetites of the curious, or even to satisfy the less objectionable zeal of the antiquarian.

The few white settlers who lived at the Stone, in 1762, partially erected a stockade fort; but before the spring of 1763 they were forced to abandon it, as well as their houses, and fly to Carlisle for protection. When the settlers returned, in 1770, the fort still stood, though partially decayed. Immediately on the breaking out of the war of the Revolution, the fort was rebuilt on a more extended scale by the few inhabitants of the town and surrounding country. It was located near where the court-house now stands, immediately on the bluff, and, according to the traces of it discovered by the present generation, must have covered ten acres of ground. It was strongly built; and, when the savages were in the midst of their depredations, it was the only reliable refuge—before the erection of the Lead Mine Fort, in Sinking Valley—for all the people residing as far west as the base of the Alleghany Mountains.

No actual attempt was ever made against Standing Stone Fort; neither were there ever any Indians seen, except on two or three occasions, very close to it. A party of lurking savages were once surprised and shot at by a number of scouts on the hill where the graveyard now stands; but they made good their escape without any injury being done.

At another time, by a display of cool courage, as well as shrewdness, that would do any general credit, the commander of the fort unquestionably saved the place from total annihilation. One morning a large body of savages appeared upon the ridge on the opposite side of the river, and, by their manœuvring, it was clearly evident that they meditated an attack, which, under the circumstances, must have proved disastrous to the settlers, for not more than ten men able to bear arms were in the fort at the time—the majority having left on a scouting expedition. The commander, with judgment that did him infinite credit, marshalled his men, and paraded them for half an hour in such a manner as to enable the Indians to see a constant moving of the middle of the column, but neither end of it, while the drums kept up a constant clatter. In addition to this, he ordered all the women out, armed them with frying-pans, brooms, or whatever he could lay his hands upon, and marched them about the enclosure after the same manner in which he did the men. The enemy could only make out the dim outlines of the people and hear the noise. The stratagem succeeded, and, after a very short council of war, the Indians disappeared.

Among those who figured about Standing Stone, at the beginning of the Revolution, were the Bradys. Hugh Brady's name appears in some of the old title-deeds; and the father of Sam. Brady (rendered famous by R. B. McCabe, Esq.) lived at the mouth of the little run opposite Huntingdon. Within the walls of Standing Stone Fort, General Hugh Brady and a twin-sister were born. All the Bradys went to the West Branch of the Susquehanna during the Revolution. Hugh entered the army at an early age, and, step by step, rose from the ranks to the exalted position he occupied at the time of his death. A characteristic anecdote is related of him. At one time he was lying ill at Erie, and his physician told him he could not survive. "Let the drums beat," said he; "my knapsack is swung, and Hugh Brady is ready to march!" He recovered, however, and died only a few years ago, at Sunbury.

The only massacre by Indians in the immediate vicinity of Standing Stone occurred on the 19th of June, 1777, at what was then known as the "Big Spring," two miles west of the fort. In consequence of hostile bands of Indians having been seen at a number of places in the neighborhood, and the general alarm which followed, people commenced flocking to the forts from every direction.

On the day above named, Felix Donnelly and his son Francis, and Bartholomew Maguire and his daughter, residing a short distance from the mouth of Shaver's Creek, placed a number of their movable effects upon horses, and, with a cow, went down the river, for the purpose of forting at Standing Stone. Jane Maguire was in advance, driving the cow, and the Donnellys and Maguire in the rear, on the horses. When nearly opposite the Big Spring, an Indian fired from ambuscade and killed young Donnelly. His father, who was close to him, caught him, for the purpose of keeping him upon the horse. Maguire urged the old man to fly, but he refused to leave his son. Maguire then rode to his side, and the two held the dead body of Francis. While in this position, three Indians rushed from their ambuscades with terrific yells, and fired a volley, one bullet striking Felix Donnelly, and the other grazing Maguire's ear, carrying away a portion of his hair. The bodies of both the Donnellys fell to the ground, and Maguire rode forward, passing (probably without noticing her) his daughter. The Indians, after scalping the murdered men, followed Jane, evidently with the intention of making a prisoner of her. The fleetest of them overtook her, and grasped her by the dress, and with uplifted tomahawk demanded her to surrender; but she struggled heroically. The strings of her short-gown gave way, and by an extraordinary effort she freed herself, leaving the garment in the hand of the savage; then, seizing the cow's tail, she gave it a twist, which started the animal running, and

gave her an impetus which soon enabled her to pass her
father. The savage still followed, but in the mean time
Maguire had recovered from the consternation caused by
the massacre, and immediately aimed his rifle at the
Indian, when the latter took shelter behind a tree. At
this juncture, a number of men who were pitching quoits
at Cryder's Mill, on the opposite side of the river, who
had heard the firing and the whoops of the savages, put
off in a canoe to engage the Indians; but they were soon
discovered, and the Indian, shaking Jane Maguire's short-
gown derisively at them, disappeared. The men, doubtful as to the number of the enemy, returned to the mill,
to await the arrival of a greater force.

Maguire and his daughter reached the fort in a state
better imagined than described. The garrison was soon
alarmed, and a number of armed men started in pursuit
of the savages. At the mill they were joined by the men
previously mentioned; and, although every exertion was
made in their power, they could not get upon their trail,
and the pursuit was abandoned.

The dead bodies of the Donnellys were taken to Standing Stone, and buried upon what was then vacant ground;
but the spot where they now rest is pointed out in a
garden in the heart of the borough of Huntingdon.

Jane Maguire, who certainly exhibited a very fair share
of the heroism of the day in her escape from the savage,
afterward married a man named Dowling, and moved to
Raystown Branch, where she reared a family of children,
some of whom are still living.

Opposite the mouth of the Raystown Branch lived
Colonel Fee, an active and energetic man during the

Revolution. He was in Captain Blair's expedition against the tories, and for a while served as a private in the army. His widow (a sister of the late Thomas Jackson, of Gaysport) is still living, at the advanced age of eighty-seven years, and to her we are indebted for much valuable information in the construction of these pages.

The Cryders, too, are worthy of a special notice. They consisted of a father, mother, and seven sons. They built a mill at the Big Spring, which served for the people of Standing Stone and the surrounding country. They were all men suitable for the times—rugged and daring. A majority of them were constantly in service during the war of the Revolution, either as frontier-men, scouts, or fort guards. Michael Cryder, the father, used to spend his days at his mill and his nights at the fort during the troublesome times, and it was himself and five of his sons who accomplished the then extraordinary achievement of running the first ark-load of flour down the Juniata River.

The Standing Stone is frequently mentioned in the Archives, but its name is mostly coupled with rumors, grossly exaggerated, of attacks by tories, &c. There is no doubt whatever but that great distress, principally arising from a want of provisions, prevailed there during the war.

When the alarms were most frequent, and Council had been importuned time and again to send provisions to Standing Stone, as well as men for its defence, and munitions, a circular was issued to the county lieutenants, dated July 16, 1778, from which we extract the following:—

It is proper to acquaint you that Colonel Broadhead's regiment, now on a march to Pittsburg, is ordered by the Board of War to the Standing Stone; and we have ordered three hundred militia from Cumberland, and two hundred from York, to join them.

This promise to the ear of the affrighted settlers was broken to the hope. Only seventy of the Cumberland militia were taken to the Standing Stone, and thirty of them soon after removed to garrison the Lead Mine Fort.

Huntingdon was laid out previous to the commencement of hostilities—probably in 1775,—but it retained the name of Stone Town for many years. With the exception of Frankstown, it is the oldest town on the Juniata. On the formation of the county, in 1787, it took the same name. The county, during the late war with Great Britain, furnished three full companies; and, although it once was the stronghold of tories, we can now safely say that it stands among the most patriotic in the State.

SCENE BELOW WILLIAMSBURG.

CHAPTER XV.

TRIALS OF THE EARLY SETTLERS—THEIR FORTS, AND OTHER MEANS OF DEFENCE.

THE first outbreak of the war in 1775 found the frontier inhabitants few in number and without arms. Living in a remote part of the State, where no invading foe would be likely to come, many young and vigorous men went forward and joined the army. This fancied security, however, proved a sad delusion to the frontiermen; and the absence of any regular means of defence was only severely felt when the savages came down from the mountain, ripe for rapine, blood, and theft. The fact that the northwestern savages had allied themselves to the English was only fully realized by the residents of the Juniata Valley when the painted warriors came down the Kittaning War Path, and commenced their infernal and atrocious work by scalping women and innocent babes.

The first alarm and panic over, people collected together and consulted about some means of defence. The more prudent were in favor of abandoning their farms and retiring to some of the eastern settlements, which many did, especially after it was discovered that so many of the

13

king's subjects were likely to remain loyal instead of joining the cause of the patriots. The more daring would not agree to abandon their homes, but at once pledged themselves to defend their firesides at the risk of their lives.

To this end, in the fall of 1777, and in the spring of 1778, a number of fortifications were commenced, the farms abandoned, or partially so, and the inhabitants assumed an attitude of defence. These forts were generally stockades, built of logs or puncheons, with loopholes made to flare on the outside, in order to bring rifles to bear in several directions.

The first of these forts was built near where McCahen's Mill now stands, which was called Fetter's or Frankstown, about a mile above Hollidaysburg. A barn on the flat opposite the second lock, a mile below Hollidaysburg, was turned into a fort and called Holliday's. It was an old barn, but very large, and belonged to one Peter Titus. Through the energy of Mr. Holliday and a few others, it was made comfortable, but not deemed very secure. These forts served for the families in what was termed the Frankstown district, comprising not only Frankstown, but all the surrounding country. In Canoe Valley a fort was built, called Lowry's Fort, but it was small and inconvenient; and the house of Matthew Dean, a mile farther up, was also turned into a temporary fortress in 1777. These served the people of Canoe Valley and Water Street. The people of Hartslog Valley erected a fort south of Alexandria, on Cannon's mill-run, called Lytle's. A large and substantial garrison, called Hartsock's Fort, was built in Woodcock Valley, which served

for the people of that valley and also for the residents of
the middle of the Cove. The inhabitants of the lower
end of the Cove, and along Clover Creek, forted at the
house of Captain Phillips, some two or three miles above
where Williamsburg now stands, which was turned into
a temporary fortress. Anderson's Fort was erected where
Petersburg now stands, while along Shaver's Creek there
were two others—one at General McElery's, and the other
at Alexander McCormick's, toward Stone Creek. The
latter was merely a house fortified without additional
buildings, as was also the house of Captain E. Rickets, in
Warrior's Mark. Forts were also built at Dunning's
Creek, and on the Raystown Branch, while the forts at
Standing Stone and Bedford were enlarged and improved.
The year following, a very substantial fort was built at
the residence of Jacob Roller, in Sinking Valley, to accommodate the large influx of people into the valley.
In the fall of 1778, Fort Roberdeau, or as it was better
known, the Lead Mine Fort, in Sinking Valley, was completed. It was the largest as well as the best-defended
post on the frontier. It was built under the superintendence of General Roberdeau, and occupied by Major
Cluggage, with a regular company from Cumberland
county. On the ramparts two cannon were mounted,
and in the fortress there were plenty of small-arms
and ammunition. This fort was strengthened by government. Lead was exceedingly scarce, and a high
value was attached to it; and, fearing that the mines
might fall into the hands of the enemy, the most vigi-
lant watch was kept and the most rigid military discipline enforced.

During the summer of 1776, very few depredations were committed; but in the following year, as succeeding chapters will show, the incursions and massacres of the Indians were so bold and cruel that the utmost consternation prevailed, and business was in a great measure suspended. The settlers managed to get their sowing done in both fall and spring, but much was sowed that never was reaped. To add to their deplorable condition, the horrors of starvation were constantly staring them in the face.

In order to get in crops, it was necessary to have the reapers guarded and sentinels posted at each corner of a field, while half-grown boys followed in the very footsteps of the laborers, carrying their rifles loaded and primed for defence. By such means they managed to get a scant supply of grain.

The cattle were suffered to graze at large, for seldom, if ever, any of them were molested. Hogs, too, were suffered to run at large in the woods, feeding upon roots and acorns. When meat was wanted, a party ran down a hog or heifer, butchered it, and took it to the fort. As for such luxuries as coffee, tea, sugar, &c., they were among the missing, and little cared for.

It is not, we hope, to the discredit of any of the best men in the Juniata Valley now, to say that their fathers were born in forts and rocked in sugar-troughs, and their grandfathers wore entire suits, including shoes, made of buckskin, lived sometimes on poor fare, and short allowance at that. They were the men whose sinewy arms hewed down the monarchs of the forest, and, with shovel, hoe, plough, and pick, that we might enjoy the bounties of mother earth when they were mouldering in the bosom thereof, made "waste places glad" and the wilderness to blossom like the rose. Hallowed be their names! But, while we raise the tuneful lay to sing psalms of praise to the glorious old pioneers who by hardship and toil have entailed such blessings upon us, is it not a melancholy reflection to think that in but a few succeeding generations the scanty pages of *ancient* histories alone will be the monuments to chronicle their deeds?

CHAPTER XVI.

THE EARLY SETTLERS—OLD HART, THE INDIAN TRADER, ETC.

WE have been unable to procure any thing like a full and complete list of the early settlers of the entire valley; yet we deem it necessary to give what we have procured, as a necessary adjunct to our work. It will be perceived that many of the names are familiar, and the descendants are still scattered profusely over this section of the country, as well as the Union.

Mr. Bell, in his Memoir, states that, at the time of his earliest recollection, between the Stone (Huntingdon) and the mountain, the pioneers had principally settled along the streams. The prevailing religion was the Presbyterian, although there were Lutherans and Roman Catholics, "and probably as many who professed no religion at all as all the other denominations put together."

In addition to those whose names have already appeared, or will appear hereafter, we may incidentally mention, as early settlers about Lewistown, the McClays, McNitts, and Millikin; west of Lewistown, along the river, the Junkins, Wilsons, Bratton, and Stackpoles.

At Huntingdon, Ludwig Sills, Benjamin Elliot, Abraham Haynes, Frank Cluggage, Mr. Allabaugh, and Mr.

HART'S WATERING PLACE.

McMurtrie; west of Huntingdon, in the neighborhood of Shaver's Creek, Samuel Anderson, Bartholomew Maguire, General McElevy, McCormick, and Donnelly. Of course, this place was settled at a later day than the country farther east.

The first house erected where Alexandria now stands was located near a spring, and was built and occupied by two young Scotchmen, named Matthew Neal and Hugh Glover, as a kind of trading-post. They dealt in goods generally, and in whiskey particularly. The natural consequences of a free indulgence in the latter were fights innumerable, "even in them days," and the place received the euphonious title of "Battle Swamp," which clung to it for many years. Near that place, at what was called "Charles's Fording of the Big Juniata," was the celebrated log which gave rise to the name of the valley. Charles Caldwell lived in the neighborhood— was the oldest settler, and the only one residing within two miles of "Battle Swamp." In what then constituted the valley—say in 1776—lived John Tussey, Robert Caldwell, and Edward Rickets, on the banks of the Little Juniata. On the main stream, or what was then termed the Frankstown Branch, on the northwest side, resided John Bell, William Travis, James Dean, Moses Donaldson, and Thomas Johnston. On the southwest bank resided John Mitchell and Peter Grafius. George Jackson lived on the banks of the Little Juniata, probably a mile from the mouth of Shaver's Creek; and a mile farther up lived Jacob and Josiah Minor. In the neighborhood of Water Street and Canoe Valley, John and Matthew Dean, Jacob Roller, John Bell, Lowry, Beattys,

Moreheads, Simonton, Vanzant, John Sanders, Samuel Davis, Edward Milligan. Near Frankstown, and in it, Lazarus Lowry, the Moores, Alexander McDowell. West of Frankstown, Joseph McCune, McIntyre, John McKillip, McRoberts, and John Crouse. Most of the latter lived along where the Reservoir now is—the building of which destroyed the old McCune and McRoberts farms. On the flat, west of Frankstown, lived Peter Titus and John Carr; in the Loop, A. Robinson and W. Divinny; John Long, near where Jackson's farm now is; Foster, where McCahen's Mill now stands; and a little distance farther west, David Bard, a Presbyterian preacher; Thomas and Michael Coleman, Michael Wallack, James Hardin, a Mr. Hileman, and David Torrence, in the neighborhood of where Altoona now stands. Of course, this list does not comprise all the old settlers, nor probably even a majority of them, but we copy a portion of the names from Mr. Bell's Memoir. A number of them were given to us by Maguire, and some were found in an old ledger, belonging to Lazarus Lowry when he kept store in Frankstown in 1790.

The man Hart, whose name is perpetuated, in connection with his log, by the valley we have spoken of, was an old German, who followed the occupation of trading among the Indians. He was probably the first permanent white settler along the Juniata west of the Standing Stone; and, long before he settled, he crossed and recrossed the Alleghany Mountains, by the old warpath, with his pack-horses. "John Hart's Sleeping Place" is mentioned, in 1756, by John Harris, in making an estimate of the distance between the rivers Susquehanna and Alleghany. Hart's Sleeping Place is about twelve miles from the junction of the Burgoon and Kittaning Runs, and still retains its name. When he took up his residence along the river, he hewed down an immense tree, and turned it into a trough, out of which he fed his horses and cattle; hence the name, "Hart's Log."

It is stated that upon one occasion, when Hart was an old man, some savages came into his settlement on a pillaging excursion. They knew Hart, and went to his cabin, but he happened to be from home. On his log they left a tomahawk, painted red, and a small piece of slate upon which rude hieroglyphics were drawn—one resembling an Indian with a bundle upon his back, over whose head were seven strokes and whose belt was filled with scalps. In front of this drawing was the sun rising, and behind them a picture of the moon.

On Hart's return, he soon found that Indians had been about. The meaning of the articles left he could readily decipher. The red hatchet upon the log signified that Indians were about, but to him they laid down the hatchet. The picture of the rising sun signified that they were going to the east. The strokes indicated the number of warriors, and the bundle and scalps intimated that they would both plunder and murder. The moon signified that they would return at night.

Hart, although he felt safe under such an assurance, had no desire to encounter the red-skins; so he scratched upon the reverse of the slate the outline of a *heart*, and laid by the side of it a pipe—which, interpreted, meant, " Hart smokes with you the pipe of peace," and left.

On his return next day he found the Indians had returned, and passed the night at his log, where they had left a quantity of pewter platters, mugs, &c. It afterward appeared that they had been at several houses, but the inmates had fled. From one they stole a quantity of silver money, and at the house of a Dunkard they stole the pewter-ware. At the log they attempted to run the metal into bullets, but, finding it a failure, they probably left the heavy load in disgust.

TUB MILL AT BARRE FORCE, LITTLE JUNIATA.

CHAPTER XVII.

THE CONTINENTAL MILLS OF THE VALLEY.

AMONG the vicissitudes incident to the settlement of the valley was a very serious one, in the shape of sometimes an absolute want of flour—not always owing to a lack of grain, but the want of mills. Especially did this operate seriously during the Revolution. The few mills at such great distances apart rendered it necessary for parties of neighbors to join in company, arm themselves, and go to mill together—all waiting until the grain was turned into flour. The want of adequate machinery prevented the erection of mills, and those that were built prior to the Revolution, and during the continuance of the war, could scarcely do the requisite amount of work for the country, sparsely as it was settled. To look at some of the old gearing and machinery in use then would only confirm the adage that "necessity is the mother of invention."

The late Edward Bell, of Blair county, who rose to competence by his own indomitable energy and perseverance, and commanded the esteem and respect of all who knew him, once boasted to us that the first shoes he ever wore he made for himself in Fort Lowry.

"And," said he, "I made them so well that I soon became shoemaker to the fort. There is no doubt but that I could have followed the business to advantage; but I never liked it, so I served a regular apprenticeship to the millwrighting."

It is to this circumstance, then, that we are indebted for the following unique description of the old continental mill, which still stands at J. Green & Company's (formerly Dorsey's) forge, on the Little Juniata, in Huntingdon county. It was built before the Revolution,—as near as can be ascertained, in 1774,—by Jacob and Josiah Minor. Mr. Bell, in his manuscript, says:—

It was a curious piece of machinery when I first saw it. The house was about twelve feet high, and about fourteen feet square, made of small poles and covered with clapboards. There was neither floor nor loft in it. The husk was made of round logs built into the wall; the water or tub wheel was some three feet in diameter, and split boards driven into the sides of the shaft made the buckets. The shaft had a gudgeon in the lower end and a thing they called a spindle in the upper end, and was not dressed in any way between the claws. The stones were about two feet four or six inches in diameter, and not thick, and in place of a hoop they had cut a buttonwood-tree that was hollow and large enough to admit the stones, and sawed or cut it off to make the hoop. The hopper was made of clapboards, and a hole near the eye of the stone answered for the dampsil, with a pin driven in it, which struck the shoe every time the stone revolved. The meal-trough, made out of part of a gun, completed the grinding fixtures. The bolting-chest was about six feet long, two and half feet wide, and four feet high, made of live-wood puncheons, split, hewed, and jointed to hold flour, with a pair of deer-skins sewed together to shut the door. There was not one ounce of iron about the chest or bolting-reel. It had a crank or handle on one end, made of wood—the shaft, ribs, and arms, of the same material; and the cloth was leona muslin, or lining that looked like it.

Rather a one-horse concern for our day and generation! and its capacity must have been about as one to one thousand, when compared with the mills of the present age. We should like to see how some of the people of the valley *now* would relish bread baked from flour bolted through Leona muslin! It might do for dyspepsia; indeed, we doubt whether such a disease was known in the valley at so early a day.

The mill of which Mr. Bell speaks, although it may have been the first in his neighborhood, was by no means the first driven by the waters of the Juniata. William Patterson erected a mill, where Millerstown now stands, as early as 1758, which, however, was carried off by a flood a year or so after it was in operation.

The first mill in the Upper Valley was built on Yellow Creek, by the squatters, previous to the edict of the Penn family which destroyed the cabins; but in what year, or by whom built, or what its ultimate fate was, we are unable to say.

The second mill in the valley was built where Spang's Mill now stands, in Blair county, then considered a part of the Cove. It was erected by a man named Jacob Neff, a Dunkard. This mill was burned down during the Revolution by the Indians, but speedily rebuilt, and stood for many years thereafter.

The third was the " Tub" Mill, of which Mr. Bell gives a description. The term *tub* was applied to it in consequence of the peculiar formation of the water-wheel. Nearly all the mills of those days were worked with a tub-wheel.

Directly after, a mill was erected by a Mr. Fetter, near

where McCahen's Mill now stands, near Hollidaysburg. No traces whatever are left of it.

About the same period, two brothers, named Beebault, built a mill, almost the counterpart of the Minor Mill, at the mouth of Spruce Creek. Relics of this mill stood until within a few years.

The next was a small mill built by a man named Armitage, at Mill Creek, below Huntingdon.

Nathaniel Garrard built one in Woodcock Valley, about six miles from Huntingdon.

Another was built in the vicinity of Frankstown; another near where Martha Forge, in the Gap, now stands.

Cryder's Mill, above Huntingdon, was finished about 1776.

These were all the mills that existed in the upper end of the valley prior to the Revolution. Although small, they were evidently of immense value—people having sometimes been compelled to travel some forty miles to obtain their services. The vestiges of *all* are gone, like shadows that have passed away, save the old Continentaller described by Mr. Bell. It alone stands, a relic of the past.

CHAPTER XVIII.

THE COVE — EARLY SETTLEMENT BY DUNKARDS — INDIAN MASSACRES
AND CAPTIVES — MASSACRE OF ULLERY — A RESISTANT DUN-
KARD, ETC.

"THE Great Cove, Little Cove, and Canolloways," are mentioned frequently in government papers as far back as 1749, Indian traders having penetrated them at a much earlier date than that; yet they only figure prominently from that period. The Great Cove, now known as Morrison's, commences at Pattonsville, in Bedford county, and ends at Williamsburg, on the Juniata— bounded by Dunning's and Lock Mountains on the west, and Tussey Mountain on the east. For fertile limestone land, beautiful scenery, and splendid farms, few valleys in the State equal—none surpass—Morrison's Cove.

The earliest settlement of the cove was effected by Scotch-Irish, as early as 1749; but they shared the fate of the burnt-cabin folks when Secretary Peters answered the prayers of the Indians, and were expelled. Nothing daunted, however, many of them returned, and commenced improving; that, too, before the scions of "Father Onus" had acquired the right, title, and interest, to all and singular these fine lands, for the munificent sum of £400!

The greater portion of the beautiful valley, however, was almost unexplored until the Penns made the new purchase. About 1755, a colony of Dunkards took up the southern portion of the Cove, and their descendants hold possession of it to this day. They have unquestionably the finest farms, as well as the most fertile land, in the State; and right glad should we be to end *their* portion of the chapter by saying so, or even by adding that for thrift and economy they stand unsurpassed; but a sense of candor compels us to speak of them as they are,—"nothing extenuate, nor set down aught in malice."

In the first place, let it be understood that we are in no particle indebted to them for one iota of the blessings of government we enjoy. They are strict non-resistants; and in the predatory incursions of the French and Indians, in 1756–63, and, in fact, during all the savage warfare, they not only refused to take up arms to repel the savage marauders and prevent the inhuman slaughter of women and children, but they refused in the most positive manner to pay a dollar to support those who were willing to take up arms to defend their homes and their firesides, until wrung from them by the stern mandates of the law, from which there was no appeal.

They did the same thing when the Revolution broke out. There was a scarcity of men. Sixty able-bodied ones among them might readily have formed a cordon of frontier defence, which could have prevented many of the Indian massacres which took place between 1777 and 1780, and more especially among their own people in the Cove. But not a man would shoulder his rifle; they were *non-resistants!* They might, at least, have furnished money, for they always had an abundance of that, the hoarding of which appeared to be the sole aim and object of life with them. But, no; not a dollar! They occupied neutral ground, and wished to make no resistance. Again; they might have furnished supplies. And they *did* furnish supplies to those who were risking their lives to repel the invaders,—but it was only when the almighty dollar accompanied the demand.

After the massacre of thirty of them, in less than forty-eight hours, Colonel Piper, the lieutenant-colonel of Bedford county, made a stirring appeal to them. But it was of no avail; they were non-resistants, and evidently determined to remain such.

Of the peculiar religious tenets of these primitive people we do not profess to know any thing; hence our remarks are unbiassed. We are solely recording historical facts.

As a curious anomaly in the history of the present generation, it may be stated that, although they perform that part of the compact between government and a good citizen which relates to paying taxes, *they never vote*, neither can the most seductive persuasions of politicians bring them to the polls. Like their forefathers, they are non-resistants—producers, but non-consumers.

During the Indian wars of 1762, quite a number of murders were committed in the Cove, and many captives taken, but the particulars are too vague for history. Although we made every effort to ascertain the names of some of the massacred and the circumstances attending their massacre, we signally failed. It may, therefore,

14

be supposed that, in the absence of any record, there is no other method of ascertaining facts extant.

During the Great Cove massacre, among others carried into captivity was the family of John Martin. This incursion was indeed a most formidable one, led by the kings Shingas and Beaver in person. How many were killed there is no living witness to tell; neither can we conjecture the number of prisoners taken. The following petition was sent by John Martin to council:—

August 13, 1762.

The Humble Petition of Your Most Obedient Servant Sheweth, Sir, may it pleas Your Excellancy, Hearing me in Your Clemancy a few Words. I, One of the Bereaved of my Wife and five Children, by Savage War at the Captivity of the Great Cove, after Many & Long Journeys, I Lately went to an Indian Town, viz., Tuskaroways, 150 miles Beyond Fort Pitts, & Entrested in Co^l. Bucquits & Co^l. Croghan's favor, So as to bear their Letters to King Beaver & Capt. Shingas, Desiring them to Give up One of my Daughters to me, Whiles I have Yet two Sons & One Other Daughter, if Alive, Among them—and after Seeing my Daughter with Shingas he Refused to Give her up, and after some Expostulating with him, but all in vain, he promised to Deliver her up with the Other Captives to y^r Excellency.

Sir, y^r Excellency's Most Humble Servt, Humbly & Passionately Beseeches Y^r Beningn Compassion to interpose Y^r Excellencies Beneficent influence in favor of Y^r Excellencies Most Obedient & Dutiful Servt.   JOHN MARTIN.

After the march of General Forbes from Raystown, and immediately preceding it, no Indian depredations were committed in the Cove up to the commencement of hostilities between the Colonies and Great Britain. The Indians in the French interest were constantly on the alert; and their spies prowling on the outskirts did not fail to report at head-quarters the arrival at Raystown of Colonel Boquet and his army, the formidable bearing and arms of which convinced the savages that it was prudent to keep within the bounds of the French power.

The first Indian depredations of the Revolution in the Juniata Valley were committed in November, 1777. A large body of Indians—not less than thirty—armed with British rifles, ammunition, tomahawks, scalping-knives, and all other murderous appliances they were capable of using, came into the settlement with the avowed intention of gathering scalps for His Britannic Majesty's officers at Detroit. Their coming was not unlooked-for, but the settlers were unprepared for them. The constant rumors afloat that a large body of savages, British, and tories, were coming, struck the people with so much panic that there was no effort made to give any such force as might come a warlike reception, but their energies were concentrated in measures of defence.

The first Indian depredators, or at least the greater portion of them, were seen at a camp-fire by a party of hunters; and if the proper exertions had been made to cut them off, few other outrages would have followed. The supposition is that there were two parties of about fifteen each, who met at or near Neff's Mill, in the Cove. On their way thither, the one party killed a man named Hammond, who resided along the Juniata, and the other party killed a man named Ullery, who was returning from Neff's Mill on horseback. They also took two children with them as prisoners.

The alarm was spread among the inhabitants, and they fled to the nearest forts with all despatch; and on this first expedition they would have had few scalps to grace their belts, had the Dunkards taken the advice of more sagacious people, and fled too; this, however, they would not do. They would follow but half of Cromwell's advice:—they were willing to put their "trust in God," but they would not "keep their powder dry." In short, it was a compound they did not use at all.

The savages swept down through the Cove with all the ferocity with which a pack of wolves would descend from the mountain upon a flock of sheep. Some few of the Dunkards, who evidently had a latent spark of love of life, hid themselves away; but by far the most of them stood by and witnessed the butchery of their wives and children, merely saying, "*Gottes wille sei gethan.*"* How many Dunkard scalps they carried to Detroit cannot now be, and probably never has been, clearly ascertained,—not less than thirty, according to the best authority. In addition to this, they loaded themselves with plunder, stole a number of horses, and under cover of night the triumphant warriors marched bravely away.

Thomas Smith and George Woods, both, we believe, justices of the peace at the time, wrote to President Wharton as follows:—

November 27, 1777.

Gentlemen:—The present situation of this country is so truly deplorable that we should be inexcusable if we delayed a moment in

---

* "God's will be done." This sentence was so frequently repeated by the Dunkards during the massacre, that the Indians must have retained a vivid recollection of it. During the late war with Great Britain, some of the older Indians on the frontier were anxious to know of the Huntingdon volunteers whether the "*Gotswiltahns*" still resided in the Cove. Of course our people could not satisfy them on such a vague point.

acquainting you with it. An Indian war is now raging around us in its utmost fury. Before you went down they killed one man at Stony Creek; since that time they have killed five on the mountain, over against the heads of Dunning's Creek, killed or taken three at the Three Springs, wounded one, and killed some children by Frankstown; and had they not providentially been discovered in the night, and a party gone out and fired on them, they would, in all probability, have destroyed a great part of that settlement in a few hours. A small party went out into Morrison's Cove scouting, and unfortunately divided; the Indians discovered one division, and out of eight killed seven and wounded the other. In short, a day hardly passes without our hearing of some new murder; and if the people continue only a week longer to fly as they have done for a week past, Cumberland county will be a frontier. From Morrison's, Crayl's, and Friend's Coves, Dunning's Creek, and one-half of the Glades, they are fled or forted; and, for all the defence that can be made here, the Indians may do almost what they please. We keep out ranging-parties, in which we go out by turns; but all that we can do in that way is but weak and ineffectual for our defence, because one-half of the people are fled: those that remain are too busily employed in putting their families and the little of their effects that they can save and take into some place of safety, so that the whole burden falls upon a few of the frontier inhabitants, for those who are at a distance from danger have not as yet offered us any assistance. We are far from blaming the officers of the militia because they have not ordered them out, for if they had, they really can be of little or no service, not only for the foregoing reasons, but also for these:—Not one man in ten of them is armed. If they were armed, you are sensible, take the country through, there is not one fourth man that is fit to go against Indians, and it might often happen that in a whole class there might not be a single person who is acquainted with the Indians' ways of the woods; and if there should be a few good men, and the rest unfit for that service, those who are fit to take the Indians in their own way could not act with the same resolution and spirit as if they were sure of being properly supported by men like themselves. The consequence would be that the Indians, after gaining an advantage over them, would become much more daring and fearless, and drive all before them. A small number of select men would be of more real service to guard the frontiers than six times that number of people unused to arms or the woods. It is not for us to dictate what steps ought to be taken, but some steps ought to be taken without the loss of an hour. The safety of your country, of your families, of your property, will, we are convinced, urge you to do every thing in your power to put the frontiers in some state of defence. Suppose there were orders given to raise about one hundred rangers, under the command of spirited officers, who were well acquainted with the woods and the Indians and could take them in their own way. They could be raised instantly, and we are informed there are a great number of rifles lying in Carlisle useless, although the back country is suffering for the want of arms. It was a fatal step that was taken last winter in leaving so many guns when the militia came from camp; about this place, especially, and all the country near it, they are remarkably distressed for the want of guns, for when the men were raised for the army you know we procured every gun that we could for their use. The country reflect hard on us now for our assiduity on those occasions, as it now deprives them of the means of defence. But this is not the only instance in which we hear reflections which are not deserved. The safety of our country then loudly called on us to send all the arms to the camp that could be procured, and it now as loudly calls on us to entreat that we may be allowed some as soon as possible, as also some ammunition; as that which was intrusted to our care is now almost delivered out to the officers who are fortifying, and what remains of it is not fit for rifles. We need not repeat our entreaties that whatever is done may be done as soon as possible, as a day's delay may be the destruction of hundreds.

We are, in haste, gentlemen,

Your most obedient, humble servants,

GEORGE WOODS.

THOMAS SMITH.

BEDFORD, *November* 27, 1777.

The persons mentioned as having been killed belonged mostly to the Cove; but the number was greatly exaggerated, as in fact but two were killed and one wounded. The other five escaped, and did not return until after the report of their death had gone abroad. The names of the killed we could not ascertain.

The band of Indians, after the Dunkard massacre, worked their way toward the Kittaning war-path, leaving behind them some few stragglers of their party whose appetite for blood and treasure had not been satiated. Among others, an old and a young Indian stopped at Neff's Mill. Neff was a Dunkard; but he was a single exception so far as resistance was concerned. He had constantly in his mill his loaded rifle, and was ready for any emergency. He had gone to his mill in the morning without any knowledge of Indians being in the neighborhood, and had just set the water-wheel in motion, when he discovered the two Indians lurking, within a hundred yards, in a small wood below the mill. Without taking much time to deliberate how to act, he aimed through the window, and deliberately shot the old Indian. In an instant the young Indian came toward the mill, and Neff ran out of the back door and up the hill. The quick eye of the savage detected him, and he fired, but missed his aim. Nothing daunted by the mishap, the savage followed up the cleared patch, when both, as if by instinct, commenced reloading their rifles. They stood face to face, not forty yards apart, on open ground, where there was no possible chance of concealment. The chances were equal: he that loaded first would be victor in the strife, the other was doomed to certain death. They both rammed home the bullet at the same time—with what haste may well be conjectured. This was a critical juncture, for, while loading, neither took his eye off the other. They both drew their ramrods at the same instant, but the intense excitement of the moment caused the Indian to balk in drawing his, and the error or mishap proved fatal, because Neff took advantage of it, and succeeded in priming and aiming before the Indian. The latter, now finding the muzzle of Neff's rifle bearing upon him, commenced a series of very cunning gyrations and contortions to destroy his aim or confuse him, so that he might miss him or enable him to prime. To this end, he first threw himself upon his face; then, suddenly rising up again, he jumped first to the right, then to the left, then fell down again. Neff, not the least put off his guard, waited until the Indian arose again, when he shot him through the head.

Neff, fearing that others might be about, left the mill and started to the nearest settlement. A force was raised and the mill revisited; but it was found a heap of smouldering cinders and ashes, and the dead bodies of the Indians had been removed. It is altogether likely that the rear of the savage party came up shortly after Neff had left, fired the mill, and carried away their slain companions.

For the part Neff took in the matter he was excommunicated from the Dunkard society. Nevertheless, he rebuilt his mill; but the Dunkards, who were his main support previously, refused any longer to patronize him, and he was eventually compelled to abandon the business.

On the 4th of May, 1781, a band of marauding savages entered the Cove and murdered a man, woman, and two children, and took one man prisoner, within a mile of the fort of John Piper, who was then colonel of the county. Names or particulars could not be ascertained.

At another time—period not remembered—several prisoners were taken.

The name of the Cove was changed from the " Great Cove" to " Morrison's Cove," in honor of a Mr. Morris, as early as 1770.

CHAPTER XIX.

AMONG all the early pioneers of the upper end of the
Juniata Valley none was better known to the Indians
than Thomas Coleman. His very name inspired them
with terror; and, in all their marauding, they carefully
avoided his neighborhood. He was, emphatically, an
Indian-hater,—the great aim and object of whose life appeared to be centred in the destruction of Indians. For
this he had a reason—a deep-seated revenge to gratify, a
thirst that all the savage blood in the land could not
slake,—superinduced by one of the most cruel acts of
savage atrocity on record.

It appears that the Coleman family lived on the West
Branch of the Susquehanna at an early day. Their
habitation, it would also appear, was remote from the
settlements; and their principal occupation was hunting
and trapping in winter, boiling sugar in spring, and
tilling some ground they held during the summer.
Where they originally came from was rather a mystery; but they were evidently tolerably well educated,

and had seen more refined life than the forest afforded. Nevertheless, they led an apparently happy life in the woods. There were three brothers of them, and, what is not very common nowadays, they were passionately attached to each other.

Early in the spring,—probably in the year 1763,—while employed in boiling sugar, one of the brothers discovered the tracks of a bear, when it was resolved that the elder two should follow and the younger remain to attend to the sugar-boiling. The brothers followed the tracks of the bear for several hours, but, not overtaking him, agreed to return to the sugar-camp. On their arrival, they found the remains of their brother boiled to a jelly in the large iron kettle! A sad and sickening sight, truly; but the authors of the black-hearted crime had left their sign-manual behind them,—an old tomahawk, red with the gore of their victim, sunk into one of the props which supported the kettle. They buried the remains as best they could, repaired to their home, broke up their camp, abandoned their place a short time after, and moved to the Juniata Valley.

Their first location was near the mouth of the river; but gradually they worked their way west, until they settled somewhere in the neighborhood of the mouth of Spruce Creek, on the Little Juniata, about the year 1770. A few years after, the two brothers, Thomas and Michael, the survivors of the family, moved to the base of the mountain, in what now constitutes Logan township, near where Altoona stands, which then was included within the Frankstown district.

These men were fearless almost to a fault; and on the

commencement of hostilities, or after the first predatory incursion of the savages, it appears that Thomas gave himself up solely to hunting Indians. He was in all scouting parties that were projected, and always leading the van when danger threatened; and it has very aptly, and no doubt truly, been said of Coleman, that when no parties were willing to venture out he shouldered his rifle and ranged the woods alone in hopes of occasionally picking up a stray savage or two. That his trusty rifle sent many a savage to eternity there is not a shadow of doubt. *He*, however, never said so. He was never known to acknowledge to any of his most intimate acquaintances that he had ever killed an Indian; and yet, strange as it may seem, he came to the fort on several occasions with rather ugly wounds upon his body, and his knife and tomahawk looked as if they had been used to some purpose. Occasionally, too, a dead savage was found in his tracks, but no one could tell who killed him. For such reserve Mr. Coleman probably had his own motives; but that his fights with the savages were many and bloody is susceptible of proof even at this late day. We may incidentally mention that both the Colemans accompanied Captain Blair's expedition to overtake the tories, and Thomas was one of the unfortunate "Bedford Scout."

To show how well Thomas was known, and to demonstrate clearly that he had on sundry occasions had dealings with some of the savages without the knowledge of his friends, we may state that during the late war with Great Britain, on the Canadian frontier, a great many Indians made inquiries about "*Old Coley;*" and especially one, who represented himself as being a son of Shingas, pointed out to some of Captain Allison's men, who were from Huntingdon county, a severe gash on his forehead, by which he said he should be likely to remember "Coley" for the balance of his life.

In the fall of 1777, Fetter's Fort was occupied by some twenty-five men capable of bearing arms, belonging to the Frankstown district. Among these were both the Colemans, their own and a number of other settler's families.

The Indians who had murdered the Dunkards, it appears, met about a mile east of Kittaning Point, where they encamped, (the horses and plunder having probably been sent on across the mountain,) in order to await the arrival of the scattered forces. Thomas and Michael Coleman and Michael Wallack had left Fetter's Fort in the morning for the purpose of hunting deer. During the day, snow fell to the depth of some three or four inches; and in coming down the Gap, Coleman and his party crossed the Indian trail, and discovered the moccasin tracks, which they soon ascertained to be fresh. It was soon determined to follow them, ascertain their force, and then repair to the fort and give the alarm. They had followed the trail scarcely half a mile before they saw the blaze of the fire and the dusky outlines of the savages seated around it. Their number, of course, could not be made out, but they conjectured that there must be in the neighborhood of thirty; but, in order to get a crack at them, Thomas Coleman made his companions promise not to reveal their actual strength to the men in the fort. Accordingly they returned and made report—once, for a wonder, not exaggerated, but rather underrated. The available force, amounting to sixteen men, consisting of the three above named, Edward Milligan, Samuel Jack, William Moore, George Fetter, John Fetter, William Holliday, Richard Clausin, John McDonald, and others whose names are not recollected, loaded their rifles and started in pursuit of the savages. By the time they reached the encampment, it had grown quite cold, and the night was considerably advanced; still some ten or twelve Indians were seated around the fire. Cautiously the men approached, and with such silence that the very word of command was given in a whisper. When within sixty yards, a halt was called. One Indian appeared to be engaged in mixing paint in a pot over the fire, while the remainder were talking,—probably relating to each other the incidents attending their late foray. Their rifles were all leaning against a large tree, and Thomas Coleman conceived the bold design of approaching the tree, although it stood but ten feet from the fire, and securing their arms before attacking them. The achievement would have been a brilliant one, but the undertaking was deemed so hazardous that not a man would agree to second him in so reckless and daring an enterprise. It was then agreed that they all should aim, and at the given word fire. Coleman suggested that each man should single out a particular savage to fire at; but his suggestion was lost upon men who were getting nervous by beginning to think their situation somewhat critical. Aim—we will not call it deliberate—was taken, the word "*fire!*" was given, and the sharp report of the rifles made the dim old woods echo. Some three or four of the savages fell, and those who were sitting around the fire, as well as those who were lying upon the ground, instantly sprang to their feet and ran to the tree where their rifles stood. In the mean time, Coleman said—

"Quick! quick! boys, load again! we can give them another fire before they know where we are!"

But, on looking around, he was surprised to find nobody but Wallack and Holliday left to obey his order! The number proving unexpectedly large, the majority became frightened, and ran for the fort.

The Indians, in doubt as to the number of their assailants, took an early opportunity to get out of the light caused by the fire and concealed themselves behind trees, to await the further operations of this sudden and unexpected foe.

Coleman, Wallack, and Holliday, deeming themselves too few in number to cope with the Indians, followed their friends to Fetter's Fort.

Early the next morning, all the available force of the fort started in pursuit of the Indians. Of course, they did not expect to find them at the encampment of the night previous; so they took provisions and ammunition along for several days' scout, in order, if possible, to overtake the savages before they reached their own country. To this end, Coleman was appointed to the command, and the march was among those denominated by military men as *forced*.

When they reached the scene of the previous night's work, the evidence was plain that the savages had departed in the night. This the hunters detected by signs not to be mistaken by woodsmen; there was not a particle of fire left, and the coals retained no warmth. The tracks of the savages west of the fire, too, showed that they conformed to those east of the fire, in appearance, whereas, those made by the hunters in the morning looked quite differently. It was then evident that the Indians had a start of some six or eight hours.

On the spot where the fire had been the small earthen paint-pot was found, and in it a portion of mixed paint. Near the fire, numerous articles were picked up:—several scalping-knives, one of which the owner was evidently in the act of sharpening when the volley was fired, as the whetstone was lying by its side; several tomahawks, a powder-horn, and a number of other trifling articles. The ground was dyed with blood, leaving no doubt remaining in regard to their execution the night previous. They had both *killed and wounded*,—but what number was to remain to them forever a mystery, for they carried both dead and wounded with them.

This was a singular trait in savage character. They never left the body of a dead or wounded warrior behind them, if by any possible human agency it could be taken with them. If impossible to move it far, they usually buried it, and concealed the place of burial with leaves; if in an enemy's country, they removed the remains, even if in a state of partial decay, on the first opportunity that offered. To prevent the dead body of a brave from falling into the hands of an enemy appeared with them a religious duty paramount even to sepulture. As an evidence of this, Sam Brady, the celebrated Indian-fighter, once waylaid and shot an old Indian on the Susquehanna who was accompanied by his two sons, aged respectively sixteen and eighteen years. The young Indians ran when their father fell, and Brady left the body and returned home. Next morning, having occasion to pass the place, he found the body gone, and by the tracks he ascertained that it had been removed by the lads. He followed them forty miles before he overtook them, bearing their heavy burden with the will of sturdy work-horses. Brady had set out with the determination of killing both, but the sight so affected him that he left them to pursue their way unharmed; and he subsequently learned that they had carried the dead body one hundred and sixty miles. Brady said that was the only chance in his life to kill an Indian which he did not improve. It may be that filial affection prompted the young savages to carry home the remains of their parents; nevertheless, it is known that the dead bodies of Indians—ordinary fighting-men—were carried, without the aid of horses, from the Juniata Valley to the Indian burial-ground at Kittaning, and that too in the same time it occupied in making their rapid marches between the two points.

But to return to our party. After surveying the ground a few moments, they followed the Indian trail—no difficult matter, seeing that it was filled with blood—until they reached the summit of the mountain, some six or eight miles from the mouth of the Gap. Here a consultation was held, and a majority decided that there was no use in following them farther. Coleman, however, was eager to continue the chase, and declared his willingness to follow them to their stronghold, Kittaning.

This issue, successful though it was, did not fail to spread alarm through the sparsely-settled country. People from the neighborhood speedily gathered their families into the fort, under the firm impression that they were to be harassed by savage warfare not only during the winter, but as long as the Revolutionary struggle was to continue. However, no more Indians appeared; this little cloud of war was soon dispelled, and the people betook themselves to their homes before the holidays of 1777, where they remained during the winter without molestation.

It is said of old Tommy Coleman—but with what degree of truth we are unable to say—that, about twenty years ago, hearing of a delegation of Indians on their way to Washington, he shouldered his trusty old rifle, and went to Hollidaysburg. There, hearing that they had gone east on the canal packet, he followed them some three miles down the towing-path, for the express purpose of having a crack at one of them. This story—which obtained currency at the time, and is believed by many to this day—was probably put into circulation by some one who knew his inveterate hatred of Indians. An acquaintance of his informs us that he had business in town on the day on which the Indians passed through; hence his appearance there. His gun he always carried with him, even on a visit to a near neighbor. That he inquired about the Indians is true; but it was merely out of an anxiety to see whether they looked as they did in days of yore. His business led him to Frankstown, but that business was not to shoot Indians; for, if he still cherished any hatred toward the race, he had better sense than to show it on such an occasion.

He died at his residence, of old age, about fifteen years ago, beloved and respected by all. Peace to his ashes!

ARCH SPRING.

CHAPTER XX.

SINKING VALLEY — THE LEAD MINES — FORT ROBERDEAU — INDIAN MURDER, AND HEROIC CONDUCT OF A WOMAN—ENCOUNTER WITH A SAVAGE—MURDER OF ROLLER AND BEBAULT, ETC.

ONE of the most prominent points in Pennsylvania, during the Revolution, was Sinking Valley, owing, in a great measure, to the fact that it had a fort, under military discipline,—where the sentry marched upon ramparts, where the reveille aroused the inmates at the dawn of day, and where people felt secure in the immediate presence of muskets with bristling bayonets, a pair of cannon, and an abundance of ammunition, and where, for a long time, the greater part of the lead used by the Continental army was procured.

There is every reason to believe that the lead mines of Sinking Valley were known to the French as early as 1750. Although they searched extensively for minerals, it is not probable that they ventured as far into the Penn lands as Sinking Valley, unless the secret of the existence of the mines had been imparted to them by the Indians.

The Indians of the Juniata, after they had acquired the use of fire-arms, could always procure an abundance

of lead. This, they said, they procured—almost pure—
on a ridge, near where Mifflintown now stands, in Kishicoquillas Valley; and also at the foot, or in one of the
ravines, of the mountain. With true Indian craft, the
warriors kept the precise location of the lead mines a
secret. The scarcity of lead, in early days, made it a
valuable commodity to the settlers; and many an Indian's
jug was filled with whiskey on promise of showing
the lead mines—promises that were always "kept to the
ear, but broken to the hope." It is, therefore, pretty evident that all the lead-ore the savages displayed was procured in Sinking Valley;—if they obtained any at other
places along the Juniata, the mines have not yet been
discovered, and not for the lack of many thorough
searches for them, either.

The supposition that the French had been prospecting
extensively in Sinking Valley many years ago is based
upon the fact that, previous to Roberdeau's erecting the
fort, several old drifts or openings were discovered, as
well as an irregular trench, extending from the upper to
the lower lead mines,—a distance of nearly six miles.
The vestiges of this trench are still visible, and there is
no question but what the digging of it and the immense
amount of labor necessary for its construction was performed in the full confidence that they would be rewarded
by the discovery of a silver mine, or, at least, an inex-
haustible bed of pure lead-ore.

The fact that lead-ore existed in Sinking Valley was
ascertained by the settlers about 1763, and the consequence was that a number of persons took up their residence there, but without purchasing lands. The certainty

of the existence of lead, and the fabulous stories of the existence of various other precious metals, induced the proprietary family to reserve it to themselves, and to that end George Woods surveyed it for them a short time previous to the Revolution.

The earliest accounts we have of any permanent settlers in Sinking Valley bears date of 1760. There is a well-authenticated story of an occurrence that once took place in 1763, but neither names nor dates have been transmitted. Mr. Maguire had frequently heard the woman's name mentioned, who became quite a heroine, and lived in Sinking Valley until some time during the Revolution; but it had slipped his memory.

The story was that a man occupied a cabin in the upper end of the valley, and one day left it to go to the mouth of the Bald Eagle, leaving his wife and child at home. No savages had been in the neighborhood for some time, and, in fact, no friendly Indians either, except some few who resided in what is now known as Tuckahoe Valley. Fortunately, the man possessed two rifles, both of which he loaded, placed one over the chimney-piece, the other upon his shoulder, and departed on his errand. While the woman was busy attending to her household affairs, she saw two Indians, partly concealed by some bushes in front of the house. In an instant she took down the loaded gun, and watched their motions through the window. In a few minutes both of them stealthily approached the house, when she pointed the gun at the foremost savage and fired; the bullet striking him in the breast, he fell to rise no more. The other savage came directly toward the house, when the woman, still retaining in her grasp the rifle, ascended a ladder to the loft, where she stood with the gun in an attitude of defiance. The quick eye of the Indian detected her movements, and he followed, but with the usual caution of a savage; and when his head reached the opening, he peered into the dark garret to see his intended victim. Grasping one of the puncheons which composed the floor with one hand, he attempted to draw up his rifle with the other, when a discharge followed, and he fell lifeless to the floor. The woman, more dead than alive with fear, remained for a time in the loft, but, hearing no noise, she at length ventured down-stairs, and at the foot of the ladder found the savage perfectly dead, lying in a pool of blood. She took her child out of the cradle, and started for the mouth of the Bald Eagle, but fortunately met her husband but a few rods from the house.

All things taken into consideration, and especially the fact that the woman had never pulled the trigger of a gun before, this was probably one of the most heroic acts on record.

The nearest neighbors were summoned, and, on examining into the matter, it was concluded that, after the first Indian had been shot, the second one immediately cocked his rifle, and that while ascending the ladder the trigger must have been touched by a twig on the hickory rung of the ladder. The bullet had struck him under the chin, passed through his tongue, and lodged in his brain. His death was certainly an interposition of Providence in behalf of the woman and her infant child.

THE CAVE IN SINKING VALLEY.

Sinking Valley proper never could have been much of a resort of the Indians, for no traces of the existence of any villages in it have ever been discovered, neither have any relics ever been found or exhumed in it, that we can hear of, with the exception of some few arrow-heads and a skull, found near the Arch Springs.

The attention of Council was called to the existence of lead in Sinking Valley in a letter from Major-General John Armstrong to President Wharton, dated Yorktown, 23d February, 1778.   He says:—

As at present there appears to be a scarcity of the important article of lead, and it is certain a Mr. Harman Husbands, now a member of Assembly for our State, has some knowledge of a lead mine situate in a certain tract of land not far from Frankstown, formerly surveyed for the use of the proprietary family.

General Gates, President of the Board of War, having signified his earnest desire to see and converse with Mr. Husbands on the subject of the mine, and being greatly hurried with business, I have, at his instance, undertaken the present line, that you would please to use your influence with the House of Assembly and with Mr. Husbands, that he, as soon as possible, may be spared to concert with the Board of War on the best measures for making a trial of and deriving an early supply from that source.

The general is of opinion with me, that the mine ought to—or may at least for the present—be seized by and belong to the State; and that private persons, who, without right, may have sat down on that reserved tract, should neither prevent the use of the lead nor be admitted to make a monopoly of the mine.   I am of opinion that a few faithful laborers may be sufficient to make the experiment, and that the lieutenant of the county, or some other good man, may be serviceable in introducing the business.

I cannot doubt the compliance of the honorable Assembly and Council.

P.S.—It may be proper that a summary consideration be first taken, whether the State will make the effort alone or leave it to the conduct of the Board of War; that, at any rate, the salutary effects, if any, may be gained to the public. The water-carriage is a great thing. *Query*—Whether the ore should be run into portable bars at the bank, or at Middleton?

At the writing of the above, some few persons had found their way to the mines, raised small quantities of ore, and smelted it; but their operations were contracted for want of tools and the proper appliances for smelting. They confined themselves to such ore as was on or near the surface, and made small oven furnaces, and smelted with charcoal.

The Council soon took the suggestion of General Armstrong in hand; and it was resolved to give the general superintendence of the mining operations to General Daniel Roberdeau, then a member of Congress, who went forward to Carlisle to make the necessary arrangements. From that place he wrote to President Wharton, on the 17th of April, 1778, as follows :—

The confidence the honorable the representatives of our State have placed in me by a resolve, together with the pressing and indispensable necessity of a speedy supply of lead for the public service, induced me to ask leave of absence of Congress to proceed with workmen to put their business into a proper train, and have reached this place on that errand; and, having collected men and materials, and sent them forward this day, propose to follow them to-morrow. My views have been greatly enlarged since I left York on the importance of the undertaking and hazard in prosecuting it, for the public works here are not furnished with an ounce of lead but what is in fixed ammunition; on the other hand, the prevailing opinion of people, as I advance into the country, of Indian depredations shortly to commence, might not only deter the workmen I stand in need of, but affright the back settlers from their habitations, and leave the country exposed and naked. To give confidence to one and the other, I have drawn out of the public stores here twenty-five stand of arms and a quantity of gunpowder, and intended to proceed this morning, but was applied to by John Caruthers, Esq., Lieutenant of the County, and William Brown, Commissary of Provisions for the Militia, who advised me on the subject of their respective departments, and, by the account they gave of the orders from your honorable board to them as to calling out and supplying the militia, I find the State is guarding against the incursions of the savages. This confirmed me in a preconceived intention of erecting a stockade fort in the neighborhood of the mine I am about to work, if I could stir up the inhabitants to give their labor in furnishing an asylum for their families in case of imminent danger, and thus prevent the evacuation of the country. Mr. Caruthers, convinced of the necessity of the work for the above purposes, condescendingly offered one company of the militia, which he expected would consist of about forty men, under my command, to co-operate in so salutary a business,—as it consisted with the orders of Council respecting the station, being only a deviation of a very few miles,—and that one other company, of about the same number, should also join me, for the greater expedition, until the pleasure of Council was known, which he presumed might coincide with such dispositions, otherwise it might be deranged by an immediate express; and, that the pleasure of Council might be known without delay, I give this intelligence. If these measures are for the good of the public wheel, [weal,] I hope to be honored with a confirmation, and orders to the militia to exert themselves in carrying the design into immediate execution; if otherwise, I rely on the well-known candor of Council that I shall not be suspected of any sinister design in leaning to an offer freely made as above, from, I believe, the best motives, much less that I have presumed to interfere with the arrangements of Council, as this early notice is full proof to the contrary, as the whole is in their power as much as if nothing had passed between the lieutenant and myself. I have only to add, on this subject, that your design of patrolling-parties of good riflemen shall be encouraged by me. The commissary, Mr. Brown, being destitute of money, I would have spared it out of my small stock, but that, by my interference, 1200 dollars—all he asked—was supplied by a public officer here; but further sums will, he said, be soon necessary, and he expressed much concern for the scarcity of provisions. I was advised very lately, by Judge McKean, of a quantity of salted beef in the neighborhood of Harris's Ferry; and before I left York, I applied to him by letter to advise me of the quantity and quality, with a design to purchase, as I intended to employ a much greater number of men than are already employed at the lead mine, to carry on the business with vigor. If Council should think proper to order a quantity of said provisions up the Juniata for the militia, I should be glad of being favored with what I want through the same channel. I intend to build such a fort as, with sufficient provisions, under the smile of Providence, would enable me to defend it against any number of Indians that might presume to invest it. If I am not prevented, by an opportunity of serving the State eminently by a longer stay in the wilderness, I purpose to return to my duty in Congress in about three weeks. Will Council favor me with the exemption of a number of men, not exceeding twenty,—if I cannot be supplied by the adjutant-general, who has orders co-extensive with my want of smelters and miners from deserters from the British army,—to suffer such to come to this part of the country, contrary to a preceding order? If Council should think such a measure of exemption for the public good, I should be glad to receive their orders on that head. I would not intrude my sentiments on Council, but am of opinion that, besides the supplying of provisions to the militia in Bedford, it is very important that the intended stockade should be seasonably furnished with that article; therefore, if it should not be thought advisable to improve the above hint, that the provisions already mentioned in the neighborhood of Harris's should be left unnoticed until I shall have an opportunity of furnishing my own supplies from that stock. If I shall be advised by Mr. McKean, it is in my offer. My landing is at Water Street, in [on the] Juniata; but I could, on notice, receive any supply from Standing Stone.

In the mean time, the persons employed went forward to the mines, and, under the direction of a Scotch miner named Lowrie, commenced sinking shafts and raising ore at the upper mine. General Roberdeau arrived at Standing Stone after the tory expedition to Kittaning, being, as it would appear, his second visit; the first was a mere tour of observation. From this point he wrote as follows to John Carothers:—

Standing Stone, April 23, 1778.

SIR:—The enclosed was put into my hands, to be forwarded to you by express. The intelligence it contains is abundantly confirmed by several persons I have examined, both fugitives from the frontiers and some volunteers that have returned for an immediate supply of ammunition and provisions, to be sent forward to Sinking Spring Valley, as the troops will be obliged to quit the service except they are supplied without delay. Want of arms prevents those who would turn out. I shall furnish what I brought from Carlisle as soon as they come forward; but it is very unfortunate that these arms, and the ammunition, which is coming by water, have been retarded by contrary wind, and probably the lowness of the water. To remedy this, I have despatched two canoes this morning to meet them on the way. I am giving Mr. Brown, who is here, every assistance in my power; but your aid is greatly wanted to stimulate the militia, and furnish arms, ammunition, pack-horses, and every thing necessary in your line of duty. The insurgents from this neighborhood, I am informed, are about thirty. One of them (Hess) has been taken, and confession extorted, from which it appears that this banditti expect to be joined by three hundred men from the other side the Alleghany; reports more vague mention one thousand whites and savages. The supply of provisions for so great a number renders it improbable; but, in answer to this, I have been informed by the most credible in this neighborhood, that strangers, supposed to be from Detroit, have been this winter among the disaffected inhabitants, and have removed with them. If you have authority to call out the militia, in proportion to the exigence of the times, I think it of great importance that a considerable number of men should be immediately embodied and sent forward to meet the enemy; for it cannot be expected that the volunteers will long continue in service, and I find that the recruiting the three companies goes on too slowly to expect a seasonable supply from them of any considerable number. If you have not authority to call the necessary aid of militia, you, no doubt, will apply to the honorable the Council, and may furnish them with my sentiments, and to the Board of War for arms and ammunition. With ten men here, under the command of Lieutenant Cluggage, in Continental service until the 1st of December next, I intend to move forward as soon as the arms, ammunition, and other things come forward, to afford an escort to Sinking Spring Valley, where I shall be glad to meet as great a number of militia as you will station there, to enable me to erect a stockade, to secure the works so necessary to the public service and give confidence to the frontier inhabitants, by affording an asylum for their women and children. These objects, I doubt not, you will think worthy your immediate attention and utmost exertion, which, I can assure you,—making the fullest allowance for the timidity of some and credulity of others,—is a very serious matter; for without immediate aid the frontiers will be evacuated, for all that I have been able to say has been of no avail with the fugitives I have met on the roads,—a most distressing sight, of men, women, and children, flying through fear of a cruel enemy.

I am, respectfully, sir, your most obedient, humble servant,

DANIEL ROBERDEAU.

The enclosure spoken of in Roberdeau's letter was a note from Robert Smith to Robert Cluggage, of which the following is a copy:—

SIR:—Be pleased to send expresses to Lieutenant Carothers by the first opportunity, to give him some account of insurrections on the South Mountain, and likewise to inspect very closely into who is abroad at this time and upon what occasion, as there is a suspicion, by information, of other insurrections rising in other parts of the county of Cumberland; and in so doing you will oblige your friend to serve,   ROBERT SMITH.

April 23, 1778.

The letter of Gen. Roberdeau, as well as Smith's, were sent to President Wharton by Lieutenant Carothers, enclosed in another of his own dated at Carlisle, on the 27th of April.

Previous to this, however, he sent a letter to the Council,

dated on the 24th, in which he speaks of the deplorable condition of the frontier and the constant alarms from the tories. He said:—

The marching classes of the fifth battalion I have been obliged to send up to Sinking Valley and Bald Eagle, which will amount to near seventy privates. The frontiers in those parts have been greatly alarmed of late by a number of tories who have banded together, threatening vengeance to all who have taken the oath of allegiance to the States. This moment I have received an express from Kishicoquillas for a supply of arms, and that Colonel McElevy, of Bedford county, came there express himself, with an account that a body of tories, near three hundred and twenty, in and above Standing Stone, had collected themselves together and driven a number of the inhabitants from Standing Stone Town. Immediately Colonel Buchanan and Colonel Brown marched off with a few men who could be got equipped, and we are waiting with patience the issue.

General Roberdeau wrote to Council on the 27th of April, after Captain Blair's return, as follows:—

Sinking Spring Valley, April 27, 1778.

Sir :—I have little more time to refer you to the enclosed examination, taken in great haste, but correct as it respects the testimony. The confiscation of the effects of the disaffected in these parts is very irregular, and the brutality offered to the wives and children of some of them, as I have been informed, in taking from them even their wearing apparel, is shocking. I wish the magistrates were furnished with the late law respecting confiscation, and that they were more capable ministers of justice; the one I have seen is such a specimen of the popular election of these officers as I expected. I am happy to inform you that a very late discovery of a new vein promises the most ample supply; but I am very deficient in workmen. Mr. Glen is with me, to direct the making and burning of bricks, and is to come up to build a furnace, by which time I expect to be in such forwardness as to afford an ample supply to

the army. The want of provision I dread notwithstanding the
active endeavors of Mr. Brown, for it is scarcely to be got; therefore I beg leave to refer you to a hint on this subject in my letter
from Carlisle. Of forty militia, I have, at most, seven with me,
which retards building a stockade to give confidence to the inhabitants, who were all on the wing before I reached this. I send
Richard Weston, under guard, to Carlisle jail, to wait your orders.
He is conducted by Lieutenant John Means, of the militia. The
inhabitants are hunting the other insurgents, and hope they will all
be taken, but wish any other the trouble of examining them, as my
hands are full. I am, with respectful salutations to Council, sir,

Y^r most ob^t, humb^l serv^t,

DAN^L ROBERDEAU.

The general speaks of the tory Hess (in his first
letter) as if he had been forced to confess. This is
an error. Hess made a voluntary confession after the
return of Captain Blair, and after some of Blair's men
had partially hung him and let him off.

The statement that McElevy *reported* at Kishicoquillas
that three hundred and twenty tories had driven off
some of the inhabitants of Standing Stone Town is no
doubt true enough, but no such occurrence ever took
place. The fears of the people no doubt prompted Mc-
Elevy to exaggerate, in order to get aid forthwith.
Shortly after the arrival of Buchanan and Brown at
Standing Stone, the Blair expedition returned, so that
their services were not required.

General Roberdeau complained of the manner in which
confiscations were conducted. He was grossly misinformed. The facts in the case are simply these:—On the
receipt of the news of the disasters met by the tories at
Kittaning, many of the tory families fled, leaving every
thing behind them. These articles, even if wearing ap-

parel was included, could not well escape confiscation unless they were pitched into the street. There is no instance on record of the women and children of tories having any thing like wearing-apparel taken from them. If such acts were committed, they were without the sanction of the officers or the people, by outlaws who lived by plunder, who may be found in any community, and for whose acts most assuredly the patriots should not have been held accountable.

General Roberdeau's stay at the mines must have been brief. The next we hear of him is in a letter to Vice-President Bryan, dated at York, on the 30th of May of the same year. The direction of affairs at the mines was probably left in the hands of Lowrie and Cluggage.

It is altogether uncertain how long the mines were carried on by government, but not longer, probably, than till the fall of 1779; and what the total yield of lead was during that time we cannot ascertain. In one place in the Records we find an order forwarded to one of the sub-lieutenants of the county for five hundred pounds; and we also hear that quantities were issued to the militia at sundry times. There must have been some kind of a bargain existing between government and Roberdeau for taking out the lead, for, in a letter to Vice-President Bryan for some pay due him, he says, "My late engagement in the lead-works has proved a moth to my circulating cash, and obliged me to make free with a friend in borrowing." He also says, in a letter to President Reed, bearing date November 10, 1779:—

SIR:—Permit me to ask the favor of you to make my request known to the honorable Board of your Presidence that they would be pleased this day to order me payment for the ten hundred pounds of lead delivered to your order some months ago. The price of that article is so enormous that I should blush to make a demand, but my necessity keeps equal pace with the rapid depreciation of our money; and particularly as I purpose leaving the city to-morrow, dependence has been had on the money in question, for my advances are insupportably great, for my defected purpose of supplying lead to Continent, which, entirely through default of Congress in not furnishing the necessary defences, has been entirely stopped, as the honorable the Assembly have been informed. After the most diligent inquiry, I cannot find less than six dollars per pound demanded for lead by the quantity,—a price which, Mr. Peters just now informed me, the Board of War was willing to give.

This epistle near about fixes the time of the abandonment of the mines; and it also shows that lead commanded rather an exhorbitant price at that time—payable, of course, in Continental funds.

In 1779, Sinking Spring Valley contained, according to an anonymous writer, "sixty or seventy families, living in log-houses." The principal portion of these were foreigners, who were taken there to work the mines. After Roberdeau's project had fallen to the ground, in consequence of the scarcity of the ore and the immense expense of mining and melting it, these miners attempted for a while to carry on operations for themselves. Their close proximity to the Indians, and the fact that several incursions were made into the valley by the savages in search of plunder and scalps, made those men, unused to border life, quit, and seek refuge in the Atlantic cities. The fort was evacuated by the government militia. Nevertheless it was still a place of refuge, and was used by the settlers of Sinking Valley and Bald Eagle up to the close of the war.

In 1781, Jacob Roller, Jr., and a man named Bebault, were massacred by Indians in Sinking Valley. Few particulars of this massacre are known, and many contradictory stories still exist in regard to it. We give Mr. Maguire's version of it, but would at the same time state that he did not vouch for the authenticity of it, as he gathered it from the exaggerated rumors that in those days followed the recital of current events.

Roller, it appears was an active and energetic frontier-man, bold, fearless, and daring; and the common belief was that his unerring rifle had ended the days of many a red-skin. Be that as it may, however, it is certain that the Indians knew him, and marked him out for a victim long before they succeeded in despatching him. Several small roving bands were in the habit of coming down into the valley after the mines were abandoned; but no favorable opportunity offered for a long time to kill Roller.

On one occasion, four of the settlers had met at Roller's house for the purpose of going on a hunt for deer. Early in the morning, when just ready to start, Roller heard the breaking of a twig near his cabin. He peered out into the deep gloom of the misty morning, and discovered three Indians crouching near an oak-tree. It was very evident that the Indians had not been close enough to the house to ascertain the number within, and the inmates were in a state of doubt as to the number of savages. Profound silence was observed, and it was resolved to shoot from the window as soon as the light was sufficiently strong to render their aim certain. The Indians were evidently waiting for Roller to come out of his house. At length, when they thought the proper time had come, the

16

settlers gathered at the window, and thrust out their rifles as silently as possible. The quick eyes of the savages saw, even by the hazy light, that there were too many muzzles to belong to one man, and they took to the woods with all the speed they could command, leaving behind them a quantity of venison and dried corn, and a British rifle.

On another occasion, Roller had an encounter with a single Indian in the woods, which probably stands unparalleled in the history of personal encounters between a savage and a white man. Roller left home about seven o'clock in the morning, in search of deer. He had ranged along the edge of the mountain an hour or two, when he heard a rifle-shot but a short distance from him, and a minute had scarcely elapsed before a wounded doe came in the direction where he stood. To shoot it was but the work of an instant, because he supposed that one of his neighbors had wounded it; for the thought of the presence of Indians never entered his head. Yet it appears that it was an Indian who fired. The Indian mistook the crack of Roller's rifle for that of a companion left at the base of the mountain. Under this impression, the Indian, anxious to secure the doe, and Roller, intent on bleeding her, both neglected one of the first precautions of the day,—viz.: to reload their rifles. Roller was leaning over the doe, when he heard the crust of the snow breaking in a thicket near him. He jumped to his feet, and was confronted by the Indian,—a tall, muscular fellow, who was quite as large as Roller. The savage, well aware of the fact that neither of the rifles were loaded, and probably satisfied in meeting " a foeman worthy of his steel," deliberately placed his gun against a tree by the side of Roller's, and, drawing his

tomahawk, he cast a glance of savage delight at the white
man before him, which seemed to imply that he would
soon show him who was the better man of the two.   Roller, anticipating his intentions, drew his tomahawk and
stood on the defensive.   The savage made a spring, when
Roller jumped aside, and the Indian passed.   The latter
suddenly wheeled, when Roller struck him upon the elbow
of the uplifted hand, and the hatchet fell.   Fearing to
stoop to regain it, the savage drew his knife, and turned
upon Roller.   They clinched, and a fearful struggle ensued.   Roller held the savage's right arm, so as to render
useless his knife, while the Indian grasped firmly the
hand in which Roller held his hatchet, and in this manner they struggled until they were both tripped by the
carcass of the doe; still both retained their hold.   Roller
fortunately grasped his knife, lying beside the doe, with
his left hand, and thrust it into the side of the Indian.
The struggle now became terrible, and by one powerful
effort the savage loosened himself and sprang to his feet;
but Roller was as quick as he was.   In attempting to
close again, the savage stabbed Roller in the shoulder
and in the arm.   Roller had dropped his hatchet in re-
gaining his feet, and the combat was now a deadly one
with knives.   They cut and thrust at each other until
their buckskin hunting-shirts were literally cut into rib-
bons and the crusted snow was dyed with their blood.
At length, faint with the loss of blood, the combat ceased,
by mutual consent, as it were, and the Indian, loosening
himself from Roller's grasp, took his rifle and disappeared.
Roller stanched, with frozen snow and some tow, the only
dangerous wound he had, and managed to reach his home.

He was stabbed in four or five places, and it was some weeks before he fully recovered from his wounds. The skeleton of the savage, with his rifle by his side, was found the succeeding summer on the top of Warrior Ridge.

The time of Roller's death is not positively known. Mr. Maguire thought it was in the fall of 1781. From subsequent evidences, three Indians came down the mountain, avoiding the fort of Jacob Roller, Sr., which was located at the head of Sinking Valley, and passed on down through the valley to the house of Bebault, whom they tomahawked and scalped.

From thence they went to the house of Jacob Roller, Jr., who was alone at the time, his family being at his father's fort. He was murdered and scalped while at work in his corn-field. His absence from the fort at night created alarm, and early next morning a party went down to his house to see if any thing had befallen him. While searching for him, one of the men discovered blood on the bars, which soon led to the discovery of his body in the field. From the footprints in the ground, it was plain that the murder had been committed by two men and a boy between twelve and fourteen years of age. Roller had been shot and scalped, his head shockingly mangled with a tomahawk, and the region of his heart was gashed with a dozen cuts and stabs made by a sharp scalping-knife. The inference was that, after shooting Roller, the men induced the lad to tomahawk and stab him. In other words, they gave him a lesson in butchery and courage.

Bebault was found shot and scalped, although still alive,—a shocking spectacle to look upon. He was so much exhausted by the loss of blood as to be unable to give any account of the transaction.

The bodies of both were taken to the fort and buried, and, as soon as possible, a large party, consisting of the Rollers, Beattys, Rickets, &c., started in pursuit. They followed the trail for nearly fifty miles, but at last lost it, and were compelled to return without overtaking the murderers.

Every settler knew Roller, and his death cast a universal gloom over the valley. The manner of it alarmed the settlement to such an extent that such fall crops as were still out were suffered to rot upon the field, as no force could be spared from the forts, and people would no longer risk their lives to the mercy of the marauders.

Jacob Roller, Jr., was the oldest of seven brothers, all powerful fellows, and active frontier-men.

There are quite a number of the descendants of the seven brothers, who reside in various places,—some in the West, but probably a majority of them at Williamsburg, or in the neighborhood of Springfield Furnace, in Blair county.

Richard B. McCabe, Esq., in a series of reminiscences of old times, published in 1832, while speaking of the lead mines in Sinking Valley, said:—

The Upper Lead Mine, as it is called, on the lands now belonging to a German family of the name of Crissman, exhibits but the traces of former excavation, and trifling indications of ore. The lower one, about a mile in direct distance from the Little Juniata, was worked within my remembrance, under the superintendence of a Mr. Sinclair, a Scotch miner from the neighborhood of Carron Iron-works, in the "land o' cakes." The mine was then owned by two gentlemen named Musser and Wells. The former, I think, lived

and died in Lancaster county.	Mr. Wells was probably a Phila-
delphian.	Three shafts were sunk to a great depth on the side of
a limestone-hill.	A drift was worked into the bowels of the hill,
possibly a hundred yards, six feet high, and about the same width.
This was expensive.	No furnace or other device for melting the
ore was ever erected at this mine.	Considerable quantities of the
mineral still lie about the pit's mouth.	The late Mr. H———, of
Montgomery county, who had read much and practised some in
mining, (so far as to sink some thousand dollars,) visited this mine
in 1821, in company with another gentleman and myself, and
expressed an opinion that the indications were favorable for a good
vein of the mineral.	But the vast mines of lead in the West, such
as Mine a Barton and the Galena, where the manufacture of lead
can be so much more cheaply carried on, must forever prevent a
resumption of the business in Sinking Valley, unless, indeed, some
disinterested patriot shall procure the adoption of a *tariff of protection* for the lead-manufacturer of the happy valley.

Notwithstanding Mr. McCabe's prediction implied that
the lead mines of Sinking Valley would in all probability
never be worked again, some enterprising individuals
from New York prospected at the upper mine so late as
1852, and soon found, as they supposed, sufficient en-
couragement to sink shafts.	Accordingly, several were
sunk, the German heirs agreeing to take a certain per-
centage on all ore raised.	A regular company was organ-
ized, and, for a while, the "Sinking Valley Lead Mining
Company" stock figured among the bulls and bears of
Wall Street, in New York.	Extensive furnaces for smelt-
ing, and other operations on a large scale, were *talked* of;
but suddenly, one very fine day, the ore, like the Yankee's
horse, "*gin eout;*" the superintendent left, the miners followed, and the stock depreciated so rapidly that it could
have been purchased for about one cent on the dollar.
Latterly, we have heard nothing whatever of the Lead

Mining Company.   There is unquestionably lead-ore still left at the upper mine; but, in order to make the mining operations pay, foreign wars must create a demand at increased prices.

The people of Sinking Valley long entertained the idea that stores of mineral wealth still existed in it; and a legend was current that a man from the city of Phila- delphia, on the strength of a letter from Amsterdam, came there to seek for a portion of it in the shape of a canoe-load of bullion, buried by two men many years ago. The person who searched found some of the guide-marks pointed out to him, but he did not reach the bullion. The treasure, it is generally believed to this day by the older residents, was found by a Mr. Isett, while engaged in digging a mill-race.   This belief was based upon the fact that, previous to digging the race, Mr. Isett was poor, but became wealthy and abandoned the digging of the race before it was half completed.

We have incidentally mentioned the name of a Scotch miner taken to Sinking Valley by General Roberdeau, named Lowrie.   He was the head of an illustrious line of descendants, some of whom have figured in Congress, at the bar, on the bench, and in the pulpit.   One of the present Supreme Judges of Pennsylvania is a grandson of the old Scotch miner, and nearly all of the name in the Union are his lineal descendants.

Truly may it be said that Sinking Valley was once a place of note.

CHAPTER XXI.

TORIES OF THE VALLEY — THEIR UNFORTUNATE EXPEDITION TO JOIN
THE INDIANS AT KITTANING — CAPTAIN JOHN WESTON, THE TORY
LEADER—CAPTAIN THOMAS BLAIR — CAPTURE OF THE BROTHERS
HICKS — HANGING A TORY—NARROW ESCAPE OF TWO OF WESTON'S
MEN, ETC.

A SUCCESSFUL rebellion is a revolution; an unsuccessful
attempt at revolution is a rebellion. Hence, had the
Canadians been successful in their attempt to throw off
the British yoke in 1837, the names of the leaders would
have embellished the pages of history as heroes and
patriots, instead of going down to posterity as convicts
transported to the penal colonies of England. Had the
efforts of the Cubanos to revolutionize the island of Cuba
been crowned with success, the cowardly "*fillibusteros*"
would have rated as brave men, and, instead of perishing
ignominiously by the infamous garote and starving in the
dismal dungeons of Spain, they would now administer the
affairs of state, and receive all the homage the world pays
to great and successful warriors. On the other hand, had
the revolution in Texas proved a failure, Burleson, Lamar,
Houston, and others, who carved their names upon the
scroll of fame as generals, heroes, and statesmen, would

either have suffered the extreme penalty of the Mexican law, or at least occupy the stations of obscure adventurers, with all the odium which, like the poisoned shirt of Nessus, clings to those who are unsuccessful in great enterprises.

The same may be said of the American Revolution. If those who pledged their "lives, their fortunes, and their sacred honor," to make the colonies independent of all potentates and powers on earth, had lost the stake, the infamy which now clings to the memory of the tories would be attached to that of the rebels, notwith-standing the latter fought in a glorious cause, endured the heats of summer and braved the peltings of the winter's storms, exhausted their means, and shed their blood, for the sacred cause in which they were engaged.   For this reason, we should not attach too much infamy to the tories *merely* because they took sides with England; but their subsequent acts, or at least a portion of them, were such as to leave a foul blot upon their names, even had victory perched upon the cross of St. George.   The Ame-rican people, after the Revolution, while reposing on the laurels they had won, might readily have overlooked and forgiven weak and timid men who favored the cause of the crown under the firm conviction that the feeble colo-nies could never sever themselves from the iron grasp of England; but when they remembered the savage bar-barities of the tories, they confiscated the lands of all who were attainted with treason, drove them from the country, and attached black and undying infamy to their names.

To some it may appear strange—nevertheless it is true—

that, in 1777, the upper end of the Juniata Valley contained nearly as many tories as it did patriots. This is not a very agreeable admission to make by one who has his home in the valley; nevertheless, some of the acts of these tories form a part of the history of the time of which we write, and must be given with the rest. Let it be understood, however, that, as some of the descendants of those men, who unfortunately embraced the wrong side, are still alive and in our midst, we suppress names, because we not only believe it to be unprincipled in the extreme to hold the son responsible for the sins and errors of the fathers, but we think there is not a man in the valley now who has not patriotic blood enough in his veins to march in his country's defence at a moment's warning, if occasion required it.

The great number of tories in what now constitutes Huntingdon county may, in a great measure, be attributed to the fact, that, living as they did upon the frontier, they had no idea of the strength or numbers composing the "rebel" army, as they called it. They knew the king's name to be "a tower of strength;" and they knew, too, the power and resources of England. Their leaders were shrewd men, who excited the fears of the king's followers by assuring them that the rebels would soon be worsted, and all of them gibbeted.

The most of these tories, according to Edward Bell, resided in Aughwick, Hare's Valley, on the Raystown Branch, in Woodcock Valley, at Standing Stone, Shaver's Creek, Warrior's Mark, and Canoe Creek. They held secret meetings, generally at the house of John Weston, who resided a mile and a half west of Water Street, in Canoe Valley. All their business was transacted with the utmost secresy; and those who participated in their meetings did so under an oath of " allegiance to the king and death to the rebels."

These meetings were frequently attended by tory emissaries from Detroit, who went there advised of all the movements of the British about the lakes; and it is thought that one of these men at length gave them a piece of intelligence that sealed the doom of a majority of them.

It appears that a general plan was formed to concentrate a large force of Indians and tories at Kittaning, then cross the mountain by the Indian Path, and at Burgoon's Gap divide,—one party march through the Cove and Conococheague Valleys, the other to follow the Juniata Valley, and form a junction at Lancaster, killing all the inhabitants on their march. The tories were to have for their share in this general massacre all the fine farms on the routes, and the movable property was to be divided among the Indians. It would seem, however, that Providence frustrated their plans. They elected John Weston their captain, and marched away in the dead of night, without drums or colors, to join the savages in a general massacre of their neighbors, early in the spring of 1778—all being well armed with rifles furnished by the British emissaries, and abundance of ammunition. They took up the line of march—avoiding all settlements—around Brush Mountain, and travelled through the Path to Kittaning. When near the fort, Weston sent forward two men to announce their coming.

The savages, to the number of ten or twelve, accompanied the messengers; and when they met the tories, Weston ordered his men to "present arms." The order proved a fatal one; for the Indians, ever suspecting treachery, thought they had been entrapped, and, without any orders, fired a volley among the tories, and killed Weston and some eight, or probably ten, of his men, then turned and ran toward the town. The disheartened tories fled in every direction as soon as their leader fell.

Although these tories marched from the settlements under cover of night, and with the greatest possible caution, all their movements were watched by an Indian spy in the employ of Major Cluggage. This spy was a Cayuga chief, known as Captain Logan, who resided in the valley at the time,—subsequently at an Indian town called Chickalacamoose, where the village of Clearfield now stands. He knew the mission of the tories, and he soon reported their departure through the settlements. Of course, the wildest and most exaggerated stories were soon set afloat in regard to the number constituting Weston's company, as well as those at Kittaning ready to march. Colonel Piper, of Yellow Creek, George Woods, of Bedford, and others, wrote to Philadelphia, that two hundred and fifty tories had left Standing Stone, to join the Indians, for the purpose of making a descent upon the frontier,—a formidable number to magnify out of thirty-four; yet such was the common rumor.

The greatest terror and alarm spread through the settlements, and all the families, with their most valuable effects, were taken to the best forts. General Roberdeau, who had the command of the forces in the neighborhood, had left Standing Stone a short time previous, leaving Major Cluggage in command. The latter was appealed to for a force to march after Weston. This he could not do, because his command was small, and he was engaged in superintending the construction of the fort at Sinking Valley, the speedy completion of which was not only demanded to afford protection to the people, but to guard the miners, who were using their best exertions to fill the pressing orders of the Revolutionary army for lead.

Cluggage was extremely anxious to have Weston and his command overtaken and punished, and for this purpose he tendered to Captain Thomas Blair, of Path Valley, the command of all who wished to volunteer to fight the tories. The alarm was so general, that, in forty-eight hours after Weston's departure, some thirty-five men were ready to march. Twenty of them were from Path Valley, and the remainder were gathered up between Huntingdon—or Standing Stone, as it was then still called—and Frankstown.* At Canoe Valley the company was joined by Gersham and Moses Hicks, who went to act in the double capacity of scouts and interpreters. They were brothers, and had—together with the entire family—been in captivity among the Indians

---

* It is to be regretted that Mr. Maguire was so feeble, when giving us an account of this expedition, that we feared to ask him for a repetition of the names of Captain Blair's command. He knew the names of all of them, but he mentioned them in such rapid succession that we only remember Brotherton, Jones, Moore, Smith, two brothers named Hicks, Nelson, Coleman, Wallack, Fee, Gano, Ricketts, Caldwell, Moore, Holliday, and one of the Rollers.

for some six or seven years. They were deemed a valuable acquisition.

Captain Blair pushed on his men with great vigor over the mountain, by way of the Kittaning trail; and when he arrived where the path crosses the head-waters of Blacklick, they were suddenly confronted by two of Captain Weston's tories, well known to some of Blair's men, who, on the impulse of the moment, would have shot them down, had it not been for the interference of Captain Blair, who evidently was a very humane man. These men begged for their lives most piteously, and declared that they had been grossly deceived by Weston, and then gave Captain Blair a true statement of what had occurred.

Finding that Providence had anticipated the object of their mission, by destroying and dispersing the tories, Captain Blair ordered his men to retrace their steps for home. Night coming upon them, they halted and encamped near where Loretto now stands. Here it was found that the provisions had nearly run out. The men, on the strength of the reported destruction of Weston, were in high spirits, built a large fire, and passed the night in hilarity, although it was raining and exceedingly disagreeable. At the dawn of day, Gersham and Moses Hicks started out in search of game for breakfast, for some of the men were weak and disheartened for the want of food. These wood-rangers travelled three miles from the camp without anticipating any danger whatever, when Gersham shot a fine elk, which, in order to make the load as light as possible, the brothers skinned and disemboweled, shouldered the hind-quarters, and were ready to return to the camp, when five Indians suddenly came upon them and took them prisoners. They were again captives, and taken to Detroit, from which place they did not return until after peace was declared. These men unquestionably saw and experienced enough of Indian life to fill an interesting volume.

In the mean time, the company becoming impatient at the continued absence of the Hicks, several small parties were formed to go in search of them. One of these parties fell in with three Indians, and several shots were exchanged without injuring any person. The Indians took to the woods, and the men returned to the camp. The other party found the place where the elk had been skinned, and took the remains to the camp; the meat was speedily roasted and divided among the men, and the line of march again taken up. The certain capture of the guides, and the Indians seen by the party in search of them, induced the belief that a larger body of them than they wished to encounter in their half-famished condition was in the neighborhood, considerably accelerated their march.

The sufferings endured by these men, who were drenched by torrents of rain and suffered the pangs of hunger until they reached the settlements on the east side of the mountain, were such as can be more readily imagined than described. But they all returned, and, though a portion of them took sick, they all eventually recovered, and probably would have been ready at any time to volunteer for another expedition, even with the terrors of starvation or the scalping-knife staring them in the face.

The tories who, through the clemency of Captain Blair, escaped shooting or hanging, did not, it seems, fare much better; for they, too, reached the settlements in an almost famished condition. Fearing to enter any of the houses occupied, they passed the Brush Mountain into Canoe Valley, where they came to an untenanted cabin, the former occupants having fled to the nearest fort. They incautiously set their rifles against the cabin, entered it, and searched for food, finding nothing, however, but part of a pot of boiled mush and some lard. In their condition, any thing bearing resemblance to food was a godsend, and they fell vigorously to work at it. While engaged in appeasing their appetite, Samuel Moore and a companion,—probably Jacob Roller, Sr., if we mistake not,—who were on a hunting expedition, happening to pass the cabin, saw the rifles, and immediately secured them, when Mr. Moore walked in with his gun cocked, and called upon the tories to surrender; which peremptory order they cheerfully complied with, and were marched to Holliday's Fort. On the way thither, one of them became insolent, and informed Moore and his companion that in a short time they would repent arresting them. This incensed Roller, and, being an athletic man, when they arrived at the fort he fixed a rope to the tory's neck, rove it over a beam, and drew him up. Moore, fortunately, was a more humane man, and persuaded his companion to desist. They were afterward taken to Bedford; but whether ever tried or not, we have not been able to ascertain.

Captain Blair's men, while passing through what is now known as Pleasant Valley, or the upper end of

Tuckahoe, on their return, paid a visit to a tory named John Hess, who, it is said, was armed, and waiting the return of Weston to join his company. They found Hess in his house, from which they took him to a neighboring wood, bent down a hickory sapling and fastened the branches of it around his neck, and, at a given signal, let him swing. The sight was so shocking, and his struggles so violent, that the men soon repented, and cut him down before he was injured to any extent. It appears from that day he was a tory no longer, joined the rangers, and did good service for his country. His narrow escape must have wrought his conversion.

The tories who escaped the fatal error of the Indians at Kittaning never returned to their former homes. It was probably as well that they did not, for their coming was anxiously looked for, and their greeting would un-questionably have been as *warm* a one as powder and ball could have been capable of giving. Most of them made their way to Fort Pitt, and from thence toward the South. They eventually all sent for their families; but "the land [of the Juniata Valley] that knew them once knew them no more forever!"

Captain Blair, whom we have frequently mentioned, soon after or about the close of the war moved to what is known as the mouth of Blair's Gap, west of Hollidays-burg, where John Walker now lives. He was an ener-getic man, and, by his untiring exertions, succeeded in getting a pack-horse road cut through his gap at an early day.

His son, Captain John Blair, a prominent and useful

17

citizen, flourished for many years at the same place. His usefulness and standing in the community made him probably the most conspicuous man of his day in this section; and, when Huntingdon county was divided, his old friends paid a tribute to his memory in giving the new county his name.

MILL CREEK.

CHAPTER XXII.

THE TORY HARE — MURDER OF LOUDENSLAGER — ABDUCTION AND
MURDER OF MRS. EATON AND CHILDREN—TREATMENT OF HARE BY
THE SETTLERS, ETC.

DURING the troubles which followed immediately after
the declaration of war, a great many depredations were
committed by the tories, that were invariably charged to
the Indians. As we have stated in the preceding chapter, the patriots and the tories, in point of numbers, were
about equally divided in many of the settlements of what
now constitutes Huntingdon county; yet the victims of
tory wrongs could not for a long time bring themselves
to believe that they were inflicted by their neighbors.
Barns and their valuable contents were laid in ashes,
cattle were shot or poisoned, and all charged to the
Indians, although scouts were constantly out, but seldom,
if ever, got upon their trail.

In a small isolated valley, about a mile south of Jack's
Narrows, lived a notorious tory named Jacob Hare. We
could not ascertain what countryman Hare was, nor any
thing of his previous history. He owned a large tract of
land, which he was exceedingly fearful of losing. Hence
he remained loyal to the king, under the most solemn con-

viction, no doubt, that the struggle would terminate in favor of the crown. He is represented as having been a man of little intelligence, brutal and savage, and cowardly in the extreme. Although he did not take up arms positively against the Colonists, he certainly contributed largely to aid the British in crushing them.

A short time previous to the Weston Tory Expedition, a young man named Loudenslager, who resided in the upper end of Kishicoquillas, left his home on horseback, to go to Huntingdon, where Major Cluggage was enlisting men to guard the lead mines of Sinking Valley. It was young Loudenslager's intention to see how things looked, and, if they suited, he would join Cluggage's command and send his horse home. As he was riding leisurely along near the head of the valley, some five or six Indians, accompanied by a white man, appeared upon an eminence, and three of them, including the white man, fired at him. Three buckshot and a slug lodged in his thigh, and one bullet whistled past his ear, while one of the buckshot struck the horse. The animal took fright, and started off at a full gallop. Loudenslager, although his thigh-bone was shattered and his wound bled so profusely that he left a trail of blood in his wake, heroically clung to his horse until he carried him to the Standing Stone fort.

Weak and faint from the loss of blood, when he got there he was unable to move, and some of the people carried him in and cared for him as well as they could; but he was too much exhausted to give any account of the occurrence. After some restoratives were applied, he rallied, and gave a statement of the affair. His description of the white man in company with the Indians was so accurate, that the people knew at once that Hare, if not the direct author, was the instigator, of this diabolical outrage.

Loudenslager, for want of good medical attendance or an experienced surgeon, grew worse, and the commander, to alleviate his sufferings if possible, placed him in a canoe, and despatched him, accompanied by some men, on his way to Middletown,—then the nearest point of any importance; but he died after the canoe had descended the river but a few miles.

The excitement occasioned by the shooting of young Loudenslager was just at its height when more bad news was brought to Standing Stone Fort.

On the same day, the same party that shot Louden-slager went to the house of Mr. Eaton, (though probably unaccompanied by Hare,) in the upper end of the same valley; but, not finding any men about the house,—Mr. Eaton being absent,—they took captives Mrs. Eaton and her two children, and then set fire to all the buildings. The work of devastation was on the point of being completed when Mr. Eaton reached his home. He did not wait to see his house entirely reduced to ashes, but rode to Standing Stone as fast as his horse could carry him, and spread the alarm. The exasperated people could hardly muster sufficient patience to hear the particulars before they started in pursuit of the enemy. They travelled with all the speed that energetic and determined men could command, scouring the country in every direction for a period of nearly a week, but heard no tidings of Mrs. Eaton and her children, and were forced to give her up as lost.

This aroused the wrath of the settlers, and many of them were for dealing out summary punishment to Hare as the instigator; but, in the absence of proof, he was not even brought to trial for the Loudenslager murder, of which he was clearly guilty. The act, however, put people upon their guard; the most notorious known tory in the county had openly shown his hand, and they knew what to expect of him.

Mr. Eaton—broken-hearted, and almost distracted— hunted for years for his wife and children; and, as no tidings could be had of them, he was at last reluctantly forced to believe that the savages had murdered them. Nor was he wrong in his conjecture. Some years after- ward the blanched skeletons of the three were found by some hunters in the neighborhood of Warrior's Mark. The identity of the skeletons was proved by some shreds of clothing—which were known to belong to them—still clinging to their remains.

When Captain Blair's rangers, or that portion of them raised in Path Valley, came across to the Juniata, they had an old drum, and—it is fair to infer, inasmuch as the still-house then seemed to be a necessary adjunct of civili- zation—sundry jugs of whiskey accompanying them. At Jack's Narrows lived a burly old German, named Peter Vandevender, who, hearing the noise, came to his door in his shirt-sleeves, with a pipe in his mouth.

"Waas ter tuyfel ish ter meaning of all dish?" inquired old Vandervender.

"We are going to hunt John Weston and his tories," said one of the men.

"Hunt dories, eh? Well, Captin Plair, chust you go ant hunt Chack Hare. He ish te tamtest dory in Bennsylvania. He dold Weshton ash he would haff a gompany to help him after he come mit ter Inchins."

What Vandevender told Blair was probably true to the letter; for one of the inducements held out to the tories to accompany Weston was that they would be reinforced by all the tories in the county as soon as the first blow was struck; but he was *not* raising a company. He was too cowardly to expose himself to the danger attending such a proceeding.

As soon as Vandevender had communicated the foregoing, the company, with great unanimity, agreed to pay Hare a visit forthwith. The drum was laid aside, and the volunteers marched silently to his house. A portion of them went into the house, and found Hare, while Blair and others searched the barn and outbuildings to find more of the tories. On the arrival of Captain Blair at the house, some of his men, in a high state of excitement, had a rope around Hare's neck, and the end of it thrown over a beam, preparatory to hanging him. Blair interposed, and with great difficulty prevented them from executing summary vengeance upon the tory. In the mean time, one of the men sharpened his scalping-knife upon an iron pot, walked deliberately up to Hare, and, while two or three others held him, *cut both his ears off close to his head!* The tory, during these proceedings, begged most piteously for his life—made profuse promises to surrender every thing he had to the cause of liberty; but the men regarded his

pleadings as those of a coward, and paid no attention to
them, and, after cropping him, marched back to Vandevender's on their route in search of Weston.

On their arrival at the Standing Stone, they communicated to the people at the fort what they had done. The
residents at the Stone only wanted a piece of information
like this to inflame them still more against Hare, and,
expressing regrets that he had not been killed, they immediately formed a plot to go down and despatch him.
But there were tories at the Stone. Hare soon got wind
of the affair, placed his most valuable effects upon pack-
horses, and left the country.

The failure of Weston's expedition, and the treatment
and flight of Hare, compelled many tories, who had openly
avowed their sentiments, to leave this section of the
country, while those who were suspected were forced into
silence and inactivity, and many openly espoused the
cause of the colonies. Still, many remained who refused
to renounce their allegiance to the king, and claimed to
stand upon neutral ground. Those who had taken up
arms against Great Britain, however, declared that there
were but two sides to the question, and no neutral ground;—
that those who were not for them were against them.

Hare was declared and proclaimed an "attainted
traitor," and his property was confiscated and sold. Who
became the purchaser we could not ascertain; but, after
peace was declared and the treaty between the United
States and Great Britain ratified, Hare returned, and
claimed the benefit of that part of the treaty which restored
their possessions to all those of his Majesty's subjects that
had not taken up arms against the colonists. As there was

no direct evidence that he killed Loudenslager, Congress was compelled to purchase back and restore his property to him.

He lived and died on his farm. The venerable Mrs. Armitage, the mother-in-law of Senator Cresswell, of Hollidaysburg, remembers seeing him when she was quite young and he an old man. She says he used to conceal the loss of his ears by wearing his hair long.

During life he was shunned, and he died unregretted; but, we are sorry to say, his name is perpetuated: the place in which he lived, was cropped, and died, and is still called Hare's Valley. The people of Huntingdon should long since have changed it, and blotted from their memory a name linked to infamy and crime.

CHAPTER XXIII.

MOSES DONALDSON—CAPTURE AND MURDER OF HIS WIFE AND TWO
CHILDREN.

MOSES DONALDSON lived in Hartslog settlement, where
Hatfield's iron-works are now located, near Alexandria.
In 1777, after the first Indian outrages had been committed, the neighboring settlers met, and resolved for their
better protection to build a stockade fort somewhere near
the river. After the building was decided upon, the location became a subject of contention—one party wanting
the fort at Lytle's, another at Donaldson's, and for a while
party strife ran high. Lytle, however, succeeded in out-
generalling Donaldson,—not because his location was the
most eligible, but simply because he was the most popular
man. The fort was built at Lytle's, under Donaldson's
protest, who declared that he never would go into it,—that
if danger threatened he would fort at Standing Stone,—a
vow he religiously kept, at the expense of the loss of his
wife and two children, we regret to say.

He continued living at his own house until the spring
of 1778, when Indian alarms became so frequent that he
removed his family to Huntingdon. In a short time the
fears of the people were somewhat lulled, and most of them

returned to their homes again. Mr. Donaldson, finding his farm-work pressing, returned to his home about the first of June, and prepared to make hay.

On the 11th of the month, a girl who was after cows discovered in Anderson's bottom, near the mouth of Shaver's Creek, an encampment of some five or six Indians. Without their discovering her, she made her way back and communicated the intelligence, and the news was soon circulated among the settlers. The five Indians were considered the advance of a large party; otherwise they might readily have been cut off by a dozen resolute men. Instead of making the least effort to ascertain the number of the savages, the people fled to the forts in the utmost consternation.

On the same evening, a convoy of canoes landed at the mouth of Shaver's Creek, and the soldiers stopped at an old inn on the bank of the creek. They had taken a load of supplies to Water Street Landing for the Lead Mine Fort, and were returning with lead-ore, consigned to Middletown for smelting. The state of affairs was laid before the commander of the convoy, and Mr. Anderson prevailed upon him to stay a day or two, until the alarm had subsided.

On the afternoon of the 12th, Donaldson was warned that the Indians had been seen a second time, and advised to fort at Lytle's without delay. This he refused to do point-blank, but immediately packed up, put his family into a canoe, and started for Huntingdon. When he reached the mouth of Shaver's Creek, he tied the canoe to the root of a tree at the bank of the creek, and went up to transact some business with Mr. Anderson, accompanied

by his oldest child—a lad nine or ten years of age,—
leaving his wife and two younger children in the canoe.

After an absence of half an hour, the boy returned to the
canoe; but, as he came in sight of it, he observed a number
of Indians taking his mother and the children out of it.
He hastened back to the inn and told the soldiers, but
they considered it a fabrication, and paid no attention to
what he said.   From thence he hastened to Anderson's
and told his father, who immediately followed him, and
found it only too true that his family had been abducted—
that, too, within the hearing, and almost within sight, of
twelve soldiers.   Donaldson went to the inn, and appealed
to the commandant to start his force in immediate pursuit.
This, however, was found totally impracticable, as they had
been making a sort of holiday by getting drunk, and were
unfit for duty of any kind; which was to be regretted,
for the timely notice of the outrage would easily have
enabled them, had they been in condition, to overtake the
savages.

Early next morning the soldiers started in pursuit in
one direction, and the people of the settlement formed into
a strong party and went in another, and in this manner
the entire country was scoured.   Toward evening a bonnet belonging to one of the children was found in a rye-
field, near where the Maguire farm now stands, which indicated the direction the savages had taken.

Next day the search was resumed and continued until
night; but no tidings whatever could be obtained of the
route the savages had taken, and they were finally obliged
to give them up as lost.

Several years elapsed before their fate was known.

Thomas Johnston and Peter Crum, while hunting up Spruce Creek, probably a mile and a half from its mouth, came upon the camp of a friendly Indian family, near whose wigwam an old woman was engaged in boiling sugar, and who informed them that she had long been waiting for some white hunters to come up, as she had something to show them. She then led the way, and, half a mile off, showed them the skeletons of a grown person and two children. This news was communicated to Mr. Donaldson, and he had the skeletons taken to Shaver's Creek, with a view of interring them. But here a new difficulty arose. Mr. Eaton had not yet recovered his family, abducted from Kishicoquillas Valley, and there was no reason why these skeletons might not be those of his family. The matter was finally determined by a weaver, who testified to a piece of Mrs. Donaldson's short-gown, found near her remains.

When we reflect over this act of savage atrocity, we are free to confess that we look upon it as one of the most inhuman and revolting on record. The woman, with her two children, taken to a neighboring wood, and there, in all probability, tomahawked and scalped in succession,—the children witnessing the agony of the dying mother, or perhaps the mother a witness to the butchery of her helpless offspring,—the very recital chills the blood.

The son, who accompanied his father to Anderson's, died at a very advanced age, at or near Lock Haven, a year or two ago.

William Donaldson, of Hollidaysburg, is a son of Moses Donaldson by a second wife.

CHAPTER XXIV.

DEPREDATIONS AT THE MOUTH OF SPRUCE CREEK—MURDER OF LEVI
HICKS — SCALPING OF HIS CHILD.

WE have already mentioned the Hicks family in a preceding chapter, and incidentally mentioned their captivity
for a number of years among the Indians. We have
made the most unremitting exertions, yet we have failed
to ascertain any thing like a satisfactory account of this
remarkable family. The name of Gersham Hicks figures
in Miner's "History of Wyoming" as an Indian guide,
while in the Archives he is noticed as an Indian interpreter, previous to the war of the Revolution. Where
they were taken, or when released, is not positively
known. One thing, however, is quite certain: that is, that
they made themselves masters of both the habits and language of many of the Indians.

Mrs. Fee thinks they came to Water Street immediately after their release from captivity, and settled
there. During their captivity they imbibed the Indian
habit to such a degree that they wore the Indian costume,
even to the colored eagle-feathers and little trinkets
which savages seem to take so much delight in. Gersham

TUNNEL ON THE PENNSYLVANIA CENTRAL ROAD AT THE MOUTH OF SPRUCE CREEK.

and Moses were unmarried, but Levi, the elder, brought with him a half-breed as his wife, by whom he had a number of children. They all settled at Water Street, and commenced the occupation of farming. Subsequently, Levi rented from the Bebaults the tub-mill at or near the mouth of Spruce Creek.

When the Indian troubles commenced in the spring of 1778, he was repeatedly urged to go either to Lytle's or Lowry's Fort, and let the mill stand until the alarm had subsided. Hicks, however, obstinately refused, declaring that he was safe. It is thus apparent that he relied upon his intimate knowledge of the Indian character and language for safety, in case any of the marauders should find their way to what he looked upon as a sort of an out-of-the-way place,—a fatal case of misplaced confidence, notwithstanding it was asserted that the fall previous a party had attacked his cabin, and that, on his addressing them in their own language, they had desisted.

On the 12th of May, 1778, Hicks started his mill in the morning, as was his usual custom, and then repaired to breakfast. While in the house he procured a needle and thread, returned to the mill, replenished the hopper, and then seated himself near the door and commenced mending a moccasin. He had been occupied at this but a minute or two before he heard a rustling in the bushes some ten or fifteen yards in front of him. The idea of there being Indians in the vicinity never entered his head; nobody had seen or heard of any in the settlement. Consequently, in direct violation of an established custom, he walked forward to ascertain the cause of the commotion in the bushes, leaving his rifle leaning against the mill. He advanced but one or two steps before he was shot through the heart.

His wife, who was in the house at the time, hearing the report, ran to the door, and in an instant comprehended how matters stood. She opened the back door, ran down the river to a fording, crossed over, and, with all the speed she could command, hastened over the mountain to Lytle's Fort. Near Alexandria she met a man on horseback, who, noticing her distracted condition, demanded what the matter was. She explained as best she could, when the man turned back and rode rapidly toward the fort to apprise the people of what had occurred. It was then that the woman fairly recovered her senses, and, on looking around for the first time, she noticed her little son, about ten years old, who had followed her. The sight of him reminded her of her family of children at home, at the mercy of the savages, and all the mother's devotion was aroused within her. She picked up her boy, and, exhausted as she was, hastened toward the fort with him.

As it subsequently appeared, one of the children of Mrs. Hicks,—a girl between three and four years of age,— directly after her escape, went out to see her father, just while the savages were in the act of scalping him. She was too young to comprehend the act clearly, but, seeing the blood about his head, she commenced crying, and screamed, "My pappy! my pappy! what are you doing to my poor pappy?"

One of the Indians drew his tomahawk from his belt and knocked the child down, after which he scalped it; and, without venturing to the house, the savages departed. Mrs. Hicks reached the fort, and the news of the murder soon spread over the country, but the usual delays occurred in getting up a scout to follow the marauders. Some declared their unwillingness to go unless there was a large force, as the depredators 'might only be some stragglers belonging to a large party; others, that their rifles were out of order; and others again pleaded sickness. In this way the day slipped around, and in the mean time the savages got far beyond their reach, even in case the scout could have been induced to follow them.

Next morning, however, a party mustered courage and went over to the mill, where they found Hicks scalped on the spot where he fell, and his rifle gone.

The inside of the house presented one of the saddest spectacles ever witnessed in the annals of savage atrocities. Two of the children were lying upon the floor crying, and the infant in the cradle, for the want of nourishment had apparently cried until its crying had subsided into the most pitiful moanings; while the little girl that had been scalped sat crouched in a corner, gibbering like an idiot, her face and head covered with dry clotted blood!

Of course, considering the start the Indians had, it was deemed useless to follow them; so they buried Hicks near the mill, and removed the family to the fort.

It may seem a little singular, nevertheless it is true, that the child, in spite of its fractured skull and the loss of its scalp, actually recovered, and lived for a number of years after the outrage, although its wounds were never dressed by a physician. It was feeble-minded, however, owing to the fracture.

As no other family resided near the mill, no person could be induced to take it after Hicks was murdered, and it stood idle for years.

The murder of Hicks created the usual amount of alarm, but no depredations followed in the immediate neighborhood for some time after his death.

CHAPTER XXV.

STONE VALLEY—McCORMICK'S FORT—MURDER OF MRS. HOUSTON AND
JAMES McCLEES—A DEALER IN GRAIN OF THE OLDEN TIME.

IN consequence of the rumors so rife in 1778 of the country being filled with Indians, the people of Stone Valley, north of Huntingdon, determined to build a fort. While concerting the measures for its erection, a Mr. McCormick stated that, inasmuch as the population of the valley was not very large, and the labor and expense attending the erection of a fortress very great, he would agree that his house should be put into repair, pierced for defence, and that the people should fort with him. This proposition was eagerly accepted by the people, who went willingly to work; and in a very short time his house was converted into Fort McCormick, into which nearly all the settlers of Stone Valley fled at once.

Among others who took up their residence there was an old lady named Houston, who had resided some seven miles up the valley. She was a very amiable old lady, though somewhat garrulous, for which some of the settlers were disposed to ridicule her. It appears she had a small patch of flax out, which gave her more trouble than a hundred acres of wheat would occasion some men. She was constantly lamenting the certain loss of her flax, until the very word flax got to be a byword. As the time for pulling the flax approached, the old woman importuned every man in the fort to accompany her to her house only for a day, but her appeals were all in vain; some declared they would not go so far from the fort for a ten-acre field of flax, while an old soldier intimated that he would be pretty sure to be *flaxed* if he went. In short, her request was treated as a jest. Nevertheless, the old woman indulged some sort of a vague hope that somebody would help her out of her difficulty, and she continued talking about the flax.

One morning, about the middle of August, a number of men were seated in front of the fort, when some one started the ever laughable theme of the old woman's flax-patch; and, while conversing with the usual levity upon the old woman's trials, a young man, named James Mc-Clees, joined the party. After listening to them some time, he got up and said—

" Boys, it is bad enough to be too cowardly to help the old woman gather her flax; to ridicule her misfortune is a shame."

" If you think it is cowardly, why don't you go and help her pull it?" said one of the men, who was evidently piqued at what had been said.

" That is just my intention," said he. " Mrs. Houston, get ready, and I'll go with you to pull your flax."

The dream was at last to be realized, and the old woman's heart was overflowing with gratitude. In a few moments she was ready. McClees shouldered his rifle, and the two departed—alas! to return no more.

McClees was but eighteen years of age, but extremely well-proportioned, and his vocabulary knew no such word as fear. Sad fate, that his noble and generous impulses should have been the means of cutting him off in the very flower of youth!

Of the manner of his death there was no living witness to speak; but on and around his body, when found, there were unmistakable signs of such actions as are supposed to speak as plain as words.

Both had promised to return to the fort in the evening, or the evening following at farthest. The first evening passed, and they came not; the second evening, and still no sign of them. This created alarm, and the necessary arrangements were made to go in search of them.

As soon as the ordinary duty of the morning was performed, as many armed men as it was deemed safe to spare were sent up the Valley. When they arrived at Mrs. Houston's house they found all quiet, and no signs of either Mrs. Houston or McClees having been there. They then started up the hill-side, toward the flax-patch; but before they reached it they found the dead body of Mrs. Houston. She had been killed apparently by cuts from a hatchet on the forehead, and her scalp was taken off. The flax was untouched, which rendered it probable that she was attacked and killed while on her way to the patch.

A hundred yards farther on lay McClees, literally covered with blood, and stabbed and cut in every part of his body. As there were no bullet-wounds upon him, it was evident that the fight was a hand-to-hand encounter, and the struggle must have been a long, fearful, and bloody one.

That McClees had sold his life dearly was also very apparent. His rifle was gone; but by his side lay his knife, bloody, and the point broken off. Near him lay a tomahawk, also bloody, and the ground was clotted with blood for a circuit of twenty yards. In addition to these, eagle-feathers, beads, and shreds of buckskin, were found lying about where the struggle had taken place.

The nature of this fearful fight could only be guessed at by these tokens; but the true state of it was revealed in a few years after; for within a mile of where the struggle took place, on the bench of the mountain, two hunters found the remains of three Indians covered with bark. The supposition was that McClees had been attacked by five of them, and killed two outright and mortally wounded a third before they despatched him.

A hero such as this brave youth proved himself in that desperate encounter certainly deserved a better fate.

In concluding our reminiscences of Stone Valley we cannot omit giving an anecdote, characteristic of the times, told us by an old friend.

Far up Stone Creek lived an old gentleman named O'Burn. In 1777, being a thrifty farmer, he raised nearly a thousand bushels of wheat. The year following, times became very hard — wheat was high, and commanded a price which placed it almost beyond the reach of poor men. The fact that O'Burn had a large quantity of wheat attracted to his house numerous customers; and the manner in which he dealt with them may be inferred from the following:—

A man reputed to be rich rode up to his house, when Mr. O'Burn made his appearance in the doorway.

"Mr. O'Burn, have you any wheat?"

"Plenty of it. Have you the money to pay for it?"

"Certainly."

"A horse to carry it, and bags to put it in, I see."

"Oh, yes; every thing," said the stranger.

"Well, then," replied O'Burn, "you can go to Big Valley for your wheat; mine is for people who have no money to pay, no bags to put it in, and no horses to carry it off!"

We regret to say that the race of O'Burns became extinct some years ago.

CHAPTER XXVI.

TUCKAHOE — MURDER OF JOHN GUILLIFORD.

In the Valley of Tuckahoe, stretching from Altoona to the mouth of the Bald Eagle, there were some depredations committed, but never any of a very serious nature, except upon one occasion. The cause of this can be traced, in a great measure, to the fact that Thomas and Michael Coleman and Michael Wallack lived in the upper end of the valley. These men were so well known and so much feared by the Indians, that, although the Kittaning Path, leading to the Bald Eagle Valley, ran directly through Tuckahoe, they always avoided it, for fear of finding those old and experienced hunters ambuscaded along their route. Besides, Captain Logan, a friendly chief, lived for some years in what is now known as Logan's Valley. He was also known and feared, and he was constantly on the watch to guard against the incursions of hostile savages. Add to this the fact that the valley was thinly populated, and the risk attending the hunting for scalps immeasurably great, small roving parties, on but two or three occasions, made their appearance in Tuckahoe.

In the fall of 1777, two savages took captive two children while at play, near a cabin located somewhere in the neighborhood of where Mr. Hutchinson now lives. Thomas Coleman happened to be out hunting, and saw them come up the path. Each one was carrying a child, but neither of them had fire-arms, so that he felt quite at ease. From behind the tree where he stood, he might easily have shot one of the savages, but he would not run the risk for fear of hitting the child; so, waiting until they had passed him, he jumped into the path, levelled his gun at them, and shouted "*surrender!*" The affrighted savages dropped the children and disappeared in the woods.

On another occasion they entered the valley, stole three horses, and set fire to a stable. A number of pioneers tracked them through the old war-path to the top of the mountain; which was quite as far as it was prudent to venture, as that was considered the line dividing the white settlements from the Indian country.

The only massacre in Tuckahoe ever committed by the savages took place in the summer of 1778. A man named John Guilliford cleared a small patch of land a short distance south of where Blair Furnace now stands, and erected his cabin near where John Trout's house is. In the spring of 1778, he abandoned his ground and cabin after the first alarm of Indian depredations, and sought safety in Fetter's Fort. In the course of the summer, after the alarm had somewhat subsided, Guilliford went down to see how his crops were progressing. His body was found the same day by Coleman and Milligan. It was lying at the threshold of his cabin door; so that, in all probability, he was shot just as he was coming out of his house. Coleman and Milligan dug a grave near the hut, and buried him as he was, without a coffin. The most remarkable feature about this murder was that Guilliford was not scalped. When we remember that scalps were paid for at the British garrison at Detroit, the omission to scalp Guilliford appears almost inexplicable. Coleman and Milligan went in search of the Indians, but did not succeed in getting upon their trail.

CHAPTER XXVII.

EARLY SETTLEMENT OF SCOTCH VALLEY—THE MOORE FAMILY—MASSA-
CRE OF WILLIAM MOORE—INDIAN SHOT BY A BOY, ETC.

THE Moore family, whose name is identified with Scotch Valley as the original settlers, came to this country probably about the year 1768, from Scotland. It consisted of Samuel Moore, his seven sons and two daughters,—viz.: Daniel, William, John, Samuel, James, David, Joseph, Elizabeth, and Jane. Their first stopping-place in the interior was in Kishicoquillas Valley, where the hardy Scots commenced clearing land; but the yield not being such as they were led to expect, the two elder brothers, Daniel and William, were sent abroad by the old patriarch to look for better land and more of it. Accordingly, they shaped their course westward, prospecting as they went, until they reached what is now known as Scotch Valley. How they found their way to that place, an unbroken wilderness, five miles from the nearest human habitation, or what the inducements were for stopping there, were puzzling questions *then*. Let the reader *now* look at the fine farms of Scotch Valley, and he will see that, in selecting the spot, the Moores were actuated by a sagacity that enabled them to see those fine lands

blooming like the rose in the future.   They immediately
occupied a large tract of land, built a cabin, and commenced
clearing.   The year following they went to Kishicoquillas, and brought on the father and the remainder of the
family.

Beneath their sturdy blows the giant oaks fell, and the
wilderness was turned into fields of waving grain, and they
soon had a home that made them even forget the High-
lands of Scotland.

When the war broke out they were all stanch repub-
licans, active and energetic men, and were foremost in all
measures of defence for the frontier.

William Moore, second son of Samuel, a useful man,
loved and respected by all who knew him, met his death
at the hands of an Indian, in August, 1778.   It appears
that one morning two of their horses were missing, when
William and a lad named George McCartney, about fourteen years of age, started in pursuit of them—as a matter
of course not neglecting the caution of the day, to take
their rifles with them.   At that time two paths led to
Fetter's Fort from Scotch Valley,—one by way of Frankstown, through Adam Holliday's farm, fording the river
near where the plank-road bridge now crosses south of
Hollidaysburg; the other led through the flat, back of the
Presbyterian graveyard, and north of Hollidaysburg.
This was the most direct route; but, in order to make a
thorough research, they went by way of the river road,
and reached Fetter's Fort without obtaining any tidings
of the missing animals.   After remaining at the fort a
short time, they started on their way home by the back or
direct road.   No Indians having been seen in the country

for some time, they travelled on with a feeling of entire security, and never for a moment entertained the remotest idea of coming in contact with savages. When they came to a pile of drift-wood,—in what is now known as McCahen's Bottom, half a mile west of Hollidaysburg,—while Moore was in the act of trying to get over the drift, he was shot by an Indian from an ambuscade. The bullet entered his back, passed through the left ventricle of the heart, and he fell dead against the drift.

McCartney, who was some distance off, on the impulse of the moment commenced running. In the mean time the Indian had come from his place of concealment, and, seeing him, drew his tomahawk and followed. McCartney soon finding that the savage was the fleetest, and must overtake him, cocked his gun while running, suddenly wheeled, and aimed at the Indian. This unexpected defence from a mere boy rather took the Indian by surprise, and he jumped behind a tree, and McCartney did the same, still keeping the aim ready to shoot in case the Indian moved from the cover of the tree. While in this position, the Indian commenced loading his rifle, and, after ramming home the powder, he accidentally dropped his ramrod, which he stooped to pick up; in doing which he exposed his posterior, which McCartney took advantage of, and fired. The Indian gave a scream of mingled rage and pain, dropped his rifle, and ran, picking up leaves on his way, which he endeavored to thrust into the bullet-hole to stanch the blood.

Young McCartney, satisfied with the exploit, and thankful that his life had been spared, did not pursue the savage. His first impulse was to do so; but fearing that the chase might lead him into an encampment of the enemy, since it invariably turned out that where there was one more were not far off, he returned with all despatch to Fetter's Fort. The men at the fort had heard both shots, but supposed that Moore and McCartney had started game of some kind; consequently, they were unprepared for any news of the kind. Fortunately, there happened to be a very large force at Fetter's at the time, and, under the impression that there must be more Indians in the neighborhood, a strong, experienced force at once started out.

When they arrived at the drift, they found the body of Moore, stark in death, leaning against it, with his rifle grasped in his uplifted hands, as if in the very act of trying to climb over. His body was removed to the fort by some of the men, while the remainder commenced searching for the Indian. By his blood they tracked him nearly a mile up the run, and even found a place where he had evidently stopped to wash the blood off; but at length they lost all traces of his trail. They continued their march, however, to Gap Run, in order to ascertain whether there was any fresh Indian trail. In their conjectures that there were other Indians near they were not mistaken. Half a mile west of where Hutchinson's Mill now stands, they found traces of a fresh encampment of a very large party, whose trail they followed several miles up the Kittaning War-Path; but they soon abandoned all hope of overtaking them, and returned to the fort.

The dead body of the Indian shot by McCartney was found, some time afterward, by a Mr. Hileman, up Kittaning Run, where he had secreted himself by the side of of a log, under some bushes, and completely covered himself with brush and leaves previous to giving up the ghost, in order to prevent the whites from finding his body. The ruling passion was strong even in death!

His rifle, which was kept at Fetter's, as a trophy, was a brass-barrelled smooth-bore, with the British coat of arms stamped upon it,—conclusive evidence that the entire savage band had been armed and equipped by his Majesty's officers at Detroit, and were on a scalp-hunting expedition.

During the troubles of 1779–80, when the frontier-men fled before the assaults and merciless massacres of the Indians, the Moores returned to their former residence in Kishicoquillas. But the restless Scots did not remain away from their farm long. Some of them returned in a year; but the old patriarch, Samuel, did not return until after the surrender of Cornwallis. He was then accompanied by a colony of Scotchmen, consisting of the Crawfords, Irwins, Fraziers, Stewarts, and Macphersons, and others, constituting from twenty-five to thirty persons.

The late Mr. Maguire, then quite a lad, was at Shaver's Creek when they passed on their way west. They were all in full Highland costume, with bonnet and kilt, armed with claymores and Queen Anne muskets. He had seen Indians before, but never any Highlanders, and, while listening to their Gaelic dialect, he wondered to himself what tribe they belonged to.

These men settled in the upper end of the valley; hence the name—"Scotch Valley." By their sinewy arms and sturdy blows the oaks of the forest fell, and by their unremitting toil to gain a home in the New World they encountered and triumphed over the most formidable obstacles, until the valley—its natural soil taken into consideration—became one of the finest of its size in the country.

The Moore family were the first persons who conceived the idea of running arks down the river from Frankstown. This they accomplished successfully before the close of the last century, and afterward engaged in running flat-boats between Frankstown and Middletown.

Of the third generation of the Moore family but three remain in this vicinity,—viz.: T. B. Moore, in Hollidaysburg; Jesse Moore, at the old homestead, in Scotch Valley; and Johnston Moore, in Ebensburg. Others, however, live in the West; and the fourth generation, whose number we are not able to compute, are scattered over the Union.

The descendants of the men who wound their way up the Juniata, in Highland costume, nearly three-quarters of a century ago, with all their worldly possessions upon pack-horses, are also numerous; and many of them have risen to wealth and eminence by their own unaided exertions.

CHAPTER XXVIII.

WOODCOCK VALLEY — MASSACRE OF ELDER — THE BRECKENRIDGE FAMILY — FIGHT WITH, AND DESTRUCTION OF, CAPTAIN PHILLIPS'S SCOUT BY THE INDIANS—CRUEL MASSACRE OF TEN MEN.

WOODCOCK VALLEY, located north of Huntingdon, is one of the oldest-settled valleys in the county. In the days of Indian depredations, it was a favorite haunt of the savage, whose great war-path from the West to the East went through a part of it.

The first murder committed in it during the Revolutionary struggle occurred at Coffey Run, near the present residence of Mr. Entriken. The victim was a man named Elder, the husband of the woman mentioned in a preceding chapter as having been carried a captive to Detroit by the Indians. As there is no living witness who was present, the circumstances connected with his massacre are merely traditionary. He was on his way home in company with Richard Shirley, when he was shot and scalped; in which condition he was found by a scouting party a day or two after the occurrence. This was in 1778, and the same year a number of captives were taken from the valley; but the accounts are so vague that we can give no reliable data.

19

The Breckenridge family lived about three miles southeast of McConnelstown, on the road which now leads from Huntingdon to Bedford, on the farm at present occupied by Ludwig Hoover. The family consisted of the father, mother, two sons,—John and Thomas, aged respectively eighteen and sixteen years,—a girl aged fourteen, another aged three years, and an infant at the breast. They had, during the alarms of massacres, forted at Hartsock's Fort, which was almost in sight of their farm; but in the spring of 1779, the alarm having in a great measure subsided, they, as well as the rest of the settlers, went home, and the fort was abandoned, under the full impression that they would have no further use for it,—that Indian depredations were ended. In this they were most signally mistaken.

In July—probably about the middle of the month,—one morning, directly after breakfast, the sons, John and Thomas, started in search of a horse that had broken from his enclosure the night previous. After they had gone, the old lady occupied herself in her household duties, while the oldest daughter repaired to the spring-house in the meadow,—a distance of probably five hundred yards from the house,—for the purpose of churning. While engaged in this occupation, she was suddenly confronted by five Indians. Probably overcome by fright, she made no effort to escape, but screamed at the top of her voice. The father, without suspecting the real cause of the difficulty, started, unarmed, in the direction of the spring-house, and when within twenty yards of it a bullet from one of the Indian rifles struck him, and he fell dead in the path. Mrs. Breckenridge was looking out of the window at the time, and, fearing that their next move would be in the direction of the house, she snatched the infant out of the cradle, and, taking in her arms the other child, escaped. Instinctively she took the path toward Standing Stone,—a direction in which the Indians were not likely to follow. She pursued the path along Crooked Run for a few miles, and then sank exhausted upon the ground. As soon as she rallied, she endeavored to continue her way to the Stone; but to her dismay she found that she had wandered from the path and was lost. In this condition, she wandered about the woods with her children the whole day and the entire night. Next day, the oldest child complained bitterly of hunger, when the mother fortunately came to a rye-field. The rye was just beginning to head, in spots, and she gathered a number of heads, rubbed out the kernels, and gave them to the child. As the operation was a tedious one, in consequence of the scarcity of the grain, she took off her under-garment, wrapped up the infant and laid it down, and went to work to procure sufficient to appease the appetite of the child, and while so engaged she unconsciously wandered a considerable distance from the infant.

John and Thomas returned to the house with the horses late in the afternoon; and, seeing their father and sister murdered, believed that the mother, with the other children, had either met the same fate or been carried into captivity. They lost no time in making their way to Standing Stone Fort, where they communicated the sad intelligence. By that time it was nearly dark, and entirely too late to make any further effort; but at the

dawn of day, next morning, a posse of men went to Breckenridge's house, where the murdered father and daughter
lay, and, while part of the people employed themselves in
removing the bodies preparatory to burial, another party
scoured the country in search of the mother, being encouraged to do so by seeing her tracks leading toward
Crooked Run. Late in the afternoon they found her, at
the edge of the rye-field, leading her child; but the
anguish she had endured had in a measure unsettled
her mind, and she was unable to tell where she had
left the infant. It was deemed advisable to remove her
to the fort. By next day, she had so far recovered as to
be able to state that she left the infant in the field;
whereupon a party set out, and returned with it in the
evening.

The infant had apparently not suffered a great deal,
except from the annoyance of flies. *Its entire face was fly-
blown;* and yet, strange to say, she recovered, grew to be a
strong, healthy woman, got married, and was the mother
of Isaac B. Meek, Esq., formerly a member of the legislature from Centre county, and, we are told, died but a few
years ago.

John Breckenridge became a distinguished Presbyterian
preacher. Mr. Maguire was under the impression that he
located among his relatives in Kentucky; but Dr. Junkin,
of Hollidaysburg, whose knowledge of church history cannot be questioned, informs us that he officiated for many
years in the first Presbyterian church ever built in Washington City.

Woodcock Valley was the scene of the massacre of
Captain Phillips's scout,—one of the most cruel and cold-

blooded murders on record,—a massacre which hurried into eternity ten as brave men as ever ranged the woods of the Juniata Valley.

The following is Colonel Piper's official report of the massacre, made to President Reed. It contains no particulars, and is also inaccurate; nevertheless, we deem it worthy of a place, as it bears an official stamp. We copy it from the Archives of 1780:—

Bedford County, August 6, 1780.

SIR:—Your favor of the third of June, with the blank commissions, have been duly received; since which we have been anxiously employed in raising our quota of Pennsylvania volunteers, and at the same time defending our frontiers. But, in our present shattered situation, a full company cannot be expected from this county, when a number of our militia companies are entirely broken up and whole townships laid waste, so that the communication betwixt our upper and lower districts is entirely broken, and our apprehensions of immediate danger are not lessened, but greatly aggravated by a most alarming stroke. Captain Phillips, an experienced, good woodman, had engaged a company of rangers for the space of two months, for the defence of our frontiers, was surprised at his fort on Sunday, the 16th of July, when the captain, with eleven of his company, were all taken and killed. When I received the intelligence, which was the day following, I marched, with only ten men, directly to the place, where we found the house burnt to ashes, with sundry Indian tomahawks that had been lost in the action, but found no person killed at that place; but, upon taking the Indian tracks, within about one half-mile we found ten of Captain Phillips's company, with their hands tied, and murdered in the most cruel manner.

This bold enterprise so alarmed the inhabitants that our whole frontiers were upon the point of giving way; but, upon application to the Lieutenant of Cumberland county, he hath sent to our assistance one company of the Pennsylvania volunteers, which, with the volunteers raised in our own county, hath so encouraged the inhabitants that they seem determined to stand it a little longer. We hope our conduct will receive your approbation; and you'll please to approve it by sending your special order to our county commissioner to furnish these men with provisions and other necessaries until such times as other provisions can be made for our defence. As Colonel Smith will deliver this, I beg leave to recommend you to him, as he is very capable to give full satisfaction to you, in every particular, of our present circumstances.

I have the honor to be,
With all due respect,
Your Excellency's most ob't
And very humble servant,
JOHN PIPER.

Overlooking the fact that Colonel Piper, in this semi-official statement, did not even condescend to mention the name of a single one of the brave men who fell by the hands of the ruthless savages, is it not a little strange that the whole report should be filled with gross inaccuracies, not the least of which is that Captain Phillips was killed, when it is notorious that he returned after the war—having been taken prisoner,—and people are still living in the valley who saw him many years after the massacre of his scout?

Captain Phillips, previous to the disaster, resided near what is now Williamsburg. He was a man of some energy, and a skilful and experienced woodman. He had made a temporary fortress of his house, to guard against savage incursions, and his usefulness in protecting the frontier was duly appreciated by the settlers. Through the influence of some of the most prominent men about Clover Creek, Colonel Piper was induced to give Mr. Phillips a captain's commission, with authority to raise a company of rangers to serve for two months, as it was known that there was a large body of savages somewhere in the valley, unmistakeable traces of their presence having been seen at many places along the river.

Captain Phillips commenced recruiting men immediately on the reception of his commission; but, owing to the fact that it was just the beginning of harvest, he met with very little success. By the 15th of July, 1780, he had but ten men collected; but with these he determined to scout through Woodcock Valley and the Cove, in order to protect the farmers in harvesting their grain. To this end he distributed ammunition and provisions, and the party marched from the Cove across the mountain. On entering the valley, they found most of the houses abandoned, but no signs of Indians. Late on Saturday evening they arrived at the house of one Frederick Heater, which had been abandoned by its owner. The house had been pierced with loopholes, to serve as a temporary fortress in case of necessity, but the proprietor, unable to find sufficient men to garrison it, had fled to Hartsock's Fort. At this house Captain Phillips determined to remain over Sunday. The entire force consisted of Captain Phillips, his son Elijah, aged fourteen years, Philip Skelly, Hugh Skelly, P. and T. Sanders, Richard Shirley, M. Davis, Thomas Gaitrell, Daniel Kelly, and two men whose names are no longer remembered. After partaking of their supper they all stretched themselves out on the floor and slept soundly until morning. While preparing their morning meal, one of the Skellys happened to open the door, when he discovered that the house was surrounded by Indians. A glance sufficed to show Captain Phillips how matters stood. There were not less than sixty Indians, and among them two white men, dressed, decorated, and painted, the same as the savages. The captain at first supposed they were marauders, and would probably not stop; but the hope was most delusive. A small shower of rain having fallen the day previous, this savage war-party had tracked Phillips and his men to the very door of Heater's house. Phillips commanded the utmost silence, and awaited with breathless anxiety the further movements of the enemy. Through the window he discovered the savages grouped upon an eminence—some ten of them armed with rifles, and the remainder with bows and arrows—in consultation. Directly one of the savages fired his rifle, which was evidently a *ruse* to draw the men from the house; but it did not succeed. At last one of the Indians ventured within rifle-range of the house, when Gaitrell, unable to resist the temptation, thrust the muzzle of his rifle through one of the loopholes, fired, and shot him through the left shoulder. The war-whoop was then raised, and the savages ran to and fro for a while, concealing themselves behind trees, some seventy yards from the house, under the impression probably that an immediate action would take place.

No further demonstrations being made by the rangers, the Indians waited but a short time until, at a preconcerted signal, they fired a volley at the door and window of the house, both of which were riddled by the bullets, but no person was injured. The scout, in this agony of suspense, surrounded by a large body of savages, with the greatest bravery stood at the loopholes, and whenever a savage showed himself within rifle-range he was shot at. In this manner two were killed and two wounded. The Indians, in the mean time, continued firing at the door and window; and in this way the fight continued until about the middle of the afternoon, when Philip Skelly shot the chief through the left cheek at a distance of nearly a hundred yards. This so exasperated the Indians that they raised the war-whoop a second time, loud and fierce, and appeared determined to have vengeance.

At this juncture an occurrence took place which seems almost incredible; yet Captain Phillips, whose statement we are giving, vouched for the truth of it, and he was unquestionably a man of veracity. Davis had the muzzle of his rifle out of a loop-hole, and was intently watching for a chance to shoot, when he felt a sudden jarring of the rifle. He withdrew it, and found a sharp-pointed, tapering hickory arrow driven into the muzzle so tight that it took the combined efforts of four men to withdraw it. Whether this new method of spiking a gun was intentional or not, it illustrated most forcibly the wonderful power of the Indian over the bow—whether he fired at the rifle or the loop-hole.

The Indians, finding it impossible to dislodge the rangers from what appeared a stronghold in every sense of the word, by all stratagems yet used, affixed dry leaves and other combustible matter to arrows, set fire to them, and lodged them upon the roof of the house, which soon was on fire in two or three places. The men carried up all the water in the house, and subdued the flames from the inside; but the water was soon exhausted, and a fresh volley of the fire-arrows set the roof in a blaze, and there were no longer means within their reach to quench the destructive element. Still the rangers stood at the loop-holes, even when the upper part of the house was all on

fire.   Certain death stared them in the face; they dared
not go out of the house, for they would expose the weakness of their force and meet instant destruction as soon
as they passed over the threshold; on the other hand,
the fire above them was raging, and they did not know
what moment they would be buried beneath the burning
timbers.   And yet the men never flinched.   But, at last,
Captain Phillips, seeing the desperate strait to which they
were reduced, cried for quarter, and told the savages that
he would surrender, on condition that his men should be
treated as prisoners and not injured.   To this the Indians
assented, and the men escaped from the house just in time
to save their lives from fire, but only to meet a death
equally shocking.

The spokesman for the Indians—one of the white rene-
gades—demanded, in the first place, that all their arms
should be delivered up.   To this the men readily agreed;
and they handed their rifles and knives to the savages.
The next demand was that they should suffer themselves
to be pinioned, in order that none might escape.   This
degrading proposition met no favor with the men; but
they were compelled to submit, and their hands were
secured behind their backs by strong thongs.   In this condition they started—as the Indians said—for Kittaning;
but, after getting half a mile from the house, some five or
six of the Indians, who had Captain Phillips and his son
in charge, continued on their route, while the remainder
ordered a halt.   The ten men were then tied to as many
saplings, and two or three volleys of arrows were fired
into them.

The fate of the scout was not known until Tuesday.

Some persons passing Heater's house on Monday morning, seeing it in ruins, carried the news to Hartsock's Fort. An express was sent to Colonel Piper, who arrived on the ground with a small force late on Tuesday. About the house they found a number of tomahawks, knives, and other articles, which indicated that an action had taken place; but the fate of the men could not be conjectured.

Finally, some one discovered the tracks, and proposed following them, which they did, and found the men at the place designated, each man with from three to five arrows sticking in him. Some of them had not been killed outright, and it was apparent that their struggles to get loose must have been most desperate. Kelly was one of these, who, in his efforts to free himself, had buried the thong in the flesh of his arm. All of the men were scalped. They were buried on the spot where they appeased the savage appetite for blood; and their mouldering bones still repose there, without even the rudest of stones to commemorate the sad event or perpetuate their memory.

Phillips, in consequence of his rank, was taken prisoner, as at that time officers brought to the British garrison commanded an excellent price. Himself and son were taken to Detroit, and from thence to Montreal, and did not reach their home until peace was declared.

Some of the friends of the persons massacred were disposed to find fault with Captain Phillips, especially as the massacre was so general and yet he and his son had escaped. Of course, Phillips not being present to defend himself, the talk was so much on one side that some went so far as to stigmatize him as a traitor and a coward. On his return, he gave the true version of the affair; and it must be admitted by all that, under the circumstances, he did all that a brave officer could do to save the lives of his men. Their fate weighed heavily on his mind for the balance of his life; and in the thought of their untimely end he forgot all the sufferings and privations he endured while a prisoner in the camp of the enemy.

CHAPTER XXIX.

WATER STREET—THE BEATTY FAMILY—CAPTAIN SIMONTON—MASSACRE
OF THE DEAN FAMILY—CAPTIVITY OF JOHN SIMONTON, ETC.

WATER STREET is an old place, and was settled prior to
the Revolution. A stream of water from the Canoe Mountain, supposed to be the Arch Spring of Sinking Valley,
passes down a ravine and empties into the Juniata at this
place. For some distance through a narrow defile, the
road passed directly through the bed of this stream,—a
circumstance which induced the settlers to call it Water
Street when the original settlement was made.

This for a long time was an important point, being the
canoe-landing for the interior country. Hence the name
of Canoe Valley, applied to the country now known as
Catharine township, in Blair county. At this place was
General Roberdeau's landing, where he received his stores
for the lead mines, and where he shipped the lead-ore to
be taken to Middletown for smelting.

The number of persons living about Water Street and
in the lower end of Canoe Valley, during the Revolution,
was fully as great as at the present day.

Among the first settlers was Patrick Beatty. He was
the father of seven sons, regular flowers of the forest, who

never would fort during all the troubles, and who cared no more for an Indian than they did for a bear. They lived in a cabin about a mile west of Water Street.

It is related of John, the oldest son, that, coming through the woods one day, near his home, he met two Indians in his path. They both aimed at him, but by successful dodging he prevented them from shooting, and reached the house. He found one of his brothers at home; and the two, seizing their rifles, started out after the Indians, and followed them sixty miles, frequently getting sight of them, but never within shooting distance. The Indians knew the Beattys, and feared them, for a more daring and reckless party of young fellows never existed in the valley.

It is a remarkable coincidence that of the Beattys there were seven brothers, seven brothers of the Cryders, seven of the Ricketts, seven of the Rollers, and seven of the Moores,—constituting the most formidable force of active and daring frontier-men to be found between Standing Stone and the base of the mountain.

In the winter of 1778 or the spring of 1779, Lowry's Fort was erected, about two and a half or three miles west of Water Street, for the protection of the settlers of Water Street and Canoe Valley. Although built upon Lowry's farm, Captain Simonton was by unanimous consent elected the commander. Thus, during the year 1779 and the greater part of 1780, the people divided their time between the fort and their farms, without any molestation from the savages. Occasionally an alarm of Indian depredations sent the entire neighborhood to the fort in great haste; but just so soon as the alarm had subsided they all went to their farms again.

Some few of the neighbors, for some reason or other, would not fort at Lowry's; whether because they apprehended no danger, or because they felt quite as secure at home, we have no means of knowing. Among these was Matthew Dean, Esq., one of the most influential men in Canoe Valley, who lived but half a mile from the fort. His reason for not forting there, however, arose from an old personal animosity existing between himself and Lowry, and not from any fancied security at his own house, for he had several times, during the alarms of 1779, made preparations to remove his family to Huntingdon.

In the fall of 1780, on a Sunday evening, Captain Simonton and his wife, and his son John, a lad eight years of age, paid a visit to Dean's house. They spent the evening in conversation on the ordinary topics of the day, in the course of which Captain Simonton told Dean that he had heard of Indians having been seen in Sinking Valley, and that if any thing more of them was heard it would be advisable for them to fort. Dean gave it as his opinion that the rumor was false, and that there was no cause for alarm, much less forting.

The family of Mr. Dean consisted of himself, his wife, and eight children, with the prospect of another being added to the family in a day or two. The last words Mrs. Dean spoke to Mrs. Simonton were to have her shoes ready, as she might send for her before morning. When the Simontons were ready to start, the lad John was reluctant to go; and at the request of Mrs. Dean he was allowed to stay with their children until morning, at which time Mrs. Simonton promised to visit her neighbor.

In the morning, as soon as breakfast was over, Dean,

with his two boys and two oldest girls, went to a corn-field for the purpose of breaking it up preparatory to sow-ing rye in it. The boys managed the plough, while the girls made what was called "steps," or holes between the corn-hills, where the plough could not be brought to bear. Mr. Dean had taken his rifle with him, and, after directing the work for a while, he saw large numbers of wild pigeons flying in the woods adjoining the field, and he went to shoot some of them. He had been in the woods but a short time when he happened to look in the direction of his house, and saw smoke issuing from it, when he imme-diately went to his children and informed them of it. By that time the volume of smoke had so increased that they were satisfied the house was on fire, and they all started for home at their utmost speed.

In the mean time Mrs. Simonton, according to promise, came over to Dean's house. She, too, saw the smoke some distance off, and by the time she reached the gate, which was simultaneously with the arrival of the family from the corn-field, the house was in a sheet of flame. Up to this time no one had supposed that the fire was the work of Indians. Mrs. Simonton saw a little girl, about eight years of age, lying upon the steps, scalped; but she did not notice its being scalped,—merely supposing that the child had a red handkerchief tied around its head, and had fallen asleep where it lay. But when she went into the gate to get the child out, and the blood gushed up between the boards on which she trod, the fearful reality burst upon her mind; then she thought about her own little son, and for a while was almost frantic.

News of the disaster was conveyed to the fort, and in a

few hours the entire neighborhood was alarmed. A strong force, headed by the Beattys, started in pursuit, and got upon the track of the savages, but could not find them. They even waylaid the gap through which the war-path ran; but all to no purpose, for they got clear of the settlements by some other route.

Captain Simonton, at the time of the outrage, was at Minor's Mill, getting a grist ground. On his return, he heard the news at Water Street, when he threw the bag of flour from the horse, and rode as fast as the animal could carry him to the scene of the disaster, where he arrived in a state of mind bordering closely upon madness—for he passionately loved his little boy—just as the neighbors were taking the roasted and charred remains of Mrs. Dean and her three children out of the ashes. One of the neighbors so engaged was a daughter of Mr. Beatty, now Mrs. Adams, still living in Gaysport, at a very advanced age, who gave us a graphic account of the occurrence.

The remains taken out were joined together, and the skeletons of Mrs. Dean and her three children could be recognised; but no bones were found to conform to the size of Simonton's son. The Dean girls then recollected that, when last seen, he was playing near the front door with the little girl. It was then suggested that he might be killed, and that his body was perhaps lying somewhere near the house; but a most thorough search revealed nothing of the kind, and it was only too evident that the Indians had carried the child into captivity.

The murder of the Deans was the cause of universal regret, for they were known and respected by every person in the upper end of the Juniata Valley, and it did not fail to spread consternation into every settlement, even where people thought themselves beyond the reach of the merciless and bloodthirsty savages.

The reason why Simonton's child was carried into captivity, instead of being murdered and scalped, was believed to be because the Indians knew the child and expected that Simonton would follow them and pay liberally for his ransom.

The remains of the Deans were buried, and the family bore up as well as they could under the sad infliction; but it was some years before Matthew Dean fairly recovered from the blow.

The descendants of the Dean family are numerous—a majority of them living in the neighborhood of Williamsburg, Blair county. One of the young girls in the cornfield at the time of the massacre married a Mr. Caldwell, and was the mother of David Caldwell, at present one of the associate judges of Blair county.

Captain Simonton never became reconciled to the loss of his son. He made all the inquiries he could; wrote to government, and even went from his home as far as to Chillicothe, Ohio, to attend a treaty; but all to no purpose: he could obtain no tidings of him. While there, he caused proclamation to be made to the Indians, offering a reward of £10 for any information as to his whereabouts, or £100 for his recovery. This was a munificent sum for the ransom of a mere boy, considering the financial condition of the country; and the Indians promised to find him, if possible.

A year after his return home, the final treaty for the

delivery of prisoners was held in the Miami Valley. Again Captain Simonton undertook the journey — then a more formidable undertaking than traversing half the Union would be now.

But he was again doomed to bitter disappointment. The children were brought forward, but none bore the slightest resemblance to his lost boy. So the captain returned to his home, bereft of all hope. The last feeble prop was gone, and Simonton was as near being a broken-hearted man as any one could well be without giving way entirely to despair.

When the late war with Great Britain broke out, Huntingdon county, notwithstanding it had more than its proportion of tories in the time of the Revolution, furnished three companies to go to the Canadian frontier. In Captain Moses Canan's company were two, probably three, of Captain Simonton's sons. They knew they had a brother abducted by the Indians, but it never occurred to either of them that they should ever see him.

The companies of Captains Allison, Canan, and Vandevender, encamped in Cattaraugus, New York,—a country then occupied by the Seneca Indians.

These Indians were neutral at that time, although they favored the American cause and readily furnished supplies to the soldiers. Among them was a white man, who appeared to hold a very prominent position. He owned lands, cattle, horses, lived in a well-constructed house, and was married to a squaw, by whom he had several children. This was the long-lost John Simonton. After Captain Canan's company had left, two men belonging to Vandevender's company, originally from Water

Street, commenced talking about this white man among the Indians; and both of them agreed that he bore a most striking resemblance to the Simonton boys.

Next day, happening to meet him in front of his own house, one of them accosted him with the somewhat abrupt question of "What is your name?"

He answered, in broken English, "John Sims."

"Are you from the Juniata?" continued the man.

"I think I am," was Simonton's reply.

"Do you remember any thing of the country?"

"I remember my father, who used to have two big fires, and large barrels, in which he stirred with a long pole."

This answer satisfied them. Old Captain Simonton had a small distillery, and the man remembered the process of distilling very correctly.

"Wouldn't you like to go to your old house and see your relatives?" inquired one of the men.

He answered that he should like very much to do so, but that he was so much of an Indian that he doubted whether his presence would afford much satisfaction to his friends.

On being told that some of his brothers were in one of the companies, he was so much affected that he shed tears, and expressed great anxiety to see them. He evidently felt himself degraded, and saw between himself and his brothers an insurmountable barrier, built up by upward of thirty years of life among the savages; and yet he longed to see them.

While talking to the men, his wife took him away, and he was not seen again by them while they remained there.

His wife had a powerful influence over him, and she used it to the best advantage ; for she really began to suspect that the men had traced his origin.

Poor old Captain Simonton !—he never lived to learn the fate of the boy he so much doated upon.

One of the sons of Captain Simonton — a very old man — still lives several miles west of Hollidaysburg.

CHAPTER XXX.

HOLLIDAYSBURG — THE HOLLIDAY FAMILY — DEATH OF LIEUTENANT
HOLLIDAY AT THE BATTLE OF BRANDYWINE—MASSACRE OF A
PORTION OF WILLIAM HOLLIDAY'S FAMILY—JOHN HOLLIDAY, ETC.

WILLIAM and Adam Holliday, cousins, emigrated from
the North of Ireland about 1750, and settled in the
neighborhood of the Manor, in Lancaster county. The
feuds which existed between the Irish and German
emigrants, as well as the unceasing efforts of the proprietary agents to keep emigrants from settling upon their
lands, induced the Hollidays to seek a location farther
west. Conococheague suggested itself to them as a
suitable place, because it was so far removed from Philadelphia that the proprietors could not well dispossess
them; and, the line never having been established, it
was altogether uncertain whether the settlement was
in Pennsylvania or Maryland. Besides, it possessed the
advantage of being tolerably well populated. Accordingly,
they settled on the banks of the Conococheague, and commenced clearing land, which they purchased and paid for
soon after the survey. During both the French and
Indian wars of 1755–56 and the war of 1762–63 the
Hollidays were in active service. At the destruction

CHIMNEY ROCKS OPPOSITE HOLLIDAYSBURG.

of Kittaning, William Holliday was a lieutenant in Colonel Armstrong's company, and fought with great bravery in that conflict with the savages. The Hollidays were emphatically frontier-men; and on the restoration of peace in 1768, probably under the impression that the Conococheague Valley was becoming too thickly populated, they disposed of their land, placed their families and effects upon pack-horses, and again turned their faces toward the west. They passed through Aughwick, but found no unappropriated lands there worthy of their attention. From thence they proceeded to the Standing Stone, but nothing offered there; nor even at Frankstown could they find any inducement to stop; so they concluded to cross the mountain by the Kittaning Path and settle on the Alleghany at or near Kittaning. William knew the road, and had noticed fine lands in that direction.

However, when they reached the place where Hollidaysburg now stands, and were just on the point of descending the hill toward the river, Adam halted, and declared his intention to pitch his tent and travel no farther. He argued with his cousin that the Indian titles west of the mountains were not extinguished; and if they bought from the Indians, they would be forced, on the extinguishment of their titles, to purchase a second time, or lose their lands and live in constant dread of the savages. Although William had a covetous eye on the fine lands of the Alleghany, the wise counsel of Adam prevailed, and they dismounted and prepared to build a temporary shelter. When Adam drove the first stake into the ground he casually remarked to William,

"Whoever is alive a hundred years after this will see a tolerable-sized town here, and this will be near about the middle of it." This prediction has been verified to the letter long before the expiration of the allotted time.

In a day or two after a shelter had been erected for the families, William crossed the river to where Gaysport now stands, for the purpose of locating. The land, however, was too swampy, and he returned. Next day he crossed again, and found a ravine, south of where he had been prospecting, which appeared to possess the desired qualifications; and there he staked out a farm,—the one now owned by Mr. J. R. Crawford. Through this farm the old Frankstown and Johnstown Road ran for many years,—the third road constructed in Pennsylvania crossing the Alleghany Mountains.

These lands belonged to the new purchase, and were in the market at a very low price, in order to encourage settlers on the frontier. Accordingly, Adam Holliday took out a warrant for 1000 acres, comprising all the land upon which Hollidaysburg now stands. The lower or southern part was too marshy to work; so Mr. Holliday erected his cabin near where the American House now stands, and made a clearing on the high ground stretching toward the east.

In the mean time, William Holliday purchased of Mr. Peters 1000 acres of land, which embraced the present Crawford and Jackson farms and a greater part of Gaysport. Some years after, finding that he had more land than he could conveniently cultivate, he disposed of nearly one-half of his original purchase to his son-in-law, James Somerville.

Adam Holliday, too, having a large lot of land, disposed of a portion of it to Lazarus Lowry. Thus matters progressed smoothly for a time, until, unfortunately, a Scotchman, named Henry Gordon, in search of lands, happened to see and admire his farm. Gordon was a keen, shrewd fellow, and in looking over the records of the land-office he discovered a flaw or informality in Adam's grant. He immediately took advantage of his discovery, and took out a patent for the land. Litigation followed, as a matter of course. Gordon possessed considerable legal acumen, and had withal money and a determined spirit. The case was tried in the courts below and the courts above,—decided sometimes in favor of one party and sometimes in favor of the other, but eventually resulted in Gordon wresting from Adam Holliday and Lazarus Lowry all their land. This unfortunate circumstance deeply afflicted Mr. Holliday, for he had undoubtedly been grossly wronged by the adroitness and cunning of Gordon; but relief came to him when he least expected it. When the war broke out, Gordon was among the very first to sail for Europe; and soon after the Council proclaimed him an attainted traitor, and his property was confiscated and brought under the hammer. The circumstances under which he had wrested the property from Holliday were known, so that no person would bid, which enabled him to regain his land at a mere nominal price. He then went on and improved, and built a house on the bank of the river, near where the bridge connects the boroughs of Hollidaysburg and Gaysport. The very locust-trees that he planted seventy-eight years ago, in front of his door, are still standing.

During the alarms and troubles which followed in the course of the war, Adam Holliday took a conspicuous part in defending the frontier. He aided, first, in erecting Fetter's Fort, and afterward expended his means in turning Titus's stable into a fort. This fort was located on the flat, nearly opposite the second lock below Hollidaysburg, and the two served as a place of refuge for all the settlers of what was then merely called the Upper End of Frankstown District. He also, with his own money, purchased provisions, and through his exertions arms and ammunition were brought from the eastern counties. His courage and energy inspired the settlers to make a stand at a time when they were on the very point of flying to Cumberland county. In December, 1777, Mr. Holliday visited Philadelphia for the purpose of securing a part of the funds appropriated to the defence of the frontier. The following letter to President Wharton was given to him by Colonel John Piper, of Bedford county:—

Bedford County, December 19, 1777.

Sir:—Permit me, sir, to recommend to you, for counsel and direction, the bearer, Mr. Holliday, an inhabitant of Frankstown, one of the frontier settlements of our county, who has, at his own risk, been extremely active in assembling the people of that settlement together and in purchasing provisions to serve the militia who came to their assistance. As there was no person appointed either to purchase provisions or to serve them out, necessity obliged the bearer, with the assistance of some neighbors, to purchase a considerable quantity of provisions for that purpose, by which the inhabitants have been enabled to make a stand. His request is that he may be supplied with cash not only to discharge the debts already contracted, but likewise to enable him to lay up a store for future demand. I beg leave, sir, to refer to the bearer for further information, in hopes you will provide for their further support. Their situation requires immediate assistance.

I am, sir, with all due respect, your Excellency's most obedient humble servant,

JOHN PIPER.

Mr. Holliday's mission was successful; and he returned with means to recruit the fort with provisions and ammunition, and continued to be an active and energetic frontier-man during all the Indian troubles which followed.

Notwithstanding the distracted state of society during the Revolution, William Holliday devoted much time and attention to his farm. His family, consisting of his wife, his sons John, William, Patrick, Adam, and a lunatic whose name is not recollected, and his daughter Janet, were forted at Holliday's Fort; and it was only when absolute necessity demanded it that they ventured to the farm to attend to the crops, after the savage marauders so boldly entered the settlements.

James, who we believe was next to the eldest of William Holliday's children, joined the Continental army soon after the war broke out. He is represented as having been a noble-looking fellow, filled with enthusiasm, who sought for, and obtained without much difficulty, a lieutenant's commission. He was engaged in several battles, and conducted himself in such a manner as to merit the approbation of his senior officers; but he fell gloriously at Brandywine, while the battle was raging, pierced through the heart by a musket-ball. He was shot by a Hessian, who was under cover, and who had, from the same place, already dispatched a number of persons. But this was his last shot; for a young Virginian, who stood by the side of Holliday when he fell, rushed upon the Hessian, braving all danger, and hewed him to pieces with his sword before any defence could be made.

The death of young Holliday was deeply lamented by his companions-in-arms, for he was brave and generous, and had not a single enemy in the line. His friends, after the battle, buried him near the spot where he fell; and it is doubtful whether even now a hillock of greensward is raised to his memory.

About the beginning of the year 1779, the Indians along the frontier, emboldened by numerous successful depredations, came into Bedford county—within the boundaries of which Holliday's Fort then was—in such formidable bands that many of the inhabitants fled to the eastern counties. The Hollidays, however, and some few others, tarried, in the hope that the Executive Council would render them aid. The following petition, signed by William Holliday and others, will give the reader some idea of the distress suffered by the pioneers; it was drawn up on the 29th of May, 1779:—

To the Honorable President and Council:—

The Indians being now in the county, the frontier inhabitants being generally fled, leaves the few that remains in such a distressed condition that pen can hardly describe, nor your honors can only have a faint idea of; nor can it be conceived properly by any but such as are the subjects thereof; but, while we suffer in the part of the county that is most frontier, the inhabitants of the interior part of this county live at ease and safety.

And we humbly conceive that by some immediate instruction

from Council, to call them that are less exposed to our relief, we shall be able, under God, to repulse our enemies, and put it in the power of the distressed inhabitants to reap the fruits of their industry. Therefore, we humbly pray you would grant us such relief in the premises as you in your wisdom see meet. And your petitioners shall pray, etc.

N.B.—There is a quantity of lead at the mines (Sinking Valley) in this county Council may procure for the use of said county, which will save carriage, and supply our wants with that article, which we cannot exist without at this place; and our flints are altogether expended. Therefore, we beg Council would furnish us with those necessaries as they in their wisdom see cause.

P.S.—Please to supply us with powder to answer lead.
(Signed)   WILLIAM HOLLIDAY, *P. M.*
                            THOMAS COULTER, *Sheriff.*
                            RICHARD J. DELAPT, *Captain.*
                            SAM. DAVIDSON.

The prayer of these petitioners was not speedily answered, and Holliday's Fort was evacuated soon after. The Council undoubtedly did all in its power to give the frontiers support; but the tardy movements of the militia gave the savages confidence, and drove the few settlers that remained almost to despair. Eventually relief came, but not sufficient to prevent Indian depredations. At length, when these depredations and the delays of the Council in furnishing sufficient force to repel these savage invasions had brought matters to such a crisis that forbearance ceased to be a virtue, the people of the neighborhood moved their families to Fort Roberdeau, in Sinking Valley, and Fetter's Fort, and formed themselves into scouting parties, and by these means protected the frontier and enabled the settlers to gather in their crops in

1780; still, notwithstanding their vigilance, small bands
of scalp-hunters occasionally invaded the county, and,
when no scalps were to be found, compromised by stealing horses, or by laying waste whatever fell in their
way.

In 1781, when Continental money was so terribly depreciated that it took, in the language of one of the old settlers, "seventeen dollars of it to buy a quart of whiskey,"
government was in too straitened a condition to furnish
this frontier guard with ammunition and provisions, so that
the force was considerably reduced. Small scouting parties were still kept up, however, to watch the savages,
who again made their appearance in the neighborhood in
the summer, retarding the harvest operations.

About the middle of July, the scouts reported every
thing quiet and no traces of Indians in the county. Accordingly, Mr. Holliday proceeded to his farm, and, with
the aid of his sons, succeeded in getting off and housing
his grain. Early in August, Mr. Holliday, accompanied
by his sons Patrick and Adam and his daughter Janet,
then about fourteen years of age, left Fort Roberdeau for
the purpose of taking off a second crop of hay. On their
arrival at the farm they went leisurely to work, and
mowed the grass. The weather being extremely fine, in
a few days they began to haul it in on a rudely-constructed sled, for in those primitive days few wagons were
in use along the frontiers. They had taken in one load,
returned, and filled the sled again, when an acquaintance
named McDonald, a Scotchman, came along on horseback.
He stopped, and they commenced a conversation on the
war. William Holliday was seated upon one of the horses

that were hitched to the sled, his two sons were on one side of him, and his daughter on the opposite side. All of the men, as was customary then, were armed with rifles. While this conversation was going on, and without the slightest previous intimation, a volley was suddenly fired from a thicket some sixty or seventy yards off, by which Patrick and Adam were instantly killed and the horse shot from under Mr. Holliday. The attack was so sudden and unexpected that a flash of lightning and a peal of thunder from a cloudless sky could not have astonished him more. The echoes of the Indian rifles had scarcely died away before the Indians themselves, to the number of eight or ten, with a loud "*whoop!*" jumped from their place of concealment, some brandishing their knives and hatchets and others reloading their rifles.

Appalled at the shocking tragedy, and undecided for a moment what course to pursue, Holliday was surprised to see McDonald leap from his horse, throw away his rifle, run toward the Indians, and, with outstretched arms, cry "Brother! Brother!" which it appears was a cry for quarter which the savages respected. Holliday, however, knew too much of the savage character to trust to their mercy—more especially as rebel scalps commanded nearly as good a price in British gold in Canada as prisoners; so on the impulse of the moment he sprang upon McDonald's horse and made an effort to get his daughter up behind him. But he was too late. The Indians were upon him, and he turned into the path which led down the ravine. The yells of the savages frightened the horse, and he galloped down the path; but even the clattering of his hoofs did not drown the dying shrieks of his daughter, who was most barbarously butchered with a hatchet.

In a state of mind bordering on distraction, Holliday wandered about until nearly dark, when he got upon the Brush Mountain trail, on his way to Sinking Valley. His mind, however, was so deeply affected that he seemed to care little whither he went; and, the night being exceedingly dark, the horse lost the trail and wandered about the mountain for hours. Just at daybreak Mr. Holliday reached the fort, haggard and careworn, without hat or shoes, his clothes in tatters and his body lacerated and bleeding. He did not recognise either the fort or the sentinel on duty. He was taken in, and the fort alarmed, but it was some time before he could make any thing like an intelligible statement of what had occurred the day previous. Without waiting for the particulars in detail, a command of fifteen men was despatched to Holliday's farm. They found the bodies of Patrick and Adam precisely where they fell, and that of Janet but a short distance from the sled, and all scalped. As soon as the necessary arrangements could be made, the bodies of the slain were interred on the farm; and a rude tombstone still marks the spot where the victims of savage cruelty repose.

This was a sad blow to Mr. Holliday; and it was long before he recovered from it effectually. But the times steeled men to bear misfortunes that would now crush and annihilate the bravest.

The Scotchman McDonald, whom we have mentioned as being present at the Holliday massacre, accompanied the savages, as he afterward stated, to the Miami Valley, where he adopted their manners and customs, and remained with them until the restoration of peace enabled him to escape. He returned to the Valley of the Juniata; but he soon found that Holliday had prejudiced the public mind against him by declaring the part he took at the time of the massacre to have been cowardly in the extreme, notwithstanding that the cowardice of McDonald actually saved Holliday's life, by affording him means to escape. The people generally shunned McDonald, and he led rather an unenviable life; yet we might suppose, taking all the circumstances into consideration, that, in illustrating the axiom that "self-preservation is the first law of nature," he did nothing more than any man, with even less prudence than a canny Scotchman, would have done. But any thing having the least squinting toward cowardice was deemed a deadly sin by the pioneers, and McDonald soon found it necessary to seek a home somewhere else.

After the declaration of peace, or, rather, after the ratification of the treaty, Gordon came back to Pennsylvania and claimed his land under its stipulation. He had no difficulty in proving that he had never taken up arms against the colonies, and Congress agreed to purchase back his lands.

The Commissioners to adjust claims, after examining the lands, reported them worth sixteen dollars an acre; and this amount was paid to Adam Holliday, who suddenly found himself the greatest monied man in this county — having in his possession sixteen or seventeen thousand dollars.

Adam Holliday lived to a good old age, and died at his residence on the bank of the river, in 1801. He left two heirs—his son John, and a daughter married to William Reynolds.

After the estate was settled up, it was found that John Holliday was the richest man in this county. He married the daughter of Lazarus Lowry, of Frankstown, in 1803, and in 1807 he left for Johnstown, where he purchased the farm, and all the land upon which Johnstown now stands, from a Dr. Anderson, of Bedford. Fearing the place would never be one of any importance, John Holliday, in a few years, sold out to Peter Livergood for eight dollars an acre, returned to Hollidaysburg, and entered into mercantile pursuits.

William Holliday, too, died at a good old age, and lies buried on his farm by the side of his children, who were massacred by the Indians.

In the ordinary transmutation of worldly affairs, the lands of both the old pioneers passed out of the hands of their descendants; yet a beautiful town stands as a lasting monument to the name, and the descendants have multiplied until the name of Holliday is known not only in Pennsylvania, but over the whole Union.

[NOTE.—There are several contradictory accounts in existence touching the massacre of the Holliday children. Our account of it is evidently the true version, for it was given to us by Mr. Maguire, who received it from Mr. Holliday shortly after the occurrence of the tragedy.

It may be as well here to state that the original Hollidays were Irishmen and Presbyterians. It is necessary to state this, because we have heard arguments about their religious faith. Some avow that they were Catholics, and as an evidence refer to the fact that William called one of his offspring "Patrick." Without being able to account for the name of a saint so prominent in the calendar as Patrick being found in a Presbyterian family, we can only give the words of Mr. Maguire, who said:—

"I was a Catholic, and old Billy and Adam Holliday were Presbyterians; but in those days we found matters of more importance to attend to than quarrelling about religion. We all worshipped the same God, and some of the forms and ceremonies attending church were very much alike, especially in 1778, when the men of all denominations, in place of hymn-books, prayer-books, and Bibles, carried to church with them loaded rifles!"

It may be as well to state here also that the McDonald mentioned had two brothers—one a daring frontier-man, the other in the army,—so that the reader will please not confound them.]

CHAPTER XXXI.

OLD INDIAN TOWN OF FRANKSTOWN—INDIAN BURIAL-PLACES—MASSA-
CRE OF THE BEDFORD SCOUT, ETC.

FRANKSTOWN is probably the oldest place on the Juniata River—traders having mentioned it as early as 1750. The Indian town was located at the mouth of a small run, near where McCune's Mill now stands, and at one time contained a considerable number of inhabitants. The Indian name of the place was *Assunepachla,* which signifies a meeting of many waters, or the place where the waters join. This would seem to be an appropriate name, since, within a short distance of the place, the river is formed by what was then known as the Frankstown Branch, the Beaver Dam Branch, the Brush Run, and the small run near McCune's Mill.

The name of Frankstown was given it by the traders. Harris, in his report of the distances between the Susquehanna and the Alleghany, called it " Frank (Stephen's) Town." The general impression is that the town was named by the traders in honor of an old chief named Frank. This, however, is an error. It was named after an old German Indian trader named Stephen Franks, who lived cotemporaneously with old Hart, and whose post

EASTERN RESERVOIR FROM CATFISH TAVERN.

was at this old Indian town. The truth of this becomes apparent when we remember that the Indians could not pronounce the *r* in their language; hence no chief was likely to bear the name of Frank at that early day. Old Franks, being a great friend of the Indians, lived and died among them, and it was after his death that one of the chiefs took his name; hence arose the erroneous impression that the name was given to the town in honor of the chief.

How long Assunepachla was an Indian settlement cannot be conjectured, but, unquestionably, long before the Indians of the valley had any intercourse with the whites. This is evidenced by the fact that where the town stood, as well as on the flat west of the town, relics of rudely-constructed pottery, stone arrow-heads, stone hatchets, &c., have repeatedly been found until within the last few years.

The use of stone edge-tools was abandoned as soon as the savages obtained a sight of a superior article,—probably as early as 1730. The first were brought to the valley by Indians, who had received them as presents from the proprietary family.

It is stated that the first brought to Assunepachla cost a special trip to Philadelphia. Three chiefs, having seen hatchets and knives at Standing Stone, were so fascinated with their utility that they resolved to have some. Accordingly they went to work at trapping; and in the fall, each with an immense load of skins, started on foot for Philadelphia, where they arrived after a long and fatiguing march. They soon found what they wanted at the shop of an Englishman; but, being unable to talk English, they merely deposited their furs upon the counter and pointed to the tomahawks and knives. This indicated trade; and the Englishman, after a critical examination of their skins, which he found would yield him not less than £100, threw them carelessly under the counter, and gave them a hatchet and a knife each. With these the savages were about to depart, well satisfied; but the trader suddenly bethinking himself of the possibility of their falling in with the interpreters, and their ascertaining the manner in which they had been swindled, called them back, and very generously added three clasp-knives and a quantity of brass jewelry.

With these they wended their way back, proud as emperors of their newly-acquired weapons. Never did chiefs enter a place with more pomp and importance than our warriors. The very dogs barked a welcome, and the Indians came forth from their wigwams to greet the great eastern travellers. Their hatchets, knives, and trinkets passed from hand to hand, and savage encomiums were lavished unsparingly upon them; but when their practicability was tested, the climax of savage enthusiasm was reached. The envied possessors were lions: they cut, hewed, and scored, just because they could.

But—alas for all things mutable!—their glory was not destined to last long. The traders soon appeared with the same kind of articles, and readily exchanged for half a dozen skins what the warriors had spent a season in trapping and a long journey to procure.

On the point of Chimney Ridge, near Wert's farm, below Hollidaysburg, was an Indian burial-place, and another on the small piece of table-land near the mouth of Brush Run. At both places skeletons of mighty chiefs and all-powerful warriors have been ruthlessly torn from their places of sepulture by the plough, and many other relics have been exhumed.

The greater portion of the warriors residing at Frankstown went to Ohio in 1755, and took up the hatchet for their "brothers," the French, and against *Onus*, or their Father Penn. This act, the colonial government persuaded itself to believe, was altogether mercenary on the part of the savages. The real cause, as we have already stated, was the dissatisfaction which followed the purchase of the Juniata Valley by the Penns, for a few paltry pounds, from the Iroquois, at Albany, in 1754.

The town of Frankstown still continued to be a prominent Indian settlement until the army of General Forbes passed up the Raystown Branch, when the spies sent out brought such exaggerated reports of the warlike appearance and strength of the army that the settlement was entirely broken up, and the warriors, with their squaws, pappooses, and movable effects, crossed the Alleghany by the Kittaning War-Path, and bade adieu to the valley which they were only too well convinced was no longer their own.

The remains of their bark huts, their old corn-fields, and other indications of their presence, were in existence until after the beginning of the present century.

On the flat, several white settlers erected their cabins at an early day, and a few near the old town, and others where the town of Frankstown now stands.

During the Revolution, as we have stated, a stable erected by Peter Titus was turned into a fortress. In summer, the location of the fort can still be traced by the luxuriant growth of vegetation upon it. This fort was called Holliday's Fort. The fort at Fetter's, a mile west of Hollidaysburg, was known as the Frankstown garrison. In those days there was no such place as Hollidaysburg, and the Frankstown district took in a scope of country which now serves for five or six very large townships; in short, every place was Frankstown within a radius of at least ten miles.

Holliday's Fort was a mere temporary affair; while the Frankstown garrison was a substantial stockade, manned and provisioned in such a manner that a thousand savages could by no possible means have taken it. It never was assaulted except upon one occasion, and then the red-skins were right glad to beat a retreat before they were able to fire a gun.

Near this fort occurred the massacre of the Bedford scout. This was unquestionably the most successful savage sortie made upon the whites in the valley during the Revolution; and, as some of the bravest and best men of Bedford county fell in this massacre, it did not fail to create an excitement compared to which all other excitements that ever occurred in the valley were perfect calms.

We shall, in the first place, proceed to give the first report of the occurrence, sent by George Ashman, one of the sub-lieutenants of the county, to Arthur Buchanan, at Kishicoquillas. Ashman says:—

SIR:—By an express this moment from Frankstown, we have the bad news. As a party of volunteers from Bedford was going to Frankstown, a party of Indians fell in with them this morning and killed thirty of them. Only seven made their escape to the garrison of Frankstown. I hope that you'll exert yourself in getting men to go up to the Stone; and pray let the river-people know, as they may turn out. I am, in health,

GEO. ASHMAN.

Of course Colonel Ashman was not near the place, and his despatch to Buchanan is, as a natural consequence, made up from the exaggerated reports that were carried to him at the instance of the affrighted people residing in the vicinity where the massacre occurred. The following is the official report, transmitted by Ashman to President Reed:—

Bedford County, June 12, 1781.

SIR:—I have to inform you that on Sunday, the third of this instant, a party of the rangers under Captain Boyd, eight in number, with twenty-five volunteers under Captain Moore and Lieutenant Smith, of the militia of this county, had an engagement with a party of Indians (said to be numerous) within three miles of Frankstown, where seventy-five of the Cumberland militia were stationed, commanded by Captain James Young. Some of the party running into the garrison, acquainting Captain Young of what had happened, he issued out a party immediately, and brought in seven more, five of whom are wounded, and two made their escape to Bedford,—eight killed and scalped,—Captain Boyd, Captain Moore, and Captain Dunlap missing. Captain Young, expecting from the enemy's numbers that his garrison would be surrounded, sent express to me immediately; but, before I could collect as many volunteers as was sufficient to march to Frankstown with, the enemy had returned over the Alleghany Hill. The waters being high, occasioned by heavy rains, they could not be pursued. This county, at this time, is in a deplorable situation. A number of families are flying away daily ever since the late damage was done. I can assure your Excellency that if immediate assistance is not sent to this county that the whole of the frontier inhabitants will move off in a few days. Colonel Abraham Smith, of Cumberland, has just informed me that he has no orders to send us any more militia from Cumberland county to our assistance, which I am much surprised to hear. I shall move my family to Maryland in a few days, as I am convinced that not any one settlement is able to make any stand against such numbers of the enemy. If your Excellency should please to order us any assistance, less than three hundred will be of but little relief to this county. Ammunition we have not any; and the Cumberland militia will be discharged in two days. It is dreadful to think what the consequence of leaving such a number of helpless inhabitants may be to the cruelties of a savage enemy.

Please to send me by the first opportunity three hundred pounds, as I cannot possibly do the business without money. You may depend that nothing shall be wanting in me to serve my country as far as my abilities.

I have the honor to be

Your Excellency's most obedient, humble servant,

GEORGE ASHMAN, *Lieut. Bedford County.*

It would appear that even a man holding an official station is liable to gross mistakes. In this instance, Ashman, who lived remote from the scene of the disaster, was evidently misled by the current rumors, and such he transmitted; for there are still persons alive, who lived at the time of the occurrence in the immediate vicinity, who pronounce Ashman's statement as erroneous, and who give an entirely different version of the affair.

The seventy Cumberland county militia, under strict military discipline, were sent first to Standing Stone, and afterward to Frankstown, early in the spring of 1781. They were under the command of Colonel Albright and Captain Young, and were sent with a view to waylaying the gaps of the Alleghany Mountains, and preventing any savages from coming into the valley. Instead of doing so, however, they proved themselves an inefficient body of men, with dilatory officers, who chose rather the idle life of the fort than scouting to intercept the savages. In fact, these men, in the service and pay of the Supreme Executive Council of the State to protect the frontier, were never one solitary cent's worth of advantage to the inhabitants. Such a force, one would suppose, would have inspired the people with confidence, and been fully able to cope with or repel the largest war-party of savages that ever trod the Kittaning War-Path during the Revolutionary struggle.

Notwithstanding the presence of this large body of men, stationed as it were almost at the mouth of the gap through which the Indians entered the valley, the depredations of the savages were almost of daily occurrence. The inefficiency of the Cumberland militia, who either could not or would not check the marauders, at length exasperated the settlers to such an extent that they resolved to form themselves into a scouting party, and range through the county for two months.

This project was favored by Colonel Ashman, and he agreed to furnish a company of rangers to join them. The enrolment of volunteers by Captain Moore, of Scotch Valley, assisted by his lieutenant, a Mr. Smith, from the vicinity of Frankstown, proceeded; and on the second of June, 1781, these men met at Holliday's Fort, then abandoned for want of provisions. There they were joined by the rangers, under command of Captain Boyd and Lieutenant Harry Woods, of Bedford, but, instead of there being a company, as the volunteers were led to expect, there were but eight men and the two officers above named.

From Holliday's Fort they marched to Fetter's, where they contemplated spending the Sabbath. It was their intention to march through the Kittaning Gap to an old State road, (long since abandoned,) from thence to Pittsburg, and home by way of Bedford.

While debating the matter and making the necessary arrangements, two spies came in and reported that they had come upon an Indian encampment near Hart's Sleeping Place, which had apparently been just abandoned, as the fire was still burning; that, from the number of bark huts, the savages must number from twenty-five to thirty.

This raised quite a stir in the camp, as the scouts evidently were eager for the fray. The officers, who were regular woodsmen, and knew that the Indians would not venture into the settlement until the day following, were confident of meeting them near the mouth of the gap and giving them battle. They at once tendered to Colonel Albright the command of the expedition; but he refused to accept it. They then importuned him to let a portion of his men, who were both anxious and willing, accompany them; but this, too, he refused.

Nothing daunted, however, the rangers and the volunteers arose by daybreak on Sunday morning, put their rifles in condition, eat their breakfast, and, with five days' provisions in their knapsacks, started for the mountain.

We sincerely regret that the most strenuous effort on our part to procure a list of this scout proved futile. Here and there we picked up the names of a few who were in it; but nothing would have given us greater pleasure than to insert a full and correct list of these brave men. In addition to the officers named, we may mention the following privates:—James Somerville, the two Colemans, two Hollidays, two brothers named Jones, a man named Grey, one of the Beattys, Michael Wallack, and Edward Milligan.

The path led close along the river, and the men marched in Indian file, as the path was narrow. When they reached the flat above where Temperance Mill now stands, and within thirty rods of the mouth of Sugar Run, the loud warwhoop rang upon the stillness of the Sabbath morning; a band of savages rose from the bushes on the left-hand side of the road, firing a volley at the same time, by which fifteen of the brave scout were stretched dead in the path. The remainder fled, in consternation, in every direction,—some over the river in the direction of Frankstown, others toward Fetter's Fort. A man named Jones, one of the fleetest runners, reached the fort first. To screen the scout from the odium of running, he reported the number of the enemy so large that Albright refused to let any of his command go to the relief of the unfortunate men.

As the Colemans were coming to the fort, they found the other Jones lying behind a log for the purpose of resting, as he said. Coleman advised him to push on to the fort, which he promised to do.

Captain Young at length started out with a party to bring in the wounded. The man Jones was found resting behind the log, but the rest was a lasting one; he was killed and scalped. Another man, who had been wounded, was also followed a short distance and killed and scalped,—making, in all, seventeen persons who fell by this sad and unlooked-for event. In addition to the seventeen killed, five were wounded, who were found concealed in various places in the woods and removed to the fort. Some reached the fort in safety, others were missing,—among the latter, Harry Woods, James Somerville, and Michael Wallack.

It appears that these three men started over the river, and ran up what is now known as O'Friel's Ridge, hotly pursued by a single savage. Woods and Wallack were in front, and Somerville behind, when the moccasin of the latter became untied. He stooped down to fix it, as it was impossible to ascend the steep hill with the loose moccasin retarding his progress. While in this position, the Indian, with uplifted tomahawk, was rapidly approaching him, when Woods turned suddenly and aimed with his empty rifle* at the Indian. This caused the savage to jump behind a tree scarcely large enough to cover his body, from which he peered, and recognised Woods.

"No hurt Woods!" yelled the Indian; "no hurt Woods!"

This Indian happened to be the son of the old Indian Hutson, to whom George Woods of Bedford paid a small annual stipend in tobacco, for delivering him from bondage. Hutson had frequently taken his son to Bedford, and it was by this means that he had become acquainted with Harry and readily recognised him. Woods, although he recognised Hutson, had been quite as close to Indians as he cared about getting; so the three continued their route over the ridge, and by a circuitous tramp reached the fort in the afternoon.

---

* Woods shot an Indian. His rifle was the only one discharged in what Colonel Ashman termed an "engagement."

Many years afterward, long after the war, when Woods lived in Pittsburg, he went down to the Alleghany River to see several canoe-loads of Indians that had just arrived from above. He had scarcely reached the landing when one of the chiefs jumped out, shook him warmly by the hand, and said—

"Woods, you run like debble up Juniata Hill."

It was Hutson—by this time a distinguished chief in his tribe.

The fate of the unfortunate scout was soon known all over the country, expresses having been sent in every direction.

On Monday morning Captain Young again went out with a small party to bury the dead, and many of them were interred near the spot where they fell; while others, after the men got tired of digging graves, were merely covered with bark and leaves, and left on the spot to be food for the wolves, which some of the bodies unquestionably became, as Jones sought for that of his brother on Tuesday, and found nothing but the crushed remains of some bones.

In 1852, a young man in the employ of Mr. Burns exhumed one of these skeletons with the plough. It was found near the surface of the earth, on the bank of the river. The skull was perforated with a bullet-hole, and was in a remarkable state of preservation, although it had been in the ground uncoffined for a period of *seventy-one years!* It was placed in the earth again.

Immediately after the news of the massacre was spread, the people from Standing Stone and other places gathered at Fetter's; and on the Tuesday following a party of nearly one hundred men started in pursuit of the Indians. Colonel Albright was solicited to accompany this force with his command and march until they overtook the enemy; but he refused. The men went as far as Hart's Sleeping Place, but they might just as well have remained at home; for the savages, with the scalps of the scout dangling from their belts, were then far on their way to Detroit.

When the firing took place, it was plainly heard at the fort; and some of the men, fully convinced that the scout had been attacked, asked Colonel Albright to go out with his command to their relief. He merely answered by saying that he "knew his own business."

For his part in the matter, he gained the ill-will of the settlers, and it was very fortunate that his time expired when it did. The settlers were not much divided in opinion as to whether he was a rigid disciplinarian or a *coward*.

Men, arms, and ammunition, in abundance followed this last outrage; but it was the last formidable and warlike incursion into the Juniata Valley.

CHAPTER XXXII.

SHAVER'S CREEK—MYSTERIOUS DEATH OF OLD SHAVER—HEROIC CON-
DUCT OF TWO CHILDREN—ABDUCTION OF MISS EWING AND MISS
McCORMICK—PETER CRUM, THE LAST VICTIM OF THE SAVAGES, ETC.

THE original settlement at Shaver's Creek was made in
1770, by an old gentleman named Shaver. He was followed by Anderson, Maguire, the Donnelleys, and some
few others. Old Shaver met his death in a most singular
manner. One evening he left his home just at twilight,
for the purpose of putting his horse into a pasture-field.
He did not return; but his absence created no special
alarm, as this was before the war, and before any savages
had appeared in the valley with murderous intent. Next
morning, however, his family not finding him, a search
was instituted, and his body, minus the head, was found
in a lane near the pasture-field. This was regarded as a
most mysterious murder, and would have been charged to
the Indians at once, had they ever been known to take a
man's head off on any previous occasion. But as they
always found the scalp to answer their purpose, and never
encumbered themselves with the head, people shrewdly
suspected that the Indians had nothing to do with the
murder. The family offered a reward of £50 for the

22

head; and, although the country was searched in every direction, it never was found.

The most active and energetic man in the Shaver's Creek settlement during the Revolutionary war was Samuel Anderson. He succeeded, mainly by his own exertions and the aid of a few neighbors on the creek and the Little Juniata, in erecting a block-house fort on the flat near the mouth of the creek, which was more or less occupied while the war continued; and it is but a few years since the last vestiges of this old fort were swept away by a freshet.

The fort itself never was assailed; and it just happens to strike us forcibly at this time as a singular fact that the Indians, during the Revolutionary war, always kept clear of the forts. Whether they did not understand the nature of them, or feared the numbers usually congregated in them, we do not pretend to say; but they always kept at a respectful distance from them. Anderson's Fort, like the others, was frequently disturbed by alarms —sometimes real and sometimes false.

An amusing instance of a false alarm at Anderson's Fort was given the writer. In 1779, all manner of rumors and reports were afloat. Everybody was forted, and the Indians formed the entire subject of conversation. One afternoon, a half-witted, cowardly fellow was sent up the path to bring the cows to the fort. He had been out about fifteen minutes when he returned, looking wild and haggard, and almost out of breath, declaring that the Indians were coming down the creek in full force. In an instant the whole fort was in commotion: men seized their rifles, dogs barked, children screamed, and everybody swore that the audacious savages should have a warm reception. The entire force of the garrison rallied out to a hill, and, with cocked rifles, awaited the appearance of the enemy on the brow. Lo! he came; but, instead of Indians, the alarm was suddenly quieted by the appearance of *three cows!* A mock court-martial was ordered to try the half-witted chap for raising a false alarm, and the jokers of the fort convicted him and passed sentence of death upon him. The joke came near proving fatal to the poor fellow, who for a long time could not be divested of the idea that he was to be shot.

In 1779, one of the most remarkable cases on record occurred up Shaver's Creek. The particulars are vague; but of the actual occurrence of what we are about to relate there is no doubt whatever—the circumstance having been mentioned to us by two or three persons.

Late in the fall of that year, two boys, aged respectively eight and ten years, while engaged at play near a house in the neighborhood of Manor Hill, were taken captive by two lurking savages, who came suddenly upon them, and immediately started in the direction of the mountain. After travelling some eight miles, they halted, built a fire in the woods, leaned their rifles against a tree, and cooked some dried venison, of which they all partook. After the meal, one of them drew from his pouch a canteen filled with whiskey, which they drank at short intervals until it was entirely drained of its contents. By that time they had become very garrulous and very brave. They told war-stories, sang war-songs, danced war-dances, and challenged the whole settlement to mortal combat. The other

Indian then pulled out his canteen, also filled with fire-water, which was consumed in like manner; but, by the time it was drank, their mirth and boasting gave way to the stupor of inordinate intoxication, and, wrapping their blankets around them, they stretched themselves before the fire, and were soon in a deep sleep.

The eldest boy, who had feigned sleep some time previous, now got up and shook the younger, who also got upon his feet. He then took one of the rifles, cocked it, and rested it on a log, with the muzzle within a few inches of the head of one of the savages, and then motioned the younger boy to hold it. He then got the other rifle, and in like manner placed its muzzle near the head of the other savage. So far, the whole proceeding had been carried on by pantomimic action, and not a word spoken; but, every thing being now in readiness, the boy whispered "*Now!*" and both rifles went off at the same time. The elder boy killed his man outright; but the weight of the butt of the rifle in the hands of the younger threw the muzzle up, and he merely tore his face very badly. The wounded savage attempted to rise, but, before he could do so, the boys commenced running for home; nor did they stop until they reached it, which was at two o'clock in the morning and just as a party had assembled to go in search of them.

Their story was soon told; but so incredible did it appear that no person believed them. Instead of giving credit to their narrative of improbabilities, the parents were inclined to whip them and send them to bed, for getting lost in the woods and then lying about it. Next day, however, they persisted so strongly in their statement, and told such a straightforward story, that at length a party of some six or eight persons agreed to go to the place, providing the children accompanied them. To this they readily assented; and the anxiety they manifested to go soon removed all doubt as to the truth of their statement.

In due time they reached the spot, where they found a dead Indian, the two rifles and canteens; but the wounded savage was missing. Where he had lain there was a pool of blood; and, as it was probable that he had not gone far, a proposition was made to search for him, which was about being acted upon, when one of the men noticed blood upon the trunk of the tree under which they stood, which caused him to look up, and among its top branches he saw the wounded savage. The frightful wound upon his face awakened the pity of some of the men, and they proposed getting him down; but an old ranger, who was in the party, swore that he had never had a chance at an Indian in his life, especially a treed one; that he would rather lose his life than miss the opportunity of shooting him; and, before an effort could be made to prevent it, the savage received a ball through his brain, came crashing down through the limbs of the tree, and fell by the side of his dead companion. Their bodies were not disturbed; but their rifles were carried home, and given to the boys, who kept them as trophies of the event.

This daring and heroic act on the part of children so young illustrates most forcibly the kind of material people were made of who flourished in "the days that tried men's souls."

In 1782, Miss Elizabeth Ewing and Miss McCormick

were abducted by the Indians, between Shaver's Creek
and Stone Valley. They had been to the former place,
and were returning home by a path, when they were surprised and taken prisoners by a small band of roving
Indians. It was late in October, at a time when no suspicion was entertained that the Indians would ever again
enter the valley. None had been seen or heard of for
months, and all the alarms and fears of savages had subsided; hence their absence was little thought of until
they had been several days gone. It was then deemed
entirely too late to send a force to recapture them.

When captured, they had some bread with them, which
they scattered along the path they took, in hopes that if
their friends followed it would give them a clue to the
route they took. The wily savages detected the stratagem, and took the bread from them. They next broke
the bushes along the path; but the Indians saw the object
of this, too, and compelled them to desist. They then
travelled for seven days, through sleet, rain, and snow,
until they reached the lake, where Miss McCormick was
given as a present to an old Indian woman who happened
to take a fancy to her.

Miss Ewing was taken to Montreal, where, fortunately
for her, an exchange of prisoners took place soon after,
and she was sent to Philadelphia, and from thence made
her way home. From her Mr. McCormick learned the
fate of his daughter—her communication being the first
word of intelligence he had received concerning her. He
soon made his arrangements to go after her. The journey
was a long one, especially by the route he proposed to take,
—by way of Philadelphia and New York; nevertheless,

the love he bore his daughter prompted him to undertake it cheerfully.

After many days' travelling he arrived at the place where Miss Ewing and Miss McCormick parted; but, alas! it was only to realize painfully the restless and migratory character of the Indians, who had abandoned the settlement and gone into the interior of Canada. Again he journeyed on, until he finally reached the place where the tribe was located, and found his daughter in an Indian family, treated as one of the family, and subject to no more menial employment than Indian women gene-rally. The meeting of father and daughter, which neither expected, must have been an affecting one — a scene that may strike the imagination more vividly than pen can depict it.

Mr. McCormick made immediate arrangements to take his daughter with him; but, to his surprise, the Indians objected. Alone, and, as it were, in their power, he was at a loss what course to pursue, when he bethought him-self of the power of money. That was the proper chord to touch; but the ransom-money asked was exorbitantly large. The matter was finally compromised by Mr. Mc-Cormick paying nearly all the money in his possession, retaining barely enough to defray their expenses; after which they went on their way rejoicing, and, after a weary journey, reached their home in safety.

It may be as well to mention that Miss McCormick was a sister to Robert McCormick, Sr., long a resident of Hollidaysburg, who died a year or two ago in Altoona, and the aunt of William, Robert, and Alexander McCor-mick, now residents of Altoona.

And now we come to the last Indian massacre in the Valley of the Juniata. It occurred on the left bank of the Little Juniata, near the farm of George Jackson, in the latter part of August, 1781.

At that time there was a regular force of militia in the garrison at Huntingdon, another at Shaver's Creek, and another at Fetter's. The Indians were well aware of this, for they constantly kept themselves advised by spies of the progress of affairs in the valley. The settlers, feeling secure in the presence of the militia, abandoned the forts and went to their farms. During the summer of 1781, the alarms were so few that people began to consider the days of their trials and tribulations as passed away; but it appears that it was ordained that another black crime should be added to the long catalogue of Indian cruelties.

One evening George Jackson, hearing a noise in a corn-field adjoining his house, went to the door to ascertain the cause. Dark as the night was, he made out the figures of two men, who he thought were stealing corn, or at least about no good; so he let loose his dogs—a hound and a bull-dog—upon them. The hound gave tongue, and both started directly into the field, where they bayed for some time; but the men did not quit the field. In ten minutes the dogs returned, and Mr. Jackson found that the skull of the bull-dog had been wounded with a tomahawk. This circumstance led him to suspect the real character of the intruders, and he went into his house, took down his rifle, and returned to the porch. The light which shone out of the door when Jackson opened it revealed the position of affairs to the Indians, and they ran to the other end of the corn-field, closely pursued by the hound.

Peter Crum, a worthy man, well known and highly respected by all the settlers in the neighborhood, was a near neighbor of Jackson's. He had rented the Minor Tub Mill, and on the morning after the above occurrence he went to the mill a little before daylight and set it going, then raised a net he had placed in the stream the night before; after which he started leisurely on his way home to get his breakfast. In his left hand he carried a string of fish, and over his right shoulder his rifle; for, notwithstanding the great security people felt, they were so much in the habit of constantly having a rifle for a travelling companion, that many of the old pioneers carried it on all occasions during the remainder of their lives.

When Crum reached the bend of the river, a mile below his mill, at a time when an attack from Indians would probably have been the last thing he would have thought of, he heard the sharp crack of a rifle, and on looking around saw two Indians on the hill-side. He dropped his fish, and opened the pan of his rifle to look at the priming, when he noticed that he was shot through the right thumb—at least it was so conjectured. Catching a glimpse of one of the Indians, he attempted to fire, but the blood of his wound had saturated the priming. The Indians noticed his unavailing effort to shoot, and, probably thinking that he was trying to intimidate them with an empty gun, jumped into the road. One of them, it appeared, was armed with a rifle, the other with a heavy war-club. The latter, it is supposed, approached him from behind, and dealt him a blow upon the skull, which felled him, and the blow was evidently followed up until the entire back part of his head was crushed in the most shocking manner, after which they scalped him, and disappeared.

When found, (which was supposed to be within two hours after the murder,) Crum was lying with his face to the ground, his rifle by his side, and the Indian war-club, clotted with blood and brains, lying across his body,—a sad sight for his wife, who was among the first on the spot after the tragedy.

This murder, committed in open daylight on a frequented road, in the very heart of a thickly-populated country, did not fail to produce the most intense excitement, and a party of rangers started at once after the marauders. They soon got upon their trail, and followed them to the top of the mountain, getting sight of them several times; but they were always out of rifle-range. They knew they were pursued, and took such a route as the rangers could not follow, and so eluded them, and carried in triumph to the British garrison at Detroit the last scalp taken by the red men in the Juniata Valley.

PULPIT ROCKS, WARRIOR RIDGE.

CHAPTER XXXIII.

WARRIOR RIDGE — WARRIOR'S MARK — JOB CHILLAWAY, SHANEY JOHN, AND CAPTAIN LOGAN, THE LAST RED MEN IN THE JUNIATA VALLEY.

WARRIOR RIDGE, between Alexandria and Huntingdon, derives its name from an Indian path which ran along the summit of it. The Pulpit Rocks, not unlike the altars of the Druids, shaped into fantastic forms by the hand of nature, as well as the wild romantic scenery around them, at once suggest the idea of a place of meeting of the warriors,— a spot where the councils of the brave were held, with the greensward of the mountain for a carpet and the blue vault of heaven for a canopy. Were we not so well aware of the fact that the Indians preferred the lowlands of the valleys for places of abode, we could almost fancy the neighborhood of Pulpit Rocks to have been a glorious abiding-place; but of the occurrences and events that took place on the ridge we are in hopeless ignorance. Had some Indian historian of an early day transmitted to posterity, either by written or oral tradition, one-half the events of Warrior Ridge, we might add considerable interest to these pages; but as it is, we must content ourself, if not our readers, with this brief notice of the famous Warrior Ridge.

Warrior's Mark was another celebrated place for the Indians. It lies upon a flat piece of table-land, and is just the kind of a place where savages would be likely to meet to debate measures of great importance and to concoct schemes for their future movements. The name of the place originated from the fact of certain oak-trees in the vicinity having a crescent or half-moon cut upon them with hatchets, so deep that traces can still be seen of them, or, at least, could be some years ago. The signification of them was known to the Indians alone; but it is evident that some meaning was attached to them, for, during the Revolution, every time a band of savages came into the valley one or more fresh warrior marks were put upon the trees. The Indian town stood upon the highway or path leading from Kittaning, through Penn's Valley, to the Susquehanna. It was still considerable of a village when the white men first settled in the neighborhood, but immediately on the breaking out of the Revolution the Indians destroyed it, and moved to Ohio, and at this day there is not a trace of its existence left.

The first white settlers in Warrior's Mark were the Ricketts family. They were all wild, roving fellows, who loved the woods better than civilization; and their whole occupation, over and above tilling a very small patch of land, appeared to be hunting for wild game. Their arrival was followed by two or three other families; and when the Indian troubles commenced, the house of Ricketts was converted into a fortress, and the men turned their attention to protecting the frontier. One of them—Captain Elijah Ricketts—became quite an active and prominent man.

We have no record of any murder ever having been committed in the immediate vicinity of Warrior's Mark. Several captives were taken from thence, either in 1777 or 1778, but were exchanged and found their way back; we are, however, without particulars, either as to their names, capture, or release.

The three last Indians in the valley were Job Chillaway, a Delaware, Shaney John, a Mingo, and Captain Logan, a Cayuga. They were all friendly to the whites, and served the cause of liberty in the capacity of spies.

Job Chillaway is represented by the late E. Bell, Esq., in his MS., as a tall, muscular man, with his ears cut so as to hang pendant like a pair of ear-rings. He was employed as early as 1759 by the Colonial Government as a spy, and his name is frequently mentioned in the archives. Levi Trump, in writing to Governor Denny, from Fort Augusta, on April 8, 1759, when the French were using their most powerful exertions to swerve the Six Nations from their fealty to the colony, says :—

Job Chillaway, a Delaware Indian, arrived here on the 5th inst., and brought with him a message from a grand council of the Six Nations held near Onondaga, to King Teedyuscung, informing him that deputies from said council would soon be at Wyoming. On what errand they did not say; but Job says he thinks it his duty to inform his brothers what he knows of the affair:—that he was present at the opening of this council; which was by four chiefs, of different nations, singing the war-song and handing round an uncommonly large war-belt; that one of them, after some time, said: "What shall we do? Here is a hatchet from our fathers, to strike our brothers; and here is another from our brothers, to strike our fathers. I believe 'twill be best for us to do as we have done heretofore; that is, cast them both away."

In 1763, Chillaway still remained loyal to the colony, although nearly all of his tribe had taken up the hatchet against the English. Colonel James Irvine, under date of November 23, 1763, writes from "Ensign Kerns," near Fort Allen, to John Penn, as follows:—

SIR:—On the 16th instant Job Chillaway arrived here, being sent by Papunchay* to inform us that he and about twenty-five Indians (women and children included) were on their way from Weyalusing. The day after Job's arrival he delivered a string of wampum, and the following message in behalf of himself, Papunchay, John Curtis, &c., which he desired might be transmitted to your honor, viz.:

"BROTHER:—

"We are very glad that you have taken pity on us, according to the promises you made us since we had any correspondence together.

"Brother,—We are glad to hear you have pointed out two ways to us,—one to our brother, Sir William Johnson, the other to you. Our hearts incline toward you, the Governor of Philadelphia.

"Brother,—Take pity on us, and keep the road open, that we may pass without being hurt by your young men.

"Brother,—Point out the place where you intend to settle us, and we shall be glad, let that be where it will."

---

* Papunchay was the chief of the last of the Delaware warriors who remained loyal,—the great body having, by 1763, gone over to the French.

Job informed us that there were fifteen Muncy warriors, who, for three nights before he left Papunchay, encamped close by their encampment. How far they intended to proceed, or what were their intentions, he could not find out. As it was expected that Papunchay was near the frontiers, Colonel Clayton marched with fifty men, (mostly volunteers,) on the 20th inst., with Job Chillaway, in hopes of surprising the warriors. We were out three days without discovering either them or Papunchay. What hath detained the latter we know not. Job hath desired me to wait for them at this place a few days longer. On their arrival here, I purpose to conduct them to Philadelphia, unless I receive orders to the contrary from your honor.

Whether Papunchay continued loyal after 1763 is not known; but Chillaway was a spy, in the employ of Asher Clayton, at Lehigh Gap, as late as May, 1764.

About 1768, he made his way to the Juniata Valley. He first located near the mouth of the Little Juniata; but as soon as settlements were made by the whites he went up Spruce Creek; but there, too, the footprints of the white invader were soon seen, and he removed to the mountain, where hunting was good. He continued for many years after the Revolution to bring venison down into the settlements to trade off for flour and bread. In his old age he exhibited a passion for strong drink, and by the white man's baneful *fire-water* he fell. He was found dead in his cabin, by some hunters, about the close of the last century.

Of Shaney John not much is known. He came to the valley probably about the same time Chillaway did, and the two were boon-companions for many years. Shaney John moved to the Indian town called the Bald Eagle's

Nest, nearly opposite Milesburg, Centre county, where he died.

The most prominent friendly Indian that ever resided in the valley, however, was Captain Logan. This, of course, was not his proper name, but a title bestowed upon him by the settlers. He is represented as having been a noble and honorable Indian, warm in his attachment to a friend, but, like all Indians, revengeful in his character. A kindness and an insult alike remained indelibly stamped upon the book and page of his memory; and to make a suitable return for the former he would have laid down his life—shed the last drop of his heart's blood. He was a man of medium height and heavy frame; notwithstanding which he was fleet of foot and ever on the move.

He came to the valley before Chillaway did, and settled with his family in the little valley east of Martin Bell's Furnace, which is still known as Logan's Valley. He had previously resided on the Susquehanna, where he was the captain of a brave band of warriors; but, unfortunately, in some engagement with another tribe, he had an eye destroyed by an arrow from the enemy. This was considered a mark of disgrace, and he was deposed; and it was owing to that cause that he abandoned his tribe and took up his residence in the Juniata Valley.

One day, while hunting, he happened to pass the beautiful spring near the mouth of the Bald Eagle—now in the heart of Tyrone City. The favorable location for both hunting and fishing, as well as the charming scenery, fascinated Logan; and he built himself a wigwam, immediately above the spring, to which he removed his family.

Here he lived during the Revolutionary war, not altogether inactive, for his sympathies were on the side of liberty. During that time he formed a strong attachment to Captain Ricketts, of Warrior's Mark, and they became fast friends. It was to Ricketts that Captain Logan first disclosed the plot of the tories under John Weston; and Edward Bell gave it as his firm conviction that Logan was among the Indians who shot down Weston and his men on their arrival at Kittaning.

Although Logan had learned to read from the Moravian missionaries when quite a lad, he knew very little of the formula of land purchases; so he failed to make a regular purchase of the spot on which his cabin stood, the consequence of which was that, after the war, some envious white man bought the land and warned the friendly savage off. Logan was too proud and haughty to contest the matter, or even bandy words with the intruder; so he left, and located at Chickalacamoose, where Clearfield now stands, on the West Branch of the Susquehanna.

Captain Logan continued visiting the valley, and especially when any of his friends among the pioneers died. On such occasions he generally discarded his red and blue eagle-feathers, and appeared in a plain suit of citizens' clothes.

But at length Logan came no more. The Great Spirit called him to a happier hunting-ground; and all that is mortal of him—unless his remains have been

23

ruthlessly torn from the bosom of mother earth—lies beneath the sod, near the mouth of Chickalacamoose Creek.

It is to be regretted that more of his history has not been preserved, for, according to all accounts of him, he possessed many noble traits of character. Unlike Logan the Mingo chief, Captain Logan the Cayuga chief had no biographer like Thomas Jefferson to embellish the pages of history with his eloquence. Well may we say, "The evil that men do lives after them, while the good is oft interred with their bones."

CHAPTER XXXIV.

CONCLUSION.

PUSHING the light canoe on the lagoons in search of fish and lassoing the wild horse on the pampas of the South, chasing the buffalo on the boundless prairies and hunting the antlered stag in the dense forests of the West, is now the Indian's occupation; and there he may be found, ever shunning the haunts of civilization.

The Delaware Indians have been exterminated, and their very name (*Lenni Lenape*) blotted from existence, save where it appears upon the pages of history.

Of the Shawnees, once the powerful warlike tribe that was known and feared from the seaboard to the lakes, but a few degenerate families reside in the Far West.

Of the Great Confederation of the Iroquois but a remnant exists to remind us of its former greatness, its councils, its wars, and its "talks." They reside in Western New York, in a semi-civilized but degraded state, and are but sorry representatives of the once proud and stately warriors the crack of whose sharp and unerring rifles made the woods ring, and whose canoes danced upon the waves of the blue Juniata more than a hundred years ago.

But they are all gone, and the bones of their ancestors are the only relics which they have left behind them. The hand of the same inscrutable Providence that suffered them to march as mighty conquerors from the West to the East, crushing out the existence of a weaker people in their triumphant march, stayed them, blighted them in the noon-day of their glory, and, like the receding waves of the sea, drove them back in the direction whence they came, where they scattered, and the ties which bound them together as tribes dissolved even as would ice beneath the rays of a tropical sun.

The reader of the foregoing pages may sometimes think it strange that the savages committed so many depredations with impunity, killed, scalped, or carried so many into captivity, while but comparatively few of the marauders were destroyed. The cause of this can be easily explained. The savages always made covert attacks. As will be remembered, very few massacres occurred in the valley by open attack,—nearly all their depredations being committed while in ambuscade or when they had a foe completely in their power. Their incursions were always conducted with great caution, and no sooner did they strike a decisive blow than they disappeared. To guard against their ferocity was impossible; to follow them was equally futile. The settlers were too few in number to leave one force at home to guard against them and to send another in pursuit of them; for, during the Revolution, the belief was prevalent that a large force was ever ready to descend into the valley, and that the incursions of a few were only stratagems to lure the settlers to destruction by following them to where a large number were con-

cealed.   It was frequently proposed to send a strong force
to waylay the gaps of the mountain; but the settlers refused
to trust the protection of their families to the raw militia
sent by government to defend the frontier.

In extremely aggravating cases, men, driven to desperation, followed the savages to the verge of the Indian settlements; but they never got beyond the summit of the Alleghany Mountains without feeling as if they were walking
directly into the jaws of death, for no one could otherwise than momentarily expect a shower of rifle-balls from
the enemy in ambuscade.   The want of men, ammunition,
and other things, were known to and taken advantage of
by the Indians; but when an abundance of these things
was brought to the frontier they prudently kept out of
the way, for their sagacity instinctively taught them what
they might expect if they fell into the hands of the settlers.
But it may here be remarked that the savage mode of warfare, which by them was deemed fair and honorable,—such
as scalping or maiming women and children,—was held
in the utmost horror and detestation by people who professed to be Christians; and they equally detested shooting from ambuscade as an act fit for savages alone to be
guilty of.   It was only the more reckless and desperate of
the community that would consent to fight the savages
after their own mode of warfare.

It is, therefore, but a simple act of justice to the memory of the pioneers to say that the savages did not go
unpunished through any fear or lack of zeal on their part.
Their concentrated energies were used to check the frequent invasions, and many of them spent their last
dollar to protect the defenceless frontier; yet it is to be

deeply regretted that in those primitive days they lacked the knowledge of properly applying the power within their reach.

But they, too, are all gone! "Each forever in his narrow cell is laid." Beneath their kindred dust the rude forefathers of the valley sleep. We have endeavored to give a succinct account of the trials and sufferings of many of them; but, doubtless, much remains untold, which the recording angel alone has possession of. While we reflect upon the fact that it was through the privations and hardships *they* endured that *we* enjoy the rich blessings of the beautiful and teeming valley, let us hope that they are enjoying a peace they knew not on earth, in that valley "where the wicked cease from troubling and the weary are at rest."

APPENDIX.

THE VALLEY AS IT IS.

THE preceding pages fulfil the original intention of presenting to the public, as far as possible, a "History of the *Early* Settlement of the Juniata Valley." Its modern history, fraught with rare incidents, is left to the pen of some future enterprising historian, who may collect the incidents necessary to construct it when but a moiety of the generation (still numerous) who know the valley and its multifarious changes for half a century past shall be dwellers in our midst. Still, such prospect shall not deter us from giving a synopsis of the history of the valley as it is, not promising, however, to make the record complete, or even notice in detail the growth and progress of the valley during the last thirty years.

When the early settlers were apprised of the fact that some of the more enterprising contemplated cutting a pack-horse road over the Alleghany Mountains, through Blair's Gap, they shook their heads ominously, and declared that the task was one which could not be accomplished. But it *was* accomplished; and, after its completion, it was not many years until the pack-horse track was transformed into a wagon-road. People were well satisfied with this arrangement; for no sooner was there a good road along the river than some daring men commenced taking produce to the East, by the use of arks, from the Frankstown Branch, the Raystown Branch, and the Little Juniata. With these advantages, a majority of the inhabitants labored under the impression that they were keeping pace with the age; but others, endowed with a fair share of that progressive spirit which characterizes the American people, commenced agitating the project of making a turnpike between Huntingdon and Blairsville. The old fogies of the day gave this innovation the cold shoulder, spoke of the immense cost, and did not fail to count the expense of travelling upon such a road. But little were their murmurings heeded by the enterprising men of the valley. The fast friend of the turnpike was Mr. Blair, of Blair's Gap, west of Hollidaysburg. His influence was used in the halls of the Legislature until he injured his political standing; nevertheless, he persevered until the company was chartered, and he soon had the satisfaction of seeing the turnpike road completed. Once built, it was found to be rather a desirable institution, and its value soon removed all opposition to it.

Anon came the startling proposition of building a canal along the Juniata, and a railroad over the Alleghany Mountains, to connect the waters of the Juniata and the Conemaugh. To men of limited information the project seemed vague and ill-defined; while knowing old fogies shook their heads, and declared that a canal and a turnpike both could not be sustained, and that, if the former could accomplish the wonders claimed for it, the teams that carried goods between Philadelphia and Pittsburg in the short space of from fifteen to twenty days would be compelled to suspend operations! But the opposition to the canal was too insignificant to claim notice; and when the building of it was once commenced an improvement mania raged. The stately and learned engineer, Moncure Robinson, was brought all the way from England to survey the route for the Portage Road. Like a very colossus of *roads*, he strode about the mountain, and his nod and beck, like that of imperial Cæsar upon his throne, was the law, from which there was no appeal. By dint of long labor, and at a vast expense to the commonwealth, he demonstrated clearly that a road could be built across the mountain, and rendered practicable by the use of ten inclined planes. Alas! for the perishable nature of glory! Moncure Robinson had hardly time to reach his home, and boast of the honor and fame he achieved in the New World, before a Yankee engineer discovered that a railroad could be built across the Alleghany Mountain without the use of a single plane! Of course, then he was thought a visionary, and that not a quarter of a century ago; yet now we have two railroads crossing the mountain without the use of a plane, and the circumstance appears to attract no other remark than that of ineffable disgust at the old fogies who could not make a road to cross the Apalachian chain without the tedious operation of being hoisted up and lowered down by stationary engines.

The era of "flush times" in the valley must have been when the canal was building. Splendid fortunes were made, and vast sums of money sunk, by the wild speculations which followed the advent of the contractors and the sudden rise of property lying along the river. As an instance of the briskness of the times in the valley when the canal was building, an old settler informs us that Frankstown at that time contained fourteen stores, five taverns, and four roulette tables. At present, we believe, it contains but two or three stores, one tavern, and no gambling apparatus to relieve the reckless of their surplus change.

The completion of the canal was the great event of the day, and the enthusiasm of the people could scarcely be kept within bounds when the ponderous boats commenced ploughing the ditch. This will be readily believed by any one who will read the papers published at the time. From a paper printed in Lewistown on the 5th of November, 1829, we learn that a packet-boat arrived at that place from Mifflin on the Thursday previous, and departed again next day, having on board a number of members of the Legislature, as well as citizens and strangers. The editor, in speaking of the departure, enthusiastically says:—"The boat was drawn by two white horses, when she set off in fine style, with the 'star-spangled banner' flying at her head, and amid the roar of cannon, the shouts of the populace, and the cheering music of the band which was on board." Reader, this was a little over twenty-six years ago; and the jubilee was over a packet capable of accomplishing the mighty task of carrying some forty or fifty passengers at the rate of about four miles an hour.

The climax of joy, however, appears to have been reached by the editor of the *Huntingdon Gazette*, on the 15th of July, 1831, when he became jubilant over the launch of a canal-boat, and gave vent to the following outburst:—"What! a canal-boat launched in the vicinity of Huntingdon! Had any one predicted an event of this kind some years back, he, in all probability, would have been yclept a wizard, or set down as *beside himself!*"

These gushings of intensified joy, although they serve to amuse now, do not fail to convey a useful lesson. Let us not glory too much over the demon scream of the locomotive as it comes rattling through the valley, belching forth fire and smoke, or the miraculous telegraph which conveys messages from one end of the Union to the other with the rapidity with which a lover's sigh would be wafted from the Indies to the Pole; for who knows but that the succeeding generation, following in the footsteps made by the universal law of progress, will astonish the world with inventions not dreamed of in our philosophy, which will throw our electric-telegraphs and railroads forever in the shade?

For eighteen years, with the exception of the winter months, the canal packet held sway in the Juniata Valley, carrying its average of about thirty passengers a day from the East to the West, and *vice versâ*. When hoar old winter placed an embargo upon the canal craft, travel used to dwindle down to such a mere circumstance that a rickety old two-horse coach could easily carry all the passengers that offered. Who among us that has arrived at the age of manhood does not recollect the packet-boat, with its motley group of passengers, its snail pace, its consequential captain, and its non-communicative steersman, who used to wake the echoes with the "to-to-to-to-toit" of his everlasting horn and his hoarse cry of "lock ready?" The canal-packet was unquestionably a great institution in its day and generation, and we remember it with emotions almost akin to veneration. Right well do we remember, too, how contentedly people sat beneath the scorching rays of a broiling sun upon the packet, as it dragged its slow length along the sinuous windings of the canal at an average speed of three and a half or four miles an hour; and yet the echo of the last packet-horn has scarcely died away when we see the self-same people standing upon a station-house platform, on the verge of despair because the cars happen to be ten minutes behind time, or hear them calling down maledictions dire upon the head of some offending conductor who refuses to jeopardize the lives of his passengers by running faster than thirty miles an hour!

At length, after the canal had enjoyed a sixteen years' triumph, people began to consider it a "slow coach;" and, without much debate, the business-men of Philadelphia resolved upon a railroad between Harrisburg and Pittsburg. The project had hardly been fairly determined upon before the picks and shovels of the "Corkonians" and "Fardowns" were brought into requisition; but, strange to say, this giant undertaking struck no one as being any thing extraordinary. It was looked upon as a matter of course, and the most frequent remarks it gave rise to were complaints that the making of the road did not progress rapidly enough to keep pace with the progress of the age. And, at length, when it was completed, the citizens of Lewistown did not greet the arrival of the first train with drums, trumpets, and the roar of cannon; neither did any Huntingdon editor exclaim, in a burst of enthusiasm, on the arrival of the train there, "What! nine railroad cars, with six hundred passengers, drawn through Huntingdon by a locomotive! If any person had predicted such a result some years ago, he would have been yclept a wizard, or set down as one *beside himself.*"

The Pennsylvania Railroad once finished, although it failed to create the surprise and enthusiasm excited by the canal, did not fail to open up the valley and its vast resources. Independent of the great advantage of the road itself, let us see what followed in the wake of this laudable enterprise. The railroad created the towns of Altoona, Fostoria, Tipton, and Tyrone; its presence caused the building of three plank roads, and the opening of extensive coal and lumber operations in the valley, and kindred enterprises that might never have been thought of. Nor is this all. A rage for travel by railroad has been produced by the Pennsylvania Company; and there is good reason to believe that it will increase until at least three more roads tap the main artery in the Juniata Valley,— the railroad from Tyrone to Clearfield, from the same place to Lock Haven, and from Spruce Creek to Lewisburg. These roads will unquestionably be built, and at no remote period. The Pennsylvania Road has now facilities for doing business equal to those of any road of the same length in the world; and, when a second track is completed, it is destined, for some years at least, to enjoy a monopoly of the carrying trade between

Pittsburg and Philadelphia. Much as we regret it, for the sake of the Commonwealth which expended her millions without any thing like an adequate return, the canal is rapidly falling into disuse, and we see, with deep regret, that it has become entirely too slow for the age in which we live. With all the vitality forced into it that can be, we confess we can see no opposition in it to the road but such as is of the most feeble kind; yet all will agree that this opposition, trifling as it is, should continue to exist until such a time as other routes shall be opened between these points, and healthy competition established. But let us not dwell too much upon our modes of transit through the valley, lest the historian of a hundred years hence will find our remarks a fitting theme for ridicule, and laugh at us because we speak in glowing terms of a single railroad, and that road with but a single track for more than half its distance!

In order to give the reader a little insight into the progress which has been made in the valley, let us turn statistician for a time, with the understanding, however, that we shall not be held responsible for the accuracy of dates.

Less than twenty-six years ago, George Law sat upon the left bank of the Juniata, two miles west of Williamsburg, cutting stones for building two locks at that place. *Now* the aforesaid Law is supposed to be worth the snug little sum of six millions of dollars, and not long since was an aspirant for the presidential chair!

Thirty years ago, when Frankstown was a place of some note, Hollidaysburg contained but a few scattered cabins. In fact, twenty years ago it was "to fortune and to fame unknown;" yet it now contains a population (including that of Gaysport) that will not fall much short of four thousand.

Less than twenty-five years ago, Dr. P. Shoenberger, while returning from Baltimore with $15,000 in cash, fell in with the celebrated robber Lewis on the Broad Top Mountain. The intention of Lewis, as he afterward acknowledged, was to rob him; but the doctor, although he was unacquainted with his fellow-traveller, had his suspicions awakened, and, by shrewd manœuvering, succeeded in giving him the slip. Had the $15,000 in question fallen into the hands of the robber, Dr. Shoenberger would have been bankrupt, and the probability is that he would have lived and died an obscure individual. Instead of that, however, the money freed him from his embarrassments, and he died, but a few years ago, worth between four and five millions of dollars—more than one-half of which he accumulated by manufacturing iron in the Valley of the Juniata.

Less than sixteen years ago, a gentleman named Zimmerman was a bar-keeper at the hotel of Walter Graham, Esq., at Yellow Springs, in Blair county, afterward a "mud-boss" on the Pennsylvania Canal, and subsequently a teamster at Alleghany Furnace. At the present day the said Samuel Zimmerman owns hotels, palaces, a bank of issue, farms, stocks, and other property, at Niagara Falls, in Canada, which swell his income to $150,000 per annum. He is but thirty-eight years of age. Should he live the length of time allotted to man, and his wealth steadily increase, at the end of threescore-and-ten years he can look upon ordinary capitalists, who have only a few millions at command, as men of limited means.

Let it not be presumed, however, that we notice these capitalists from any adoration of their wealth or homage to the men, but merely because their history is partially identified with the valley, and to show in what a singular manner the blind goddess will sometimes lavish her favors; for hundreds of men without money, but with brighter intellects and nobler impulses than ever were possessed by Zimmerman, Law, or Shoenberger, have gone down to the grave "unwept, unhonored, and unsung," in the Juniata Valley. Neither will the soughing of the west wind, as it sweeps through the valley, disturb their repose any more than it will that of the *millionaires* when resting from "life's fitful fever" in their splendid mausoleums.

Less than ten years ago a railroad from Huntingdon to Broad Top was deemed impracticable. Since then, or, we may say, within the last four years, a substantial railroad has been built, reaching from the borough of Huntingdon to Hopewell, in Bedford county, a distance of thirty-one miles; and the cars are now engaged in bringing coal from a region which, but a few years ago, was unexplored. In addition to the main track, there is a branch, six miles in length, extending to Shoup's Run. The coal-field contains eighty square miles of territory; and from the openings made at Shoup's Run and Six Mile Run semi-bituminous coal has been taken the quality of which cannot be surpassed by any coal-fields in the world. Along the line of the road quite a number of villages have sprung up. The first is Worthington, some thirteen miles from Huntingdon. The next is Saxton, twenty-six miles from Huntingdon. Coalmont is the name of a flourishing village growing up on Shoup's Run, about a mile below the lowest coal-veins yet opened. Barret is located about two miles farther up; and Broad Top City is located upon the summit of the mountain, at the terminus of the Shoup's Run Branch, at which place a large three-story stone hotel has been built, and a number of lots disposed of, on which purchasers are bound to build during the summer of 1856.

Less than eight years ago the author of these pages, while on a gunning expedition, travelled over the ground where Altoona now stands. It was then almost a barren waste. A few fields, a solitary log farm-house and its out-buildings, and a school-house, alone relieved the monotony of the scene; yet now upon this ground stands a town with between three and four thousand inhabitants, where the scream of the engine is heard at all hours of the day and night,—where the roar of fires, the clang of machinery, and the busy hum of industry, never cease from the rising to the setting of the sun, and where real estate commands a price that would almost seem fabulous to those not acquainted with the facts. But of this enough.

Let us now proceed to examine the products of the valley. The lower end of it is a grain-growing region, the upper an iron-producing country; and it is owing to the mineral resources alone that the valley maintains the position it does and boasts of the wealth and population it now possesses. The Juniata iron has almost a worldwide reputation; yet we venture to say that many of our own neighbors know little about the immense amount of capital and labor employed in its manufacture. The following is a list of the iron establishments in the valley:—

BEDFORD COUNTY.

Name.	Location.	Owner.
Bloomfield Furnace	Middle Woodbury	John W. Duncan.
Lemnos "	Hopewell	John King & Co.
Lemnos Forge	"	" "
Bedford "	"	" "
Bedford Foundry and Machine-shop	Bedford	Michael Bannon.
Keagy's Foundry	Woodbury	Snowden & Blake.
West Providence Foundry	Bloody Run	George Baughman.

BLAIR COUNTY.

Alleghany Furnace	Logan township			Elias Baker.
Blair "	"	"		H. N. Burroughs.
Elizabeth "	Antes	"		Martin Bell.
Bald Eagle "	Snyder	"		Lyon, Shorb & Co.
Etna "	and Forge Catharine	"		Isett, Keller & Co.
Springfield "	Woodberry	"		D. Good & Co.

Name.	Location.	Owner.
Rebecca Furnace	Houston township	E. H. Lytle.
Sarah "	Greenfield "	D. McCormick.
Gap "	Juniata "	E. F. Shoenberger.
Frankstown "	Frankstown	A. & D. Moore.
Harriet "	Alleghany township	Blair Co. Coal & Iron Co.
Hollidaysburg Furnace	Gaysport	Watson, White & Co.
Chimney Rock "	Hollidaysburg	Gardener, Osterloh & Co.
Gaysport "	Gaysport	Smith & Caldwell.
Portage Works (rolling-mill, &c.)	Duncansville	J. Higgins & Co.
Maria Forges (two)	Juniata township	J. W. Duncan.
Lower Maria Forge	" "	D. McCormick.
Gap "	" "	Musselman & Co.
Elizabeth "	Antes "	John Bell.
Tyrone Forges (two)	Snyder "	Lyon, Shorb & Co.
Cove Forge	Woodberry "	J. Royer.
Franklin Forge	" "	D. H. Royer.
Cold Spring Forge	Antes "	Isett & Co.
Alleghany "	Alleghany "	E. H. Lytle.
Hollidaysburg Foundry and Machine-shop	Hollidaysburg	J. R. McFarlane & Co.
Gaysport Foundry and Machine-shop	Gaysport	McLanahan, Watson & Co.
Tyrone Foundry	Tyrone City	J. W. Mattern & Co.
Williamsburg Foundry	Williamsburg	Loncer & Hileman.
Martinsburg "	Martinsburg	Crawford & Morrow.
Penn'a Railroad "	Altoona	Penna. Railroad Co.
Duncansville "	Duncansville	Mr. Gibboney.
Axe and Pick Factory	Alleghany township	J. Colclesser.

HUNTINGDON COUNTY.

Huntingdon Furnace	Franklin township	G. K. & J. H. Shoenberger.
Monroe "	Jackson "	George W. Johnston & Co.
Greenwood "	" "	A. & J. Wright.
Rough and Ready Furnace	Hopewell "	Wood, Watson & Co.
Paradise Furnace	Tod "	Trexler & Co.
Mill Creek "	Brady "	Irvin, Green & Co.
Edward "	Shirley "	Beltzhoover & Co.
Rockhill "	Cromwell "	Isett, Wigton & Co.
Matilda " and Forge	Springfield "	Shiffler & Son.

24

Name.	Location.	Owner.
Coleraine Forges (two)	Franklin township	Lyon, Shorb & Co.
Stockdale Forge..................	" "	John S. Isett.
—— "	" "	G. K. & J. H. Shoenberger
Elizabeth "	" "	Martin Gates's heirs.
Rolling Mill and Puddling Forge...............................	Porter "	S. Hatfield & Son.
Juniata Rolling Mill and Forge	West "	B. Lorenz, (Lessee.)
Barre Forge....................... ...	Porter · "	Joseph Green & Co.
Alexandria Foundry		J. Grafius.
Water Street "		Job Plympton.
Spruce Creek "		H. L. Trawly.
Petersburg "		H. Orlady.
Huntingdon "		J. M. Cunningham & Co.
Shirleysburg "		John Lutz.
Eagle "	Tod township..............	J. & D. Hamilton.

MIFFLIN COUNTY.

Lewistown Furnace..............	Lewistown	Etting, Graff & Co.
Hope "	Granville township.....	W. W. Happer & Co.
Matilda "	Wayne "	W. Righter.
Brookland "	McVeytown	Huntingdon, Robison & Co.
" Rolling Mill	"	" " "
Freedom Forge...................	Derry township	J. A. Wright & Co.
Juniata Foundry and Machine-shop...............................	Lewistown	Zeigler & Willis.
Logan Foundry	"	A. Marks & Co.
McVeytown Foundry.............	McVeytown...............	Faxon & Co.
Axe Factory......................	Near Reedsville...........	A. Mann.
Plough Foundry..................	" "	J. & M. Taylor.

In addition to these, there may be some few foundries in Juniata and Perry counties, but no furnaces or forges in that portion of them which lies in the valley proper.

It may be as well here to mention that the furnace of Watson, White & Co. is just completed; the Chimney Rock Furnace will be completed during the summer of 1856, as well as the furnace of Messrs. Smith & Caldwell, in Gaysport. These three furnaces follow the discovery of immense fossil ore-veins immediately back of Hollidaysburg, which are supposed to extend, in irregular strata, from the river east as far as the basin extends. In addition to this, in the Loop,—a basin lying between points of the Cove Mountain, south of Frankstown,—mines capable of the most prolific yield have also been opened. The ore, smelted with coke, is said to produce the best iron in market, and commands a ready sale at excellent prices. From the discoveries of ore-deposits already made, and those that will follow future explorations, it is but reasonable to infer that, during the next four or five years, the number of furnaces will be considerably augmented; and at this time there is a project on foot for building an extensive rolling-mill and nail-factory at Hollidaysburg.

The foregoing list of iron establishments numbers seventy-three, (and we are by no means certain that we have enumerated all,) and employ some six or seven thousand men, directly or indirectly, and the capital invested cannot possibly fall far short of five millions of dollars. And all this vast source of wealth and happiness is drawn from the bosom of mother earth in a valley a little over a hundred miles in length. We say it boldly, and challenge contradiction, that the iron-mines of the Juniata Valley have yielded more clear profit, and entailed more blessings upon the human family, than ever the same extent of territory did in the richest diggings of California.

But, great as the valley is, unquestionably half its resources have not yet been developed. Along the base of the mountain are vast seams of coal that have never been opened, and forests of the finest timber, which only await capital and enterprise to show the real extent of our coal and lumber region. Of the extent of the ore-fields of the valley no man can form any conception. Time alone can tell. Yet we are not without hope that ore will be found in such quantities, before the present generation shall have passed away, as shall make the valley a second Wales in its iron operations.

From De Bow's Census Compendium of 1850 we copy the following, set down as an accurate statement of the amount of capital, hands employed, and amount produced, in all the counties of the valley, by manufactures, in that year :—

Counties.	Capital.	Hands employed.	Amount produced.
Bedford	$212,500	427	$561,339
Blair...........	1,065,730	1383	1,385,526
Huntingdon...	1,335,525	1218	1,029,860
Mifflin	129,235	300	310,452
Juniata.	309,300	182	467,550
Perry	336,992	609	845,360
Total...	$3,389,282	4119	$4,600,087

This is manifestly an error; for we are satisfied that more capital and hands were employed in the iron business alone in 1850, leaving out Perry county, only a portion of which belongs to the valley proper. The gatherers of the statistics evidently did not enumerate the wood-choppers, charcoal-burners, teamsters, ore-diggers, and others, who labor for furnaces. Yet, granting that the statistics of the manufactures of the valley, as given in the census report, are correct, and we deduct a tenth for manufactures other than iron, we are still correct; for since then new furnaces, forges, and foundries have been built, the capacity of old ones greatly enlarged, and many that were standing idle in 1850 are now in successful operation. In Altoona alone, since then, 600 hands find steady employment in working up the Juniata iron at the extensive machine-shops and foundries of the Pennsylvania Railroad Company.

The following shows the population in 1840, and in 1850, together with the number of dwellings :—

Counties.	Pop. in 1840.	Pop. in 1850.	Dwellings.
Bedford.............................. 29,335		23,052	3,896
Blair, (formed out of Huntingdon and Bedford, 1846).........21,777			3,718
Huntingdon 35,484		24,786	4,298
Mifflin........................ ... 13,092		14,980	2,591
Juniata.......... 11,080		13,029	2,168
Perry. 17,096		20,088	3,412
Total.............................. 106,085		117,712	20,083

If we add to Bedford the 7567 inhabitants taken from it to form Fulton county, we shall find that the population increased 19,192 in the valley, between 1840 and 1850. This may be rated as an ordinary increase. To the same increase, between 1850 and 1860, we may add the extraordinary increase caused by the building of the Pennsylvania and the Broad Top Railroads, which, we think, will increase the population to double what it was in 1840 by the time the next census is taken.

The number of dwellings in the valley, it will be observed, amounted, in 1850, to 20,083. Since then, five hundred buildings have been erected in Altoona, one hundred and fifty in Tyrone, five hundred in the towns and villages along the line of the Broad Top Road, a hundred along the line of the Pennsylvania Road, while the towns of Hollidaysburg, Huntingdon, McVeytown, Lewistown, Mifflin, and Newport, and, in fact, all the villages in the valley, have had more or less buildings erected during the past five years. A corresponding number erected during the next five years will, we venture to predict, bring the census return of buildings up to 40,000.

Let it also be remembered that the increase of population between 1840 and 1850 was made when the mania for moving to the West was at its height; when more people from the Juniata located in Iowa, Wisconsin, Illinois, and Indiana, than will leave us during the next twenty years, unless some unforeseen cause should transpire that would start a fresh tide of western emigration. The fact that many who have taken up their residences in the Far West would most willingly return, if they could, has opened the eyes of the people, in a measure; and many have become convinced that a man who cannot live and enjoy all the comforts of life on a fine Pennsylvania farm can do little better upon the prairies of Iowa or the ague-shaking swamps of Indiana. As an evidence that money may be made at home here by almost any pursuit, attended with perseverance, we may incidentally mention that a gentleman near Frankstown, who owns a small farm,—probably one hundred and sixty acres,—not only kept his family comfortable during the last year, but netted $1400 clear profit, being half the amount of the original purchase. Is there a farm of the same size in Iowa that produced to its owner so large a sum over and above all expenses? But, more than this, we can safely say, without fear of contradiction, that every acre of cultivated land in the Juniata Valley has, during the last two years, netted as much as the same amount of land in the most fertile and productive Western State in the Union. A large proportion of the people who have located in the West, actuated by that ruling passion of the human family—the accumulation of money, (mostly for dissipated heirs to squander,)—are engaged in speculating in lands. Now, we venture to say that the increase in the price of some of the lands in the Juniata Valley will vie with the rapid rise in the value of Western lands; and we are prepared to maintain our assertions with the proof. Some years ago a gentleman in Huntingdon county took a tract of timber-land, lying at the base of the mountain in Blair county, for a debt of some four or five hundred dollars. The debt was deemed hopelessly bad, and the land little better than the debt itself.

Right willingly would the new owner have disposed of it for a trifle, but no purchaser could be found. Anon the railroad was built, and a number of steam saw-mills were erected on lands adjoining the tract in question, when the owner found a ready purchaser at $2500 cash. A gentleman in Gaysport, in the summer of 1854, purchased twelve acres of ground back of Hollidaysburg for seven hundred dollars. This sum he netted by the sale of the timber taken off it preparatory to breaking it up for cultivation. After owning it just one year, he disposed of it for $3000! A gentleman in Hollidaysburg, in the fall of 1854, bought three hundred and eighty acres of ground, adjoining the Frankstown Ore Bank, for three hundred and eighty dollars. The undivided half of this land was sold on the 22d of February, 1856, for $2900, showing an increase in value of about 1400 per cent. in fifteen months; and yet the other half could not be purchased for $5000. By this the land speculator will see that it is not necessary for him to go to the Far West to pursue his calling while real estate rises so rapidly in value at home.

Within a few years past, the Juniata country has been made a summer resort by a portion of the denizens of Philadelphia, Baltimore, and Pittsburg. From either city it is reached after but a few hours' travel. The romantic scenery, the invigorating air, and the pure water of the mountains, are attractions that must eventually outweigh those of fashionable watering-places, with their customary conventional restraints. The hotels erected along the line of the Pennsylvania Railroad are admirably adapted, and have been built with a view to accommodate city-folks who wish to ruralize during the summer months. Prominent among them we may mention the Patterson House, kept by General Bell; the House, kept by Mrs. C. C. Hemphill, at the Lewistown station; the Keystone Hotel, at Spruce Creek, kept by Colonel R. F. Haslett; the City Hotel, Tyrone City; the large hotel at Tipton; the

Logan House, in Altoona; the two large hotels lately erected at Cresson, by Dr. Jackson, (capable of accommodating five hundred guests;) and Riffle's Mansion House at the Summit. In addition to these, all the larger towns contain excellent hotels. In short, we may say that the hotels of the valley, collectively, cannot be surpassed by country hotels anywhere.

The valley is not without its natural curiosities to attract the attention of the man of leisure. The Arch Spring and the Cave in Sinking Valley are probably among the greatest curiosities to be found in any country. The spring gushes from an opening arched by nature in such force as to drive a mill, and then sinks into the earth again. The subterranean passage of the water can be traced for some distance by pits or openings, when it again emerges, runs along the surface among rocky hills, until it enters a large cave, having the appearance of an immense tunnel. This cave has been explored as far as it will admit—some four hundred feet,—where there is a large room, and where the water falls into a chasm or vortex, and finds a subterranean passage through Canoe Mountain, and emerges again at its southern base, along which it winds down to Water Street and empties into the river.

Another of these subterranean wonders is a run back of Tyrone City, where it sinks into the base of a limestone ridge, passes beneath a hill, and makes its appearance again at the edge of the town.

The most remarkable spring, however, is one located on the right bank of the river, some seven miles below Hollidaysburg. The peculiar feature about this spring is the fact that it ebbs and flows with the same regularity the tides do. The admirer of natural curiosities may arrive at it when it is brimming full or running over with the purest of limestone water; yet in a short time the water will commence receding, and within an hour or two the hole in the ground alone remains. Then a rumbling noise is heard up the hill-side, and soon the water pours down until the spring is again overflowed.

In the town of Williamsburg, on the property of John K. Neff, Esq., there is a remarkable spring. It throws out a volume of water capable of operating a first-class mill, together with other machinery, although the distance from the spring to the river does not exceed the eighth of a mile.

At Spang's Mill, in Blair county, is by far the largest spring in the upper end of the valley. It has more the appearance of a small subterranean river breaking out at the hill-side than that of a spring. It is about three hundred yards long, varying in width from one hundred to one hundred and fifty feet. The water has a bluish-green tinge, and is so exceedingly pure that a drop of it placed under a microscope would show fewer animalculæ than a drop of river-water would after being filtered. Formerly it contained thousands upon thousands of the finest brook trout; but of late years the number has been considerably diminished by the sportsmen who could obtain permission from Mr. Spang to entice them from their element with the tempting fly. A hundred feet from what is considered the end of the spring, there is a large grist-mill driven by its waters, which empty into the eastern reservoir of the Pennsylvania Canal, after traversing a distance of about three miles. Within two miles from the head of the spring, its waters furnish motive-power to two grist-mills, a saw-mill, and four forges.

As a singular circumstance in connection with this subject, we may mention that, within the memory of some of the older inhabitants, a considerable stream of water ran through the upper end of Middle Woodbury township, Bedford county; but the spring at the head of it gave out, as well as several other springs which fed it, and now scarcely any traces of it remain.

In facilities for teaching the rising generation the counties composing the valley are not behind any of their sister counties in the State, as the Common School Report for 1855 proves.

Ever mindful of the Giver of all good and his manifold mercies to mankind, the people of the Juniata region have reared fully as many temples to the worship of Almighty God as the same number of inhabitants have done in any land where the light of the gospel shines. The following table, compiled from the census statistics, shows the number of churches in 1850:—

SECTS.	Bedford.	Blair.	Huntingdon.	Mifflin.	Juniata.	Perry.	Total.
Baptist.............................	5	5	6	1	......	4	21
Christian.	......	......	......	......	......	1	1
Congregational	......	......	......	1	......	......	1
Episcopal.........................	......	......	1	2	......	......	3
Free.	......	......	3	......	......	......	3
Friends.	2	......	......	......	......	......	2
German Reformed.............	7	5	5	......	......	10	27
Lutheran.	14	10	5	5	9	8	51
Mennonite	......	3	......	......	......	......	3
Methodist.	10	6	22	8	7	14	67
Moravian.	2	2	1	1	......	1	7
Presbyterian	6	6	13	11	10	8	54
Roman Catholic.	1	3	1	1	......	......	6
Tunker............................	......	1	1	......	......	......	2
Union	5	......	2	......	1	1	9
Minor Sects.....................	......	1	......	2	......	......	3
Total...................	52	42	60	32	27	47	260

During the six years that have elapsed since the above statistics were taken, quite a number of new churches have been erected—probably not less than twenty. Of this number four have been erected in Altoona and three in Tyrone City alone.

And now, worthy reader, our voluntarily-assumed task is ended. As we glance over the pages of our work, we are made painfully aware of the fact that many of the narratives given are too brief to be very interesting. This is owing altogether to the fact that we chose to give unvarnished accounts as we received them, broken and unconnected, rather than a connected history garnished with drafts from the imagination. In thus steering clear of the shoals of fiction,—on which so many historians have wrecked,—we conceive that we have only done our duty to those who suggested to us this undertaking.

We are strongly impressed with the idea that a history of the early settlement of the valley should have been written a quarter of a century ago. Then it might have made a volume replete with all the stirring incidents of the times, for at that period many of the actors in the trials and struggles endured were still among us, and could have given details; while we were compelled to glean our information from persons on the brink of the grave, whose thoughts dwelt more upon the future than on the past.

The modern history of the valley will be a subject for the pen of the historian a quarter of a century hence. We have given him a hint of some occurrences during the last half century; and for further particulars, during the next twenty-five years, we would refer him to the twenty newspapers published in the seven counties, from whose columns alone he will be able to compile an interesting history, sparing himself the trouble of searching among books, papers, and old inhabitants, for incidents that, unfortunately, never were recorded.

The future of the valley no man knoweth. We even tax the Yankee characteristic in vain when we attempt to guess its future. Many yet unborn may live to see the fires of forges and furnaces without number illuminating the rugged mountains, and hear the screams of a thousand steam-engines. They may live, too, to see the day when population shall have so increased that the noble stag dare no longer venture down from the mountain to slake his thirst at the babbling brook, and when the golden-hued trout, now sporting in every mountain-stream, shall be extinct. But, before that time, there is reason to believe that the present generation, including your historian, will have strutted upon the stage the brief hour allotted to them, performed life's pilgrimage, and, finally, arrived at

THE END.

STEREOTYPED BY L. JOHNSON & CO.
PHILADELPHIA.

EVERYNAME INDEX